The Language of Ontology

MIND ASSOCIATION OCCASIONAL SERIES

This series consists of carefully selected volumes of significant original papers on predefined themes, normally growing out of a conference supported by a Mind Association Major Conference Grant. The Association nominates an editor or editors for each collection, and may cooperate with other bodies in promoting conferences or other scholarly activities in connection with the preparation of particular volumes.

Director, Mind Association: Daniel Whiting
Publications Officer: Eliot Michaelson

The Language of Ontology

Edited by

J. T. M. MILLER

OXFORD

UNIVERSITY PRESS

OXFORD

UNIVERSITY PRESS

Great Clarendon Street, Oxford, OX2 6DP,
United Kingdom

Oxford University Press is a department of the University of Oxford.
It furthers the University's objective of excellence in research, scholarship,
and education by publishing worldwide. Oxford is a registered trade mark of
Oxford University Press in the UK and in certain other countries

© Oxford University Press 2021

The moral rights of the authors have been asserted

First Edition published in 2021

Impression: 1

Published in the United States of America by Oxford University Press
198 Madison Avenue, New York, NY 10016, United States of America

British Library Cataloguing in Publication Data
Data available

Library of Congress Control Number: 2021934452

ISBN 978-0-19-289533-2

DOI: 10.1093/oso/9780192895332.001.0001

Printed and bound in the UK by
TJ Books Limited

Contents

Acknowledgements

The papers in this volume were presented at 'The Language of Ontology', a conference held in September 2017 at Trinity College Dublin. I am very grateful for funding for that event from the Irish Research Council (New Foundations Award), the Mind Association (Major Conference Grant), the Trinity Arts and Social Sciences Benefactions Fund, and the Analysis Trust.

Huge thanks must, of course, also go to all the speakers and participants at that event who made it a success. I would also like to thank Una Campbell, Keith Begley, Kenneth Pearce, and Peter Larsen for their help and advice on various aspects of organizing the conference; and to Thomas Hughes, Sarah Sawyer, and Peter Momtchiloff, for their support and advice in bringing this volume together. Lastly, I would like to thank Anna Bortolan for her advice and support throughout the entire process, from initial thoughts about organizing a conference to the final production of this volume.

List of Contributors

Delia Belleri is a FCT Junior Researcher and a member of LanCog (Language, Mind and Cognition Research Group), at the Centre for Philosophy of the University of Lisbon. Her research interests include philosophy of language, metaontology, and metaphilosophy.

Matti Eklund is Chair Professor of Theoretical Philosophy at Uppsala University. His publications are mainly in metaphysics, philosophy of language, philosophy of logic, and metaethics.

Vera Flocke is an Assistant Professor in the Department of Philosophy at Indiana University, Bloomington. She studied philosophy in Berlin, Pittsburgh, and St Andrews before completing her PhD at New York University in 2019.

Eli Hirsch is Professor of Philosophy, Brandeis University. He has generally worked on metaphysics, but more recently wrote a book on epistemology, and has also been teaching courses on normative and metaethics.

Thomas Hofweber is Professor of Philosophy at the University of North Carolina at Chapel Hill. He works mostly in metaphysics, philosophy of language, and philosophy of mathematics, and is the author of *Ontology and the Ambitions of Metaphysics* (OUP, 2016), as well as numerous articles.

James (J. T. M.) Miller is Assistant Professor of Philosophy at Durham University. His work covers topics in metaphysics, philosophy of language, and linguistics, particularly questions at the intersection of those domains. He recently co-edited the *Routledge Handbook of Metametaphysics* (2020).

Friederike Moltmann is Research Director at the French Centre Nationale de la Recherche Scientifique and in recent years has been Visiting Researcher at New York University. Her research focuses on the interface between natural language semantics and philosophy, often in relation to generative syntax. One particular interest of hers is natural language ontology, the branch of metaphysics whose subject matter is the ontology implicit in natural language. She received a PhD in 1992 from MIT and taught both linguistics and philosophy at various universities in the US, the UK, France, and Italy. She is the author of *Parts and Wholes in Semantics* (OUP, 1997) and *Abstract Objects and the Semantics of Natural Language* (OUP, 2013).

Alessandro Torza is a Fellow of the Institute for Philosophical Research at the National Autonomous University of Mexico. He specializes in metaphysics and its interaction with logic and language. His published work covers such topics as modality, laws and counterfactuals, indeterminacy, metametaphysics, and assorted Lewisiana. He is editor-in-chief of *Crítica: Revista Hispanoamericana de Filosofía*.

Richard Woodward works at the Humboldt University in Berlin. His research interests are located in metaphysics (especially modality, fictionalism, indeterminacy, and metaontology), the philosophy of language (especially vagueness, conditionals, and metasemantics), and aesthetics (photography, fiction, and the imagination).

Stephen Yablo is David W. Skinner Professor of Philosophy in the Department of Linguistics and Philosophy at MIT. He specializes in metaphysics, philosophy of math, and philosophy of mind and language.

Introduction

The Language of Ontology

J. T. M. Miller

Metametaphysics and metaontology are not new domains of inquiry. For as long as there has been metaphysical theorizing, there has been debate about the scope, methods, and limits of metaphysics. However, in the last two decades, the previously often sporadic and isolated interest in metametaphysics has consolidated into a lively and growing domain which includes, but is not limited to, historical work on various key figures in the history of philosophy, the analysis of a number of foundational concepts of metaphysical inquiry, reflection on the relationship between metaphysics and science, and direct debate about whether or not metaphysics is a substantive domain.[1]

In recent years, it has also become common to talk about metaphysical and ontological theories as 'languages'.[2] Disputing metaphysicians are, under this way of framing the issue, engaged in a dispute about which 'language' is the 'best' (or 'fundamental' or 'privileged')—a debate about which language accurately describes reality (or whose terms 'carve nature at its joints' or are 'reference magnets'). One advantage of this way of conceiving of metaphysics is that it allows the metaphysician to avoid concerns about how we ordinarily use language. For example, it does not matter whether 'Tables exist' is true in English as English is not the ontologically best language. What matters is whether 'Tables exist' is true in the best language (or 'Ontologese', or the language of the ontology room, or the privileged language). The job of the metaphysician therefore becomes one of working out what is true in *the* language of ontology—the language that only includes terms that carve nature at its joints.[3]

Understanding metaphysics in this way faces a number of issues. For example, it is not obvious how the variety of metaphors employed in the above characterization should be cashed out. What does it mean to say that a language is 'privileged', or that it 'carves nature at its joints'?

---

[1] See Bliss and Miller (2020) for an overview of the range of topics within contemporary metametaphysics.

[2] Though there are older traditions that would accept this way of phrasing ontological talk, in my experience the recent trend towards using 'language' in this way often links back to Dorr (2005).

[3] Or, perhaps more precisely, the language whose non-logical terms carve nature at its joints; cf. Sider (2011).

J. T. M. Miller, *Introduction: The Language of Ontology* In: *The Language of Ontology*. Edited by: J. T. M. Miller, Oxford University Press (2021). © Oxford University Press. DOI: 10.1093/oso/9780192895332.003.0001

Furthermore, the approach seems to do little to assuage concerns about our epistemic access to reality, or, put another way, our ability to know what is true in the metaphysically best language. How could we know that we are stating truths in the best language, and how do we know that we even could express truths in such a language? After all, it cannot simply be through an act of will that we come to speak Ontologese, just as much as stating that I am speaking Italian does mean that I am.

The chapters in this volume address issues related to these concerns and various others arising from a focus on the language of ontology. The chapters focus on questions about whether the nature of language itself restricts, shapes, or otherwise influences the ontological theories and debates expressed in that language. It seems necessary for creatures such as us that ontological questions are expressed in language (be that natural languages such as English, French, or Swahili, or formal languages such as those of logic, mathematics, or 'Ontologese'). The chapters in this volume (in various ways) aim to reflect on the nature of language as a way to reveal something about the nature of metaphysics itself, and potentially the substantivity (or non-substantivity) of ontological debates.

The centrality of questions about the nature of language when considering the substantivity of metaphysics can be seen by considering one prominent divide in the literature (and one that will arise in some form in many of the contributions to this volume). On one side are those that endorse a substantive (or metaontological realist) account of metaphysics wherein metaphysical questions and statements are substantive claims about the structure of the world. On the other are those that support a more deflationary view of metaphysics which takes those same metaphysical and ontological questions and statements as unable to live up to such rigorous demands.

To give a better sense of these positions, albeit far too briefly, consider the idea that is implicit in many, if not most, first-order ontological disputes that certain ways of speaking, terms, or entire languages are 'objectively better' than others. This idea, for many, seems to imply that there could be a language that is not merely 'better', but is *the* 'objectively best' (or is the metaphysically 'privileged', or 'fundamental', language).

However, deflationary accounts argue that metaphysical statements are ultimately only (or merely) about our concepts, our language, or our view of the world. Metaphysics would then be about the ways that we contingently happen to speak and think about the world, not about reality itself. Such views draw inspiration from, in particular, the work of Carnap (1950, 1959) and Putnam (1975). They argue, for a variety of reasons, that there cannot be an objectively best language that accurately describes the objective similarities and differences in reality. Many would reject the idea that natural language could just happen to be the objectively best language, but the principle carries over to the more formal languages of the physicist, biologist, economist, and metaphysician, making all-encompassing questions about existence, and the nature of those things that exist, non-substantive.

It is worth stressing, though, that for these arguments to run counter to a substantive account of metaphysics, there must be at least two of these different languages, or different sets of ontological expressions, that are expressively equal, or truth-conditionally equivalent. Without this, the thesis would only be the claim that there are these different languages or sets of ontological expressions, and we could still hold that one could be privileged. The deflationist must admit of no hierarchy of expressive richness in relation to the world (as opposed to pragmatic reasons for choosing one language over another). A harmless (to substantive metaphysics) view that few would find controversial is that there are many different, potentially infinitely many, sets of ontological expressions, or languages within which to express metaphysical claims. The controversy lies in the denial of any privileged set amongst those sets of ontological expressions, and importantly, privileged in a metaphysical sense, rather than some pragmatic or other sense.

If the deflationists are right, metaphysical debates lack the significance that metaphysicians generally take them to have. Metaphysical debates are non-substantive, merely verbal, in some sense 'easy' to solve, or even nonsensical. Some of the most notable examples, and that will be discussed in the chapters in this volume, are arguments from 'quantifier variance' (see Hirsch 2011), 'easy ontology' (see Thomasson 2015) and the related neo-Fregean view (see Hale and Wright 2001, 2009), and (global) expressivism (see Price 2011).

This is just to give a taster of one strand of debate arising from the language of ontology. This volume brings together new work from established and emerging authors that discusses these and various related questions connected to the possibility and coherency of a privileged language, what the consequences for metaphysical debates are if we deny the existence of an objectively best language, and the relationship between natural language and any putative 'objectively best' language. Together, these collected essays illustrate the strong connection between the nature of language and metametaphysics, and will provide inspiration for future research on these and related topics. In what remains of this Introduction, I will briefly summarize the main themes and questions in each of the chapters.

In 'Ontology by Stipulation', Eli Hirsch builds upon his highly influential previous work on 'quantifier variance' through a new deflationary line of argument. Hirsch argues that in cases where we observe an ontological dispute, we can introduce by stipulation languages for each disputant in such a way that it allows us to express all of the facts that are relevant to that debate. In this way, Hirsch argues that those engaging in ontological disputes need not disagree about what facts hold, and explains how this is the case even in situations where we posit fine-grained facts.

In 'Are Ontological Questions Meaningless?', Delia Belleri argues that even a Carnapian should accept that ontological statements are meaningful. Belleri argues that we can respond to a semantic critique of ontology through conceiving of Ontologese as a Carnapian framework itself. This move renders ontological claims meaningful, even to the Carnapian. However, Belleri goes on to argue that this may not vindicate ontology in the way that most metaontological realists want, and that ontology may still face serious deflationary concerns, such as from epistemic critiques.

In 'Collapse and the Varieties of Quantifier Variance', Matti Eklund distinguishes between the different theses that might all be called 'quantifier variance', and considers the significance of these different theses. Eklund goes on to consider how these different versions of quantifier variance fare with respect to the collapse argument, and the Eklund-Hawthorne argument. Eklund also suggests the need to distinguish between variance theses that concern actual languages, and those that concern possible languages, and considers how this distinction might affect how we interpret those variance claims.

In 'Ontological Expressivism', Vera Flocke outlines the thesis of 'ontological expressivism' as the view that ontological existence claims express non-cognitive states of mind. Flocke's aim is not to defend ontological expressivism, but to show how there is a coherent version of expressivism to be applied to ontological discourse. Under this view, speakers do not make a factual mistake by asserting the truth or falsity of ontological existence propositions, but instead express a non-cognitive disposition to assess the truth of propositions by considering those worlds at which numbers exist.

In 'Why Our Natural Languages Are Ideal Languages for Metaphysics', Thomas Hofweber argues that, contra how they are often supposed, natural languages are perfectly matched to the facts and thus ideally suited to describe reality. Importantly, Hofweber argues that we have reason to think that natural languages perfectly fit reality without first knowing what reality is like. Central to Hofweber's view is the argument that if internalism is true for our own talk about facts, then there cannot be ineffable facts. This means that our natural language can represent all of the facts within the domain of metaphysics, and is ideal for metaphysics.

In 'What Counts as a "Good" Metaphysical Language?', J. T. M. Miller focuses on the deflationist claim that there are 'equally good' languages for describing reality, and on how we might understand the normativity of 'good' in this context. Miller argues that for languages to be compared to see if one is better (or that they are equally good), they must share the same semantic purpose. After distinguishing coarse- and fine-grained semantic purposes for languages, Miller argues that we can identify a semantic purpose against which we can compare putative 'privileged' metaphysical languages, and that, contra deflationism, claims that languages are equally good relative to this purpose rely on substantive first-order metaphysical claims.

In 'The Questions of Ontology', Richard Woodward responds to the recent critique of Quine's metaontological views from Kit Fine. Woodward argues that a Quinean approach can, contra Fine, both accommodate the apparent triviality of many existential questions and secure the autonomy of ontological existence questions from ordinary language. In this way, Woodward argues that the

Quinean ontological inquiry can continue beyond the point at which we have answered existence questions in ordinary language.

In 'What "X Does Not Exist" Says About We Who Do Exist', Stephen Yablo takes up the question of what it means to say that something does *not* exist, taking as his starting point a worry about the overdetermination of why negative existentials are true, and Kripke's discussion of negative existential statements such as *Holmes does not exist*. Yablo considers various ways in which we might account for the cognitive content of these sorts of sentences, in particular stressing that we need a view that allows us to adequately distinguish between why *Holmes does not exist* is distinct from other true negative existentials, such as *Vulcan does not exist*. The solution, for Yablo, is to hold that singular nonexistence claims, when true, are true because of facts like: $\forall x$ (*x is not Holmes, even if Holmes exists*).

In 'Structural Pluralism', Alessandro Torza outlines and defends the position of 'structural pluralism'—the view that there is a plurality of primitive notions of 'structural'. This view is particularly important in the context of Sider's defence of the notion of structure as central to metaontological realism. Torza argues that structural pluralism can avoid various problems associated with structural monism, and leads to a novel form of ontological deflationism—pluralistic quantifier variance. However, Torza argues that this form of deflationism, whilst compatible with the possibility of non-substantive ontological disagreement, is more moderate than other forms of deflationism derived from quantifier variance.

In 'Levels of Ontology and Natural Language: The Case of the Ontology of Parts and Wholes', Friederike Moltmann argues for the need to recognize a level of ontology—'language-driven ontology'—that is distinct from both the ontology of fundamental entities and the ontology of ordinary objects. The argument for this level of ontology comes from a linguistic analysis of how we talk about parts and wholes. This creates a new way that ontology and language might be connected, with this language-driven ontology being tied to the functional part of language, not the semantic part. Moltmann argues that this new level of ontology has significant consequences for our notion of unity, especially given the (in Moltmann's view) mandatory acceptance of language-driven ontology when we use language.

References

Bliss, R. and Miller, J. T. M. (eds.) 2020. *The Routledge Handbook of Metametaphysics.* London: Routledge.

Carnap, R. 1950. 'Empiricism, Semantics, and Ontology', *Revue Internationale de Philosophie*, 4: 20–40. Reprinted in the *Supplement to Meaning and Necessity: A Study in Semantics and Modal Logic*, 1956, University of Chicago Press.

Carnap, R. 1959. 'The Elimination of Metaphysics Through Logical Analysis of Language', trans. A. Pap. In A. J. Ayer (ed.), *Logical Positivism*, 60–81. Glencoe, IL: Free Press.

Dorr, C. 2005. 'What We Disagree About When We Disagree About Ontology'. In M. E. Kalderon (ed.), *Fictionalism in Metaphysics*, 234–286. Oxford: Oxford University Press.

Hale, B. and Wright, C. 2001. *The Reason's Proper Study: Essays Towards a Neo-Fregean Philosophy of Mathematics*. Oxford: Oxford University Press.

Hale, B. and Wright, C. 2009. 'The Metaontology of Abstraction'. In D. J. Chalmers, D. Manley, and R. Wasserman (eds.), *Metametaphysics: New Essays on the Foundations of Ontology*, 178–212. Oxford: Oxford University Press.

Hirsch, E. 2011. *Quantifier Variance and Realism: Essays in Metaontology*. New York: Oxford University Press.

Price, H. 2011. *Naturalism Without Mirrors*. New York: Oxford University Press.

Putnam, H. 1975. *Mind, Language and Reality: Philosophical Papers, vol. 2*. Cambridge: Cambridge University Press.

Sider, T. 2011. *Writing the Book of the World*. New York: Oxford University Press.

Thomasson, A. L. 2015. *Ontology Made Easy*. Oxford: Oxford University Press.

1

Ontology by Stipulation

Eli Hirsch

In previous work I suggested that many ontological disputes can be viewed as merely verbal, in that each side can be charitably interpreted as speaking the truth in its own language. Critics have objected that it is more plausible to view the disputants as speaking the same language, perhaps even a special philosophy-room language, sometimes called Ontologese.[1] In this chapter I want to suggest a different kind of deflationary move, in a way more extreme (possibly more Carnapian) than my previous suggestion. Let's suppose we encounter an ontological dispute between two sides, the A-side and the B-side, and we assume that they are speaking the same language so that (at least) one of them is mistaken (perhaps the common language is Ontologese). My suggestion is that we can introduce by stipulation two languages, one for each side, such that in speaking the A-side stipulated language we capture whatever facts might be expressed in the A-side's position, and in speaking the B-side stipulated language we capture whatever facts might be expressed in the B-side's position. In this way we get whatever facts there might be in this ontological area without risking falsehood. This can be accomplished even if we believe in fine-grained facts. Let me try to explain how this works.

1.1

Suppose that language L1 and language L2 have the same sentences (phonetically individuated) and any sentence, relative to any context of utterance, has the same truth conditions in L1 and L2 (where sameness of truth conditions is sameness of truth-value with respect to any possible world).[2] I'll then say that L1 and L2 are *truth-conditionally indiscernible*. And let's say that L1 and L2 are *referentially indiscernible* if any expression (relative to any context of utterance) has the same

---

[1] See especially Dorr (2005); Sider (2011), p. 171.

[2] Since the ontological disputes do not directly concern either meta-level sentences or sentences attributing intentional states, let it be understood that such sentences are excluded from the definitions and principles that I formulate in this section. I think they could be accommodated, but they introduce irrelevant complications.

Eli Hirsch, *Ontology by Stipulation* In: *The Language of Ontology*. Edited by: J. T. M. Miller, Oxford University Press (2021).
© Oxford University Press. DOI: 10.1093/oso/9780192895332.003.0002

intension—the same reference with respect to any possible world—in L1 and L2. Now consider the following thesis:

Referential Supervenience. It is necessarily the case that if L1 and L2 are truth-conditionally indiscernible, then L1 and L2 are referentially indiscernible.

The thesis of referential supervenience makes a claim about a necessary relationship between truth and reference. It should not be taken to say anything about whether reference or truth is in some sense more fundamental.

The thesis of the inscrutability of reference entails the thesis of referential supervenience, but the converse entailment does not hold. A *reference scheme* for a anguage is an assignment of (n-tuples of) objects to the expressions of the language in a way that generates the correct truth conditions of the sentences of the language. It's well known that there must be an indefinite number of different reference schemes for any language. The inscrutability thesis says that, amongst these reference schemes, there isn't a privileged one that is the real reference relation; any reference scheme can count as the reference relation.[3] Referential supervenience trivially follows, because it is necessarily the case that if L1 and L2 are truth-conditionally indiscernible, then L1 and L2 have the same reference schemes.

Inscrutability, however, is not at all entailed by referential supervenience. The latter can perfectly well allow that there is for any language a privileged reference scheme, determined perhaps by considerations of causality or property naturalness, but that the truth conditions of the sentences settle which is the privileged reference scheme for the language.

To be clear, referential supervenience does not imply that it is impossible for a sentence to belong to two languages, and to have the same truth conditions in both languages, but to contain an expression that has a different reference in the different languages. Imagine a version of English, English*, in which the word 'seller' refers to any buyer and the word 'buyer' refers to any seller (where I'm here taking sellers and buyers to be people who, respectively, succeed in selling and buying). Since the English sentence 'There exists a seller' is truth-conditionally equivalent to the English sentence 'There exists a buyer', the sentence 'There exists a seller' has the same truth conditions in both English and English*. But the word 'seller' does not have the same reference in English and English*. This is evidenced by the fact that numerous other sentences containing the word 'seller' do not have the same truth conditions in English and English*. That kind of evidence of a difference of reference is absent where languages are truth-conditionally indiscernible. And absent that kind of evidence, it seems difficult to make any sense of the idea that there is a difference of reference. What could explain a

---

[3] This view seems to be held at times by Quine (1960) and Davidson (1984).

difference of reference that has no connection to truth conditions? What could such a difference amount to?

Given these clarifications, I would expect referential supervenience to be acceptable to many philosophers. And here, finally, is the thesis on which my stipulation maneuver will depend:

> *Propositional Supervenience.*   It is necessarily the case that if L1 and L2 are ruth-conditionally indiscernible, then any sentence (relative to any context of utterance) expresses the same proposition in L1 and L2.

Discussions of propositions in the literature sometimes lean inward toward cognitive states and meanings-in-the-head and sometimes outwards toward non-linguistic and non-mental facts in the world. It is always the latter sense that should be understood in the present discussion, since ontological controversy, at least in the sorts of examples I want to consider, is thought by the ontologists engaged in the controversy to be aiming for the objective mind-independent facts or truths; these are not supposed to be controversies about our cognitive states. (I will say something more about this in section IV.) Propositional supervenience is the thesis that true sentences in L1 and L2 express the same objective facts, where a fact can be roughly identified with a true proposition (and any proposition might be roughly identified with a fact that may or may not obtain).

There are two main views about the nature of propositions in this objective-fact sense. On the coarse-grained view, championed by Lewis and Stalnaker, propositions are identified with truth conditions or with possible worlds. On this view, propositional supervenience is trivially correct. It follows, I think, that, on this view, the stipulation maneuver that I'm going to describe is also trivially correct. But my interest here is in satisfying philosophers who believe in fine-grained (hyperintensional) propositions.[4]

The fine-grained view of objective propositions has many exotic twists and spins, but one quite central version holds that a proposition is a structured item whose structure matches the structure of some sentence that expresses it, and whose constituents are the referents of the terms of the sentence.[5] Fine-grained theorists who reject the letter of the structured-proposition version will often accept the following principle: if two sentences have the same logical form, and corresponding words refer (at any context of utterance) to the same referents (with respect to any world), then the sentences express the same proposition (the same fact).[6] The clause 'at any context of utterance' is intended to leave room for

---

[4] There is, most assuredly, nothing in this chapter to discourage skepticism about the notion of objective fine-grained propositions. My aim, however, is to argue that, even if one accepts this notion, the stipulation maneuver may succeed.

[5] Seminal formulations are in Russell (1903), Kaplan (1989), and Salmon (1986).

[6] An alternative to the above principle might be to hold that in order for two sentences to express the same proposition it is required not only that corresponding words, as used in any context of

arguing that co-extensional proper names or kind-names do not have the same reference in other possible contexts of utterance. (And note that the principle says 'if', not 'only if': the stated conditions are sufficient but may not be necessary.) It immediately follows from this principle that referential supervenience implies propositional supervenience, since, if L1 and L2 are referentially indiscernible, any sentence in L1 and that same sentence in L2 trivially satisfy the conditions in the principle. I would therefore expect that many fine-grained theorists who are thinking of propositions in the objective-fact sense will be attracted to propositional supervenience.

It is certainly not my aim here to elaborate, let alone defend, some specific conception of fine-grained objective propositions or facts. I've given a broad and flexible formulation that seems to cover many familiar versions of the conception, and from which propositional supervenience seems to follow.

It should be understood that referential and propositional supervenience do not necessarily imply that truth-conditionally indiscernible languages L1 and L2 are one and the same language. There is, first, the obvious point that some utterances are instances of speech acts that do not have truth conditions, and L1 and L2 may differ in the meanings of such utterances. But, also, there may be some kinds of hyperintensional differences in the cognitive states expressed in L1 and L2 beyond the objective propositions or facts expressed. The only assumption required in what follows is that, if L1 and L2 are truth-conditionally indiscernible, any sentence expresses the same objective proposition or fact in L1 and L2.

1.2

Let me now begin to explain the stipulation maneuver. Suppose we come across the organicist van Inwagen debating the four-dimensionalist Lewis. In the background of their dispute is a large body of *uncontroversial sentences*—sentences that they would both acknowledge to be outside the range of their dispute. These would include many sentences about simples, about living things, and about sets and perhaps other abstract things. One kind of uncontroversial sentence is, 'There is a set of table-wise interrelated simples'. A controversial sentence is, 'There is something composed of a set of table-wise interrelated simples'.

For my purposes here I'll count a sentence S as controversial iff it satisfies one of the following three conditions: (a) there is disagreement about the truth-value of S (where disagreement might consist in one side being committed to a certain truth-value of S while the other side is agnostic); (b) there is disagreement about

---

utterance, have the same reference in any possible world, but also that the words stand in some putatively stronger relation of *synonymy*. I will here assume, however, that an account of propositions that aims outwards toward non-linguistic and non-mental facts in the world will not appeal to synonymy (insofar as the latter involves sameness of cognitive states).

whether S is contingent; or (c) S is a compound sentence one of whose components is a sentence that satisfies (a) or (b).[7]

This dispute between Lewis and van Inwagen satisfies the following *equivalence condition*: for any controversial sentence C, each disputant is prepared to specify an uncontroversial sentence U such that this disputant claims that C and U are *truth-conditionally equivalent*; that is, C and U, relative to any context of utterance, hold true in the same worlds. What the disputants disagree about is which controversial and uncontroversial sentences are truth-conditionally equivalent to each other.

I will now stipulate into existence two versions of English that I'll call 'S-Inwagen' and 'S-Lewis'. 'S' is for 'stipulation'. These are my stipulated languages; I'm not at this point suggesting that either of them is used by van Inwagen or Lewis. It's stipulated that in both S-Inwagen and S-Lewis the uncontroversial sentences function in the manner agreed upon by van Inwagen and Lewis. In S-Inwagen it's stipulated that the truth conditions of the controversial sentences stand to the truth conditions of the uncontroversial sentences in just the way that is claimed by van Inwagen; and in S-Lewis it's stipulated that the truth conditions of the controversial sentences stand to the truth conditions of the uncontroversial sentences in just the way that is claimed by Lewis. For example, in S-Inwagen it's stipulated that the controversial sentence 'There is something composed of a set of table-wise interrelated simples' is truth-conditionally equivalent to the uncontroversially false sentence 'There is a living thing that is composed of a set of table-wise interrelated simples'; and in S-Lewis it's stipulated that the controversial sentence 'There is something composed of a set of table-wise interrelated simples' is truth-conditionally equivalent to the uncontroversially true sentence 'There is a set of table-wise interrelated simples'.[8]

Suppose now that van Inwagen is right about which uncontroversial and controversial sentences are truth-conditionally equivalent to each other; in the language he is using his claims about the equivalences are correct. Given that van Inwagen is right in his claims about the equivalences, it follows that, since his claims about the equivalences are stipulated to be correct in my S-Inwagen language, the language he is using is truth-conditionally indiscernible from my S-Inwagen language. Therefore, if I assert in S-Inwagen the same sentences van Inwagen asserts, I am asserting the same facts he is asserting. So, if he is right, I am right, and right about the same facts he is right about. And if he is wrong (the equivalences do not hold in his language), I'm still right, since in my S-Inwagen language the equivalences hold by stipulation.[9]

---

[7] A more inclusive definition of 'controversial' might require some changes of formulations in what follows but would not, I think, make any substantive difference.

[8] I am here ignoring the possibility of gunk, which would complicate the equivalences but not alter the essential point.

[9] To be more accurate, I am right on the assumption that the 'uncontroversial sentences' agreed on by the disputants are true. Let that assumption be understood in all that follows.

The corresponding point holds for Lewis's position. If he is right in what he asserts about the equivalences, then my corresponding assertions in my S-Lewis language express the same facts he asserts. And if he is wrong, I am anyway right. This is for me a win-win situation. If either of these philosophers have the facts, I have those same facts in one of my languages, and I suffer no risk of error.[10]

Of course, I have not determined which, if either, of these philosophers is right. And I have not ruled out that they are in fact speaking different languages and both are right. But these questions, though they might understandably be of interest to the philosophers involved, do not seem to be ontological questions about the facts, about objective reality. As regards objective reality, it seems that I have by way of stipulation secured whatever facts in this area these philosophers might be asserting.

The success of the stipulation maneuver doesn't seem threatened by the possibility that both philosophers are using Ontologese, the special philosophy-room language. If either one of them is asserting facts in Ontologese, then I am asserting those facts in one of my languages, and that language, I suppose, would have a claim to being itself Ontologese.

But, it may be objected, isn't it a matter of philosophical importance *which* language is Ontologese? The facts expressed in Ontologese are supposed to be in some sense *fundamental*; they are supposed to be in some sense the ground of facts expressed in lesser languages. Insofar as I don't know which, if either, of my two stipulated languages is Ontologese, the objection goes, I don't know which facts are fundamental.

My answer is that questions about fundamentality are just further grist for the stipulative maneuver. Let's imagine a kind of organicist O who agrees with a four-dimensionalist F that there are such things as (non-living) tables but holds that facts about the existence of non-living composite things are not fundamental, whereas F holds that such facts are fundamental. Their dispute, then, concerns sentences like 'It is fundamental that there exists a (non-living) table'.[11] I assume that O will consider this sentence (relative to any context of utterance) to be not

---

[10] It might be objected that there cannot be a stipulation on behalf of the side that is wrong. If Lewis, say, is wrong and van Inwagen is right, then there is no structured fact that could play the role of corresponding to the structure of the allegedly true sentence 'This table is brown' in S-Lewis. I will suggest three answers to this objection. The third is the hardest but the one that I think goes to the heart of the matter. (1) It must be possible to stipulate truth conditions for sentences. The stipulation can at least allow 'This table is brown' to be true by virtue of correctly expressing a coarse-grained fact. (2) Even if it were the case that one of my stipulations does not come off, I have 'no risk of error' at least in the sense of 'no risk of making any false assertion (and no risk of missing out on any facts)'. (3) What counts as a 'structured fact' varies from language to language, and the question whether the S-Lewis sentence 'This table is brown' expresses a structured fact can itself be answered by stipulation. In the S-Lewis language it is correct to say, 'The sentence "This table is brown" expresses the structured fact that this table is brown'. There is no linguistically neutral standpoint from which to declare what are the 'structured facts'.

[11] This seems to be the sort of ontological dispute envisioned in Dorr (2005).

just false, but necessarily false, and therefore truth-conditionally equivalent to such uncontroversial impossibilities as 'Something is not identical with itself', whereas F will hold the sentence to be truth-conditionally equivalent to the uncontroversially true 'There exists a (non-living) table'.[12] The stipulation maneuver, therefore, applies to this dispute: in my stipulated language on behalf of O, I can without risk of error assert whatever facts O may be asserting; and in my stipulated language on behalf of F, I can without risk of error assert whatever facts F may be asserting.

Let's look at another example related to fundamentality. Fine and Sider seem to agree that it is fundamental that there exists an electron, but they disagree about whether it is fundamental that either there exists an electron or there exists an electron.[13] I take it that Fine claims that such disjunctions are necessarily non-fundamental; so Fine holds that the sentence 'It is fundamental that either there exists an electron or there exists an electron' is truth-conditionally equivalent to some uncontroversial impossibility. Sider, on the other hand, presumably holds that the sentence is truth-conditionally equivalent to the uncontroversial sentence 'It is fundamental that there exists an electron'. I can therefore easily stipulate that in my S-Fine language the equivalence held by Fine holds, whereas in my S-Sider language the equivalence held by Sider holds. Although the details would have to be carefully examined, I think it is plausible to suppose that the same maneuver can work for any other dispute between Fine and Sider about what is fundamental. Then, if I assert in my S-Fine language the sentences Fine asserts and I assert in my S-Sider language the sentences Sider asserts, I have asserted whatever facts about fundamentality these philosophers might have asserted; and I do so without any risk of error. Bringing fundamentality into the story does not clearly change anything.

A different kind of example concerns issues of modal metaphysics. In Williamson's book on that topic he defends the doctrine of necessitism, which says that whatever exists, exists by necessity.[14] Kripke, throughout all of his work, rejects necessitism.[15] Here the stipulation maneuver seems to apply straightforwardly, at least on the plausible assumption that Williamson presents his doctrine as being necessarily true and Kripke rejects it as being necessarily false. In my S-Williamson language the doctrine of necessitism is stipulated to be truth-conditionally equivalent to an uncontroversial necessity, whereas in my S-Kripke language the doctrine is stipulated to be truth-conditionally equivalent to an uncontroversial impossibility. My risk-free assertions in these languages will then deliver whatever facts there might be about necessitism.

---

[12] In order for 'p' to be truth-conditionally equivalent to 'q', it is not enough that the sentence, 'Necessarily p iff q' is true; it must be true relative to any possible context of utterance. In what follows, for ease of exposition, I will often omit mention of contexts of utterance.

[13] Sider (2011), pp. 148ff.; Fine (2013).   [14] Williamson (2013).

[15] For example, Kripke (1980).

It must be understood that the stipulation maneuver is meant to undermine the significance of certain metaphysical *disputes*; it does not undermine the significance of any *statements* made on either side of the dispute, let alone any of the uncontroversial statements. (Each stipulated language may in some sense embody a different and potentially interesting 'framework'.) Moreover, it is meant to apply to certain *actual* disputes that have occurred within philosophy. I claim, for example, that the particular dispute between Sider and Fine about disjunctive facts is vulnerable to the stipulation maneuver. And I suggest that any other dispute between them about fundamentality can in all likelihood be treated in the same way. And, I would say, the same holds for disputes about fundamentality between Fine and Schaffer or between Sider and Schaffer, or between the various other philosophers who have been arguing about fundamentality. But I am not able to rule out the possibility that there could be a dispute about fundamentality that cannot be treated in this way. Everything depends on there being uncontroversial sentences in terms of which each side can stipulate the equivalences required to construct a language for the other side. It is most emphatically not being claimed that the concept of fundamentality can be analyzed or defined in other terms. The same points hold for all of the other examples I discuss in this chapter.

In all of these examples I could have directly stipulated that in the S-languages certain sentences have certain truth conditions, instead of doing this indirectly by stipulating that certain equivalences hold. It's seems, however, a bit easier to start out with certain uncontroversial sentences whose truth conditions are taken as understood, and then to stipulate that certain other sentences are truth-conditionally equivalent to the ones whose truth conditions are understood. Of course, there are an indefinite number of relevant equivalences, and it's not possible to simply list them all in introducing my different S-language. I'm not going to take that problem very seriously, however. The equivalences can be roughly indicated, as I have done. That should be enough, I think, to introduce the different S-languages. Alternatively, one can think of the equivalences as not being directly stipulated, but rather as deriving from other stipulations. In the example of the dispute between organicists and four-dimensionalists, one can arrive at the two S-languages by stipulating differences in the way the quantifier operates in the languages.[16] (The S-Inwagen and S-Lewis languages will certainly exhibit some form of *quantifier variance* regardless of where the focus of the stipulations is.) In the examples pertaining to fundamentality the stipulation might be to different intensions of the word 'fundamental', and here it might be possible to give a finitary list of the different basic categories of truths that Fine or Sider count as fundamental. In the modal example the stipulation might again be

---

[16] The stipulations might be accomplished in the manner of Dorr (2005), Hirsch (2011), pp. 234–243, and especially Hirsch and Warren (2019).

about the quantifiers. Having mentioned this problem, I will ignore it in what follows, and talk about stipulating equivalences.

Something needs to be said about the notion of stipulation itself. Certainly, stipulating that one is using language in a certain way amounts to nothing unless one actually goes on to use the language in that way. This is why the relevant stipulations could not be of the general form, for example, 'Let the sentences of the S-Inwagen language have the truth conditions corresponding to van Inwagen's beliefs'; the stipulations must specify certain sentences and stipulate what their truth conditions are in a manner that would allow the sentences actually to be used in accordance with those truth conditions. It might then be asked what the semantic force is of making a stipulation: one's use of the language will determine by interpretive charity what one means, with or without the stipulation. I think, however, that stipulating specific equivalences has some significant force. For example, suppose you stipulate in the introduction to a book, 'I will always use "fish" as equivalent to "aquatic creature that has a fish-like shape"'. Given this stipulation, the statement 'Whales are big fish' is true. Considerations of reference magnetism, or of Burgean communal pressures, do not cancel the stipulation, so long as your use of 'fish' accords with the stipulation. If later in the book you start saying, 'It's necessary for a fish to have a certain kind of internal structure', I don't think we should say that because of 'charity to retraction'[17] you were wrong when you initially said, 'Whales are big fish'. Rather, we should say that you have (carelessly, inadvertently) changed your language and given up the stipulation, but that your sentence 'Whales are big fish' was true in your previous stipulated language. I don't know if 'charity to stipulation' brings something essentially new into the story besides 'use', but I think it can count significantly. The example I just mentioned shows that stipulation can render as ineffectual appeals (a) to future charity to retraction, (b) to reference magnetism, and (c) to Burgean considerations about the community language. In this new stipulation maneuver that I'm trying to explain, I hope to satisfy some of the people who have rejected my previous appeal to charity as showing that each side speaks the truth in its own language. These critics have often appealed to consideration of (a), (b), or (c). I think even these critics should agree that the assertions I make in one of my S-languages are true by stipulation.

If it seems shocking that I can arrive by stipulation at the same true propositions that ontologists arrive at with intuitive insights and arguments, it must be borne in mind that stipulating is not waving a magic wand that produces facts; it is rather a speech act that tilts the force of interpretive charity in a certain direction. When the ontologists assert their favored equivalences and the various ontological sentences coming out of those equivalences, there is a charitable presumption that

---

[17] See Hirsch (2011), pp. 151, 180.

they are speaking a language in which those assertions are true. The same holds for the assertions I make in my S-languages, except that the effect of my stipulations is that the charitable presumption is virtually indefeasible. (In my previous work, which I'm putting aside here but by no means retracting, I suggested that the charitable presumption suffices even for the ontologists.) It does not seem so surprising that the ontologists and I arrive at the same true propositions, the same facts, by somewhat different semantic routes.

But here is a general caveat. I'm not sure exactly what is involved in 'adopting a language'. I think we can distinguish between a weaker and stronger sense. I can adopt one of my stipulated S-languages in the sense that I intend to use the sentences of the language in accordance with the stipulated truth conditions. But there is a sense in which I continue to *think* in my original language. Perhaps this can change after a time, but I cannot immediately adopt the S-language in the sense of having this be the language that corresponds to my cognitive activity. I'm assuming, however, that adopting the S-language in the weaker sense suffices for me to be able to assert all the objective propositions, all the facts, asserted by the ontologist who is right, and that is all that matters for my argument. That my cognitive states are in a sense different from those of the ontologist does not seem crucial. (Again, see section IV for more on this point.)

1.3

Let me now consider what limits there are on the stipulation maneuver. The most basic constraint (possibly not the only one) is what I will call the *equivalence constraint*. This constraint requires that, in order for the stipulation maneuver to succeed, the previously mentioned equivalence condition must by satisfied, that is, for any controversial sentence C, each disputant is prepared to specify an uncontroversial sentence U that is truth-conditionally equivalent to C.

I will illustrate this constraint by considering a dispute about the Goldbach conjecture. This is a dispute about the Goldbach sentence G: 'Any even number greater than 2 is the sum of two primes'. Suppose that the Acceptance-side affirms G and the Rejection-side denies G. I assume that both the affirmation and the denial are intended as necessities. I can stipulate that in the S-Acceptance language the sentence G is truth-conditionally equivalent to an uncontroversial necessity, and that in the S-Rejection language the sentence G is truth-conditionally equivalent to an uncontroversial impossibility. Would this have the effect that, whichever side is right, I can without risk of falsehood assert the facts of that side in one of my stipulated languages? No, this cannot be done. Let me try to explain why.

In applying the stipulation maneuver, one must leave the uncontroversial sentences alone; otherwise one won't wind up with an S-language that is truth-conditionally indiscernible from the language being used by the side that is right. Moreover, the maneuver must be applicable on neutral grounds; that is, without begging any questions as to which side is right. What that amounts to is that the two S-languages, one for each side, can be stipulated from the standpoint of either side.

A dispute about the Goldbach sentence G must carry over to a dispute about such 'applied sentences' as the sentence H: 'If the number of stars is even (and greater than two), then the number of stars is the sum of two primes'. The Acceptance-side will consider H to express a necessity, while the Rejection-side will consider H to express a contingency. Suppose I adopt the Acceptance-side. Could I then stipulate that in the S-Rejection language the sentence H has the contingency truth conditions claimed by the Rejection-side? The problem is that I have no way, given my Acceptance-standpoint, of specifying what those contingency truth conditions are. The source of the problem is that the equivalence condition is not satisfied by this dispute, for the Rejection-side does not hold that sentence H is truth-conditionally equivalent to any uncontroversial sentence. I am therefore unable, from the Acceptance-side, to stipulate relevant contingency truth conditions for many such sentences as H. Therefore, I cannot achieve the effect of making the S-Rejection language truth-conditionally equivalent to the language used by the Rejection-side, if that side is right.

The fact that I cannot, from the Acceptance-side, successfully stipulate an S-Rejection language suffices to show that the stipulation maneuver cannot apply to the Goldbach conjecture. It would be puzzling, however, if I could so much as successfully stipulate, from the Rejection-side, an S-Acceptance language. For, if I could do that, I would at least acquire in the S-Acceptance language a risk-free method of asserting whatever fact the Acceptance-side might be asserting. However, this is actually not possible. I can indeed stipulate that in my S-Acceptance language the sentence H is equivalent to an uncontroversial necessity, which is the equivalence claimed by the Acceptance-side. But this is not enough to successfully stipulate an S-Acceptance language. Consider that the Acceptance-side would endorse an inference from the uncontroversial sentence 'The number of stars is even (and greater than two)' to the uncontroversial sentence 'The number of stars is the sum of two primes'. (These sentences are uncontroversial insofar as both sides are uncertain of their truth-values.) I cannot, on neutral grounds, endorse any such inference. I can, on neutral grounds, stipulate that the conditional sentence H is a necessary truth, but I cannot without risking error commit myself to following the Acceptance-side in asserting 'The number of stars is the sum of two primes' in an imagined epistemic circumstance in which we have reason to assert 'The number of stars is even (and greater than two)'.

My S-Acceptance language cannot, therefore, achieve the desired result of allowing me without risk of error to assert whatever facts the Acceptance-side would be prepared to assert.

The point that I made before about why I cannot, on neutral grounds, successfully stipulate an S-Rejection language is reinforced by the point just made about inferences. The two sides differ not only on what they assert in the current epistemic circumstance but also in what they are committed to asserting on the basis of inference in other epistemic circumstances. The equivalence constraint should be understood as including a clause about inference, so that the constraint is satisfied by a dispute only if, for any controversial sentence (or inference) C, each disputant is prepared to specify an uncontroversial sentence (or inference) U that is truth-conditionally equivalent to C (where two inferences are truth-conditionally equivalent if their respective premises and conclusions are truth-conditionally equivalent).

It is obvious that typical empirical disputes do not satisfy the equivalence constraint and are therefore not vulnerable to the stipulation maneuver. If there is a dispute, for example, about whether there is life on Mars, neither disputant holds that 'There is life on Mars' is truth-conditionally equivalent to some uncontroversial sentence. Our discussion of Goldbach's conjecture suggests that controversies in basic mathematics do not satisfy the equivalence constraint, and these controversies too are not vulnerable to the stipulation maneuver. The reason for this, as suggested in the above discussion, is that controversies in basic mathematics have a certain kind of application to contingencies in the world. Ontology seems to have no such applications that would prevent questions of ontology from satisfying the equivalence constraint and being vulnerable to the stipulation maneuver. Can we say in general terms what the relevant kind of application to contingencies is that mathematics has and that ontology lacks? A characterization that fits many (perhaps not all) examples is this: a controversy in basic mathematics implies a controversy about what the entailment relations are between uncontroversial contingencies (for example, the contingencies 'The number of stars is the sum of two primes' and 'The number of stars is even (and greater than two)'). Our stipulations cannot affect these uncontroversial sentences or their entailment relations, and therefore our stipulations cannot resolve the mathematical controversy. By contrast, controversies in ontology seem to have no bearing on the entailment relations between uncontroversial contingencies.[18]

---

[18] I am suggesting here that in typical examples (a) violation of the equivalence constraint goes together with (b) disagreement about the entailment relations between non-controversial contingencies. It's clear that (b) entails (a), but I do not rule out the possibility of there being examples in which (a) holds but not (b). It is (a) that determines whether the stipulation maneuver is feasible.

It may turn out to be provable what the truth-value is of the Goldbach sentence G. It might be suggested that this would be another reason why the stipulation maneuver could not work for G. If the truth-value of G is provable, it might be said, then there is no room for stipulations with regard to G, since the fixed background of uncontroversial sentences settles what the truth-value is of G.[19] I think this suggested 'non-provable constraint' is important, but it is not easy to work out with clarity. For it is unclear how the relevant meta-level *rules* of proof can be included in the background of uncontroversial *sentences*, or, to put it another way, it's unclear exactly what the connection is between rules of proof and truth conditions of sentences, the latter being what defines truth-conditional indiscernibility. These are important questions, but I will not here pursue them further. I bring in the non-provable constraint mainly to note that the answers to questions of ontology are surely not provable in any relevant sense, so such questions would satisfy any non-provable constraint that might be formulated.

We know that neither the truth nor the falsehood of the continuum hypothesis is provable from standard set theory, so a controversy about it would presumably satisfy a non-provable constraint, if such a constraint could be formulated. I think this point might encourage some people to feel that we could successfully stipulate languages on behalf of both sides of this controversy. It appears, however, that the equivalence constraint blocks this. The two sides will disagree about the inference from 'The number of angels is less than the number of reals' to 'The number of angels is not more than the number of integers', and it seems that neither side will consider this inference to be truth-conditionally equivalent to an uncontroversial inference. To be clear, it's no part of my claim in this chapter that the stipulation maneuver is the only way to deflate an ontological controversy. It may be that the controversy about the continuum hypothesis can be undermined in some other way related to the non-provability results.

Let me mention another problematical example. If we consider a sentence from physics that purports to refer to numbers, such as the force law 'F = m × a', a nominalist might view the sentence as truth-conditionally equivalent to an uncontroversial impossibility, whereas the platonist will regard it as a contingency. Can the platonist specify an uncontroversial sentence truth-conditionally equivalent to the force law? This is debatable. Only if the answer is yes is the controversy between platonism and nominalism vulnerable to the stipulation maneuver. But I have tried to show that various other kinds of examples of ontological controversy are vulnerable to the stipulation maneuver, and I now want to return to those examples.

---

[19] Intuitively, it seems that it must be the case that the truth-value of G is somehow settled by the uncontroversial background.

1.4

Since the language L1 of the ontologist who is right is truth-conditionally indiscernible from my stipulated language L2, it follows that any sentence expresses the same fact in both languages. That has been the gist of my argument. I think that a natural reaction is that, if merely stipulating different languages can guarantee us possession of whatever facts might be asserted by the correct side in an ontological controversy, then it follows that ontological controversies are in some important sense empty and insignificant.[20]

As indicated earlier, it is not being claimed that the ontologist's language L1 and my stipulated language L2 are one and the same language. Indeed, since it's correct to say that the relevant sentences of L2 are governed by stipulation, and it's not correct to say this of L1, it seems to follow immediately from Leibniz's Law that L1 is not L2. A correlative point is that, even if I could get myself to think in terms of the stipulated language, the cognitive states expressed in that language may not be the same as those expressed by the ontologist.

It would be implausible, however, to try to appeal to these differences of language or cognitive states to explain the significance of the ontological controversies. As I have said from the outset, the ontologists under consideration are concerned with propositions in the sense of objective facts; their debates do not concern cognitive sates. We can't readily imagine Williamson, for example, making a speech like the following: 'Sure, you can stipulate into existence your S-Williamson language, and since what I assert about necessitism is true, and you replicate my assertions, you are expressing the same true propositions I'm expressing. But your assertions, arrived at by stipulation, don't *mean* the same as mine; they don't express the same *cognitive states* that I'm expressing. And it's the truth of those cognitive states, the truth of those very thoughts expressed in my language, that interests me. I care about what is true in the language that I'm speaking, and your stipulated language is not my language'.

A speech like that might be suitable coming from a 'descriptive metaphysician' like Peter Strawson, who thought of metaphysics as essentially a species of linguistic or conceptual analysis. Descriptive metaphysicians might indeed say that what matters to them is what the truth is of the cognitive states or thoughts expressed in the natural language they are speaking. Williamson, however, seems generally unfriendly to such orientations; and the same, I think, is true of Lewis, van Inwagen, Sider, and many other prominent ontologists in the recent literature. Let me, in fact, quote something from a recent piece by Williamson in which

---

[20] Obviously, this does not preclude the Carnapian idea that some languages might be more practical than others. The ontological controversies under consideration are not supposed to be about which language is more practical.

he characterizes a dominant tendency in current philosophy of which he himself is certainly a leading representative:

> [C]ontemporary practitioners [of metaphysics] tend to see themselves as inves-
> tigating the most general and fundamental nature of the world in which human
> minds play only a very minor role…[W]hen you are doing the philosophy of X,
> you are primarily interested in X itself…and only secondarily in the word 'X', or
> our concept of X. You are not surreptitiously doing the philosophy of language
> or thought or mind or knowledge.[21]

Philosophers like Williamson, Lewis, van Inwagen, and Sider are akin to what was once called speculative metaphysicians; they are theory-driven ontologists who base themselves not primarily on linguistic or conceptual analysis, but on highly theoretical arguments. (I don't include Kripke in this list, since I consider him to play the role of defending pre-theoretical intuitions and concepts against the theory-driven speculations of the other side.[22]) The focus of the theory-driven ontologists is surely not on their particular language or cognitive states, but on the facts that their sentences express. But I express those same facts in my stipu-lated languages. It ought not matter to these philosophers whether these facts are expressed in their languages or in my stipulated languages.[23]

The takeaway from all of this, I think, is that the kind of ontological controversies that have dominated much of the recent literature seem largely meaningless. We can meaningfully engage in inquiries about how ontological concepts operate within the natural languages we speak, and these inquiries, which are essentially exercises in linguistic or conceptual analysis, may sometimes spawn meta-level controversies as to whether an ontological sentence is true or false in the language we speak; such meta-level controversies are not subject to the stipulation maneuver.[24] But the theory-driven object-level ontological controversies that have dominated much of the recent literature—controversies between nihilists, organicists, mereological essentialists, four-dimensionalists; controversies about which things exist funda-mentally; controversies about whether things exist by necessity—such controversies seem pointless. They can be resolved, or circumvented, by stipulation.[25]

---

[21] Williamson (2014).

[22] See also Fine's warning against excessive appeal to theory in metaphysics in Fine (2013), p. 729.

[23] Might Sider be an exception? He might say, 'It's not enough to express all the facts—both coarse-grained and fine-grained, including facts about fundamentality. You're required to do it in the lan-guage of the book of the world, and that cannot be a stipulated language'. But what is the nature of this surprising requirement to do something beyond stating the facts? According to my argument, the stipulated languages allow me to state all the facts that can be stated in the so-called language of the book of the world. How could that not be good enough? Cf. Hirsch (2013).

[24] If the controversy is over the sentence (T) 'The sentence (S) is true in the language we speak', neither side holds that (T) is truth-conditionally equivalent to some uncontroversial sentence.

[25] I am much indebted to Jared Warren for help with this, and thanks also to Matti Eklund, and to the members of the Dublin Language of Ontology conference in 2017.

References

Davidson, D. 1984. *Inquiries into Truth and Interpretation*. Oxford: Oxford University Press.

Dorr, C. 2005. 'What We Disagree about When We Disagree about Ontology'. In M. Kalderon (ed.), *Fictionalism in Metaphysics*. Oxford: Oxford University Press.

Fine, K. 2013. 'Fundamental Truth and Fundamental Terms', *Philosophy and Phenomenological Research*, 84(3): 725–732.

Hirsch, E. 2011. *Quantifier Variance and Realism: Essays in Meta-Ontology*. New York: Oxford University Press.

Hirsch, E. 2013. 'The Metaphysically Best Language', *Philosophy and Phenomenological Research*, 84(3): 709–716.

Hirsch, E. and Warren, J. 2019. 'Quanitifer Variance and the Demand for a Semantics', *Philosophy and Phenomenological Research*, 98(3): 592–605.

Kaplan, D. 1989. 'Demonstratives'. In J. Almog, H. Wettstein, and J. Perry (eds.), *Themes from Kaplan*. Oxford: Oxford University Press.

Kripke, S. 1980. *Naming and Necessity*. Oxford: Blackwell.

Quine, W. V. 1960. *Word and Object*. Cambridge, MA: MIT Press.

Russell, B. 1903. *Principles of Mathematics*. New York: Norton.

Salmon, N. 1986. *Frege's Puzzle*. Cambridge, MA: MIT Press.

Sider, T. 2011. *Writing the Book of the World*. Oxford: Oxford University Press.

Williamson, T. 2013. *Modal Logic and Metaphysics*. Oxford: Oxford University Press.

Williamson, T. 2014. 'How Did We Get Here from There? The Transformation of Analytic Philosophy', *Belgrade Philosophical Annual*, 27: 7–37.

2

Are Ontological Questions
Really Meaningless?

Delia Belleri

A well-known critique of ontology has it that ontological questions and statements are devoid of sense, or meaningless. In his *Pseudoproblems of Philosophy* (1928), Rudolf Carnap originally proposed this critique in verificationist terms, arguing that given a typical ontological claim (like 'There are numbers'), since there is no empirical evidence that could either confirm it or confirm its negation, the claim is devoid of factual content; that is, it is devoid of meaning. Later on, in his 'Empiricism, Semantics and Ontology' (1950), Carnap presents a different critique, which avails itself of the distinction between internal and external questions. The ontological question 'Are there numbers?' could be asked either within a framework containing number-terms and variables, in which case the answer to this question is positive, but also trivial; or it could be asked (purportedly) outside of a framework, in the way of an inquiry as to what there is independently of any linguistic system.[1] In the latter case, however, the question makes no sense and therefore can receive no answer. Given that answers to internal questions are rather uninteresting, philosophers cannot reasonably be taken to ask those questions, and should be interpreted as asking the external ones. Yet, these are meaningless and unanswerable questions.

The extent to which the critique from 1950 still relies on the verificationist arguments presented by Carnap in 1928 is nowadays debated (see Bradley 2018). Yet, the received view seems to treat 'Empiricism, Semantics and Ontology' as offering a purely semantic critique of this practice, whereby the problem for ontological questions lies mainly in their semantic defectiveness, independently of evidence-related issues. Several contemporary authors interpret Carnap this way or hold metaontological theories that owe much to his interpretation. These theorists include Huw Price (2009), Amie Thomasson (2009, 2015, 2016), David Chalmers (2009), and Jared Warren (2016a).

The aim of this chapter is to assess the threat posed by this semantic critique for some contemporary practitioners of ontology. Just like the ontologists

---

[1] This passage presupposes an interpretation of Carnap's text whereby frameworks are languages or language-fragments; for a defence of this reading, see Eklund (2009).

Delia Belleri, *Are Ontological Questions Really Meaningless?* In: *The Language of Ontology.* Edited by: J. T. M. Miller, Oxford University Press (2021). © Oxford University Press. DOI: 10.1093/oso/9780192895332.003.0003

criticized by Carnap, these authors purport to find out about what there is in a distinctly mind- and language-independent sense, so they would seem vulnerable to the charge of asking external and therefore meaningless questions. Ted Sider (2009, 2011), for instance, holds that the world has an objective, fundamental structure that language should appropriately mirror. Similarly, Jonathan Schaffer (2009) conceives of ontology as the business of identifying the fundamental constituents of reality, which he calls 'substances'. Also Kit Fine (2001, 2009) conceives of ontology as investigating what there is in reality; that is, what ultimately and intrinsically characterizes the world. Let us call all these theorists 'serious ontologists'. The question I will tackle is whether the Carnapian, purely semantic critique poses a significant threat for them.[2]

In what follows, I will first present a contemporary version of the Carnapian semantic critique, due to Price and Thomasson, aptly formulated so as to remain wholly independent of verificationism. I will then counter this critique by arguing that, given the terms in which it is cashed out, a number of avenues seem open to vindicate the meaningfulness of ontological questions as today's serious practitioners of this discipline view them. I will then suggest that the importance of this critique should be downplayed, and that theorists eager to attack serious ontology should focus on other kinds of challenges, for example epistemic ones.

2.1 Carnapian Charges of Meaninglessness

In Amie Thomasson's view (2015, 2016), ontological questions are devoid of sense simply because *they do not comply with any rules of correct linguistic usage*. This idea is hinted at by Putnam (1987), when he points out that 'what is wrong with the notion of objects existing "independently" of conceptual schemes is that there are *no standards for the use of even the logical notions* apart from conceptual choices' (pp. 35–36, my italics).

Thomasson (2015) develops this insight in much closer detail. She first endorses Huw Price's (2009, p. 234) interpretation of Carnap's internal/external distinction, whereby internal questions are appropriately asked by *using* key terms like 'number' or 'material object', while external questions are not appropriately asked by using these terms. Thomasson's only assumption at this stage seems to be that a sentence is meaningful just in case it complies with rules for correct use. With this assumption in mind, we may reconstruct her view as follows: (i) internal

---

[2] It should be considered accidental (although by no means unimportant for the purposes of this chapter) that these authors all use special terminologies—such as 'structure', 'substance', 'reality'—in order to formulate ontological questions and answers. Whether the Carnapian critique poses a threat for them would still be a relevant issue even if they asked questions using plain English sentences like 'Are there numbers?' or 'Do numbers exist?', as long as these could be interpreted as external questions.

questions are asked while using the terms (e.g. 'number') according to the rules of use that are internal to a linguistic framework. Because their use conforms with the rules, the sentences employed are meaningful; but also, thanks to our mastery of the rules, we are in a position to obtain an answer to existence questions by either employing empirical methods or by appealing to framework-internal analytic entailments. For example, suppose the question to be answered is 'Are there properties?'. According to Thomasson:

> the very rules for introducing property language (combined with 'customary deductive rules') license us to infer from an ordinary truth like 'the house is red' that 'the house has the property of being red' and so to provide an easy affirmative answer to the general question (asked internally).   (2015, p. 37)

By contrast, (ii) external questions are asked while using the terms, but not in accordance with the rules of any particular framework (since the point of the question is supposedly that of inquiring into the existence of a certain class of objects *independently* of our language and concepts). Because no rules can be appealed to in order to determine whether or not the terms are correctly used, the question is devoid of sense. Thomasson thus illustrates the point:

> A question like 'Are there huasadoes?' cannot be answered, as 'huasadoe' is a meaningless term, without rules of use that would determine under what conditions 'huasadoe' is to be applied or refused. So similarly, if we take a familiar term but strip it of its rules of use (not using it in a way governed by those rules), the term is left meaningless, and the existence question unanswerable.
>
> (2015, p. 40)

The problem about pseudo-questions, Thomasson says, is that they feature uses of terms without these uses being governed by any rule. If the terms were simply *mentioned*, though, one could form meaningful and answerable questions, even though one could only ask whether a certain linguistic form would be *pragmatically convenient* to use—for instance: 'Is it pragmatically expedient to use the word "number"?'

The Carnapian point is therefore revived by Thomasson while supposedly avoiding slipping into verificationism: ontological questions qua external questions are devoid of meaning not because we lack verification conditions for them, but because *we lack application conditions* for the terms occurring in them, something that prevents us from formulating an answer. In what follows, I aim to show that the serious ontologist is in a position to address the Carnapian critique as it is formulated by Thomasson. If this is the best version of the semantic critique that a detractor of serious ontology can formulate, then showing that answers to this critique are available after all will reduce the threat it poses to the practice of contemporary, 'heavyweight', or serious ontology.

2.2 Providing a Rule of Use

The Carnapian critique presented by Thomasson links pseudo-questions with expressions not being employed according to framework-internal rules of usage. Provided this is the only source of the semantic problem for ontological questions, I wish to argue that it is possible for the serious ontologist to remedy this lack of rules, thus moving towards an account of the meaningfulness of ontological questions that the Carnapian could in principle accept.

As a first stab, we may begin by specifying a rule of use for ontological statements by considering which conditions permit the assertion of sentences like 'There (really) are Fs'. I propose to treat these sentences as devices for signalling that a certain stage in inquiry has been reached, namely a stage where the theorist believes that, in light of the methods applied and the evidence collected, *she has reached the end of her inquiry*. Although, at first sight, this does not seem to be what serious ontologists use existence statements for, in the course of the section I hope to show that this may be, at least for the time being, a fruitful, Carnapian-friendly way of reconstructing the meaningfulness of their discourse, in light of evidence drawn from some of their texts.

So, let us ask: when is it okay for the serious ontologist to go ahead and signal that her inquiry has come to an end (at least for the time being)? Based on the methodology adopted by prominent ontologists, one could suggest that such a stage is reached once the theorist has conducted what the philosophical community regards as a satisfactory ontological inquiry. I take it that, in the field of ontology, this requires critically engaging[3] with either (1) the results, arguments, and methods of a common-sense-based ontological inquiry; or (2) the results, arguments, and methods of an ontological inquiry based on at least some special sciences. The disjunction of (1) and (2) should be read as inclusive. This broad characterization of what it is to conduct an ontological inquiry (at least nowadays and in a number of academic circles) is borne out by the work of leading figures in analytic ontology. For instance, Quine's realism about mathematical entities is the result of his critically engaging with ontological inquiry as informed by the

---

[3] 'Critically engaging' should be understood, along standard lines, as the activity of analysing and producing arguments, paying attention to aspects like the truth of their premises, the justification we have to hold them, the acceptability of the background assumptions that underlie them (if any), etc. The evidence the philosophers are allowed to rely on ranges from empirical (including scientific results, experimental-philosophy results) to a priori evidence (including intuitions, reasoning from cases, thought experiments, etc.); also comparing theoretical virtues such as simplicity, integration, explanatory power, etc. is an increasingly common move.

special sciences, where his conclusion is famously to admit the existence of numbers based on their indispensability for science (cf. Quine 1981, pp. 149–150); and conversely, his physicalism about mental states results from his critically engaging with the ontology that underlies psychological explanation (in common sense and some sciences), where his conclusion is that we have no reason to maintain a distinctive ontological commitment to mental states (Quine 1960, pp. 264–265). Sider's realism about structure results from engaging critically with the way in which, in scientific discourse, we think about the world; he argues that the notion of an objective worldly structure affords us a number of theoretical benefits (fix meanings for the ideal interpreter, set the goal of inquiry, illuminate the notion of 'projected' properties); plus, he counters the opposite idea that the world is a mere construction (Sider 2009, pp. 401–402). Kit Fine, too, critically engages with the methods and results of ontological inquiry as informed by scientific methodology; however, his investigation leads him to posit a dimension of 'the real' that goes *beyond* the range of commitments of the special sciences (Fine 2009, pp. 159–161). In all these cases, I suggest we say that meaningful usage (in *some* sense of the word 'meaningful'!) of a sentence like 'There (really) are Fs' obtains whenever it is appropriate, in light of certain epistemic and methodological standards dictated by the philosophical community, to assert 'There (really) are Fs'.

If these considerations correctly reflect the practice of serious ontologists, then it is possible to formulate the following rule of usage:

[ONT]   It is permitted to use a sentence like 'There (really) are Fs' just in case use of this sentence is supported by the speaker's prior application, in her inquiry, of the methodology commonly accepted by ontologists.

[ONT] seems to meet the Carnapian's requirement by allowing to distinguish between uses that are permitted by the rule (call them 'rule-abiding') and uses that are not permitted by the rule (call them 'non-rule-abiding'). That this distinction is enabled should at least bring us closer to an attribution of meaningfulness to the expressions under exam.[4]

So, to illustrate, suppose the ontologist's inquiry aimed to answer the question 'Are there (really) numbers?'. The serious ontologist conducts an analysis whereby

---

[4] One may suspect that [ONT] fails to fully comply with Thomasson's characterization of a term's application conditions (I am grateful to an anonymous OUP reviewer for pointing this out). This characterization has it—among other things—that a term's application conditions should not merely be conditions 'under which we would have *evidence* that the term applies, but rather [they should be conditions] under which the term *would be correctly applied*' (2015, p. 91). Yet, nothing in the formulation I have given suggests that [ONT] merely specifies when we would have *evidence* of correct application; the formulation rather specifies when *it would be correct* to use a sentence like 'There (really) are Fs'— namely, whenever the philosopher's inquiry meets certain criteria. So, [ONT] is in line with Thomasson's conception of a term's application conditions in this respect. This being said, I grant that the correctness it deals in does not coincide with *truth*; this is why, in the following sections, I will also propose how to specify the truth-conditions of ontological sentences like 'There (really) are Fs'.

she thoroughly critically engages with both the deliverances of ontological inquiry based on common sense and ontological inquiry based on (at least some) special sciences. She reaches a conclusion which she articulates linguistically, e.g. 'There (really) are numbers'. [ONT] allows us to judge her use as rule-abiding. Had the philosopher executed a method which, by the lights of the relevant philosophical community, did not sufficiently critically engage with either common-sense ontology or with an ontology based on the special sciences, she would have used the sentence 'There (really) are numbers' in an illicit, non-rule-abiding way. If [ONT] is an acceptable rule which allows us to discern between uses that are appropriate and inappropriate in the sense just sketched, this seems to mark a step in the direction of vindicating the meaningfulness of ontological statements.

Notice that for present purposes, it does not matter whether the methodology mentioned by [ONT] is truth-conducive—although the serious ontologist will presumably believe that it is. For, I contend, what sustains the meaningfulness of these statements is simply the rule-governed practice of employing a methodology approved by a certain community in order to reach certain answers, whatever the epistemic merits of the practice. The Carnapian is free to object that the meaningfulness produced by such practice is not enough, or not relevant. Yet, it is her task at this point to explain what sense of 'meaningful' she has in mind and why it should be cared about.[5]

One possible objection is that [ONT] is circular. It presupposes that the ontologist is conducting an inquiry, where presumably the question 'Are there (really) Fs?' is asked; but this question surely had to be meaningful before the ontologist started her quest for an answer! If it was meaningful, then [ONT] does not help after all; if it was not meaningful, or even if it is not clear that it was, then the Carnapian can reiterate her point that an unanswerable question had been asked. My answer to this objection is the following: suppose the first serious ontological question ever asked was indeed meaningless—at least in the sense that it was not governed by any rule of use. It is perfectly possible that, in trying to answer that question, the ontologist *worked out the rules for answering the question while answering it*, so that at the end of the inquiry, the question was meaningful after all. This process then made it the case that, from that moment on, all subsequent ontological questions and their attendant answers were meaningful. So, although [ONT] does seem to presuppose that an antecedent meaningful question precedes the answer, such a presupposition can be seen as innocent in light of the possibility of the 'primigenial' story sketched above.

---

[5] The Carnapian may require that genuinely meaningful talk, besides being governed by a rule of use, has certain pragmatic advantages, or is sufficiently connected with talk that is already well established within our linguistic practices. In the following sections, I will argue that the serious ontologist has something to say to meet both these requirements. In any event, the considerations run so far could be taken as suggesting that Carnapian theorists pose too weak a criterion of meaningfulness. At the very least, more work needs to be done in order to enrich and strengthen it.

Although [ONT] seems to be in good enough standing to provide the rule of use demanded by the Carnapian, it admittedly returns only a partially faithful picture of what serious ontologists purport to be doing when they utter sentences of the form 'There (really) are Fs'. For of course the serious ontologist wants to utter a sentence like 'There are Fs' in order to accurately represent the world 'out there', and not just to say that the conclusion of her inquiry (modulo such-and-such alleged epistemically and methodologically appropriate considerations) is that there are Fs. So, for the serious ontologist, accounting for the meaningfulness of ontological statements by *simply* linking them with the conditions in which it would be acceptable to state 'I have reached the answer that *p*' is to misrepresent what the practitioner aims to communicate.

A strategy that promises a greater faithfulness to the realist aspirations of serious ontologists is trying to specify, again in a Carnapian-friendly way, *which conditions in the world* would have to obtain in order for an existence statement issued by the serious ontologist to be true. The next section will be devoted to such an attempt.

2.3 Providing Truth-Conditions

In this section, I will try to cast some light on the meaningfulness of serious-ontology statements by articulating truth-conditions for them. Of course, the challenge here is that of executing this task in a way that is acceptable to the Carnapian.

2.3.1 Introducing a Carnapian Framework for Serious Ontology

The first step towards this aim is that of specifying the truth-conditions of sentences like 'There (really) are Fs' via a biconditional whose right-hand side is either a paraphrase or translation of the relevant sentence that can either directly or indirectly reveal the conditions that would have to obtain in the world in order for that sentence to be true.

The first option is that of formulating a biconditional of the form 'S is true iff P' whose right-hand side offers *an ordinary English paraphrase* of the serious-ontology sentence S. If the terms occurring in S are semantically analysable, or even just if there is a clear way to non-analytically trace talk in-certain-terms to talk in-certain-other-terms, then obtaining a paraphrase on the right-hand side should be no problem. In a number of cases, however, one of the ontologically relevant terms *t* occurring in S may be understood as *primitive*, and hence as not amenable to semantic analysis; plus, there may be no obvious, non-analytic way to relate talk in terms of *t* to talk in terms of something else within the natural language. This indeed seems to be the case with the modifier 'really' (cf. Kitsik 2020), or with the notion of ground (see Rosen 2010; Schaffer 2009). Furthermore, as Sider (2011, §5.3) notes, the mechanisms that determine the extension of certain terms in ordinary English might be the wrong ones, for instance they might be internalistic despite our belief that they are, or expectation that they be, externalistic. For all these reasons, we might want to engineer our own linguistic resources and move away from an ordinary language paraphrase.

Whence the second option—what Sider (2011) might want to call 'Plan B'—where the biconditional specifying the truth-conditions of 'There (really) are Fs' displays on the right-hand side a translation *in some other language/idiolect* of our own establishment. My suggestion at this point is that the serious ontologist could *create a Carnapian framework*, which she can employ in order to formulate the truth-conditions of 'There (really) are Fs' on the right-hand side of the biconditional. Note that when I say that the serious ontologists may construct something akin to a Carnapian framework, I only mean that they may introduce a number of new linguistic expressions which carry with them a number of metaphysical or ontological commitments; and I will for the sake of simplicity ignore the fact that, for Carnap (1950), introducing a framework seemed to only imply introducing new predicates and variables.

Basically, then, I want to encourage the serious ontologist to introduce Ontologese (to borrow Dorr's (2005) term) as a Carnapian framework. How could this be done? The biggest challenge is surely that of justifying such introduction in terms that are acceptable to the Carnapian. In the next section, I will look at how the serious ontologist could invoke pragmatic considerations in order to render this option palatable by Carnapian lights. But let's proceed one step at a time. The purpose of this section is to review a number of linguistic proposals inspired by the current literature which seem compatible with the strategy just sketched.

Ted Sider (2011, §6.3) introduces a structure operator $\mathscr{S}$ which can be combined with items of various grammatical categories. Thus, for instance, we can form the sentence '$\mathscr{S}$ (and)', meaning that the conjunction-sign is structural or fundamental or joint-carving; we can form the sentence '$\mathscr{S}$ (electron)', meaning that the concept of electron is structural; or we can form the sentence '$\mathscr{S}$ (there is)', meaning that the existential quantifier is structural; or we can form the sentence '$\mathscr{S}$ (There are tables)', meaning that the sentence 'There are tables' is structural or carves at the joints. This proposal can be adapted to the Carnap-style format set forward above. Then, the truth-conditions of a sentence like 'There are numbers' as uttered by the serious ontologist can be formulated via the following biconditional:

'There are numbers' is true iff $\mathscr{S}$ (There are numbers)

where this means that the sentence 'There are numbers' is structural; that is, it latches onto some fundamental aspect of reality.

A second potential way of implementing the proposal just advanced draws inspiration from the linguistic resources introduced by Kit Fine. Fine introduces a reality operator R which attaches to propositions and allows us to say that the objects to which the ontological realist is committed are 'real'; that is, fundamental or part of the intrinsic structure of the world (their existence as expressed through the existential quantifier is, in Fine's view, inconsequential to their ontological status, as the anti-realist can agree about existence statements too). Thus, the mathematical realist will maintain that numbers are real, and she will express this by saying that it is part of reality that numbers have such-and-such features. In symbols: $Rx =_{df} \exists \phi R[\phi x]$ (Fine 2009, p. 172). The truth-conditions of a sentence like 'There (really) are numbers'—or perhaps more accurately, 'Numbers are real'—could therefore be rendered via the following biconditional:

'There (really) are numbers' is true iff there are features ϕ such that it is part of reality that numbers have ϕ.

The third potential implementation draws on Jonathan Schaffer's work. Schaffer (2009) introduces the metaphysically charged notion of grounding, which he treats like a predicate (p. 375) whose relata can be entities of any kind. The grounding relation is denoted by the symbol '\' which can be flanked by symbols of any grammatical (or ontological) category. The sentence '$x\backslash y$' is to be interpreted as meaning that x (partially) grounds y. The notion of fundamentality is tied to the idea that the world is arranged hierarchically, with the more fundamental entities grounding the less fundamental ones. At the bottom of the hierarchy lie what Schaffer calls *substances*, which provide the basis for all the derivative layers of being. Schaffer's specific view is that there is just one substance, the Cosmos, which can then be de-composed to form a hierarchy of particular concrete objects. These details won't concern us here, since the focus is on how the serious ontological claims Schaffer wishes to issue are to be rendered within a Carnap-style linguistic framework. Providing the truth-conditions of 'There are numbers' in Schaffer's framework would imply employing the grounding-language to locate numbers in the 'big chain of being', thus stating a biconditional that could take the following form:

'There are numbers' is true iff numbers are substances or grounded in a substance.

I have reviewed three ways in which the serious ontologist could specify the truth-conditions of sentences like 'There (really) are numbers' via a biconditional where the right-hand side is a translation of the sentence at issue into a language introduced as a Carnapian framework. There is much to be discussed about the feasibility of this project, starting with the question: 'How is the Carnapian deflationist, who is proverbially opposed to serious ontology, ever going to accept the language of the serious ontologist *as a Carnapian framework?*'. The next section is devoted to answering this question.

2.3.2 Justifying the Serious Ontologist's Carnapian Framework

I have reviewed three possible ways of introducing special linguistic resources in order to inquire about matters of serious ontology. The second step is that of appropriately motivating the introduction of these frameworks by appealing to considerations that could be shared by a Carnapian as well. This will be my suggestion: the serious ontologist could invoke the well-connectedness of her favourite notions within a web of already established conceptual and methodological resources as evidence of their expediency and fruitfulness.

This way of operating can again be inspired by strategies already present in the literature. Sider (2011), for instance, emphasizes the way in which the notion of structure may be linked to a number of already fairly well-accepted ideas. The notion of structure, he argues, helps better to understand the notion of objective similarity; it is connected with reference magnetism as a way of solving the problem of radical underdetermination; it helps constrain the assignment of prior probabilities in inductive (Bayesian) inferences; it helps understand talk about the 'intrinsic' nature of space, time, and spacetime. Furthermore, it helps to articulate and comprehend the idea that disputes, both within and outside metaphysics, are in some sense 'substantive', as well as to flesh out the seemingly widely accepted idea that there is an epistemically 'privileged' aim to inquiry (both in and outside of metaphysics). This wealth of connections can be exhibited as evidence that the notion of structure is expedient, or fruitful.

Similar strategies can be adopted with respect to the terms 'reality' and 'ground'. To the extent that these notions are well connected and well integrated within a sufficiently established network of ideas, practices, and assessments (see e.g. Fine 2009, pp. 175–176; Schaffer 2009, pp. 373–375), this could be evidence of their expediency and fruitfulness.

Notice how these considerations originally have a different epistemic significance for the serious ontologist. For the serious ontologist, the fact that the notions of structure, or reality, or ground, are so well integrated within our web of beliefs and practices is evidence that 'we are onto something', as it were; that we are representing mind-independent reality in the right way, by making reference to or otherwise tracking certain aspects of it. We could say that, in this case, the serious ontologist reasons abductively from the high integration of their favourite notions to their ontological fit or joint-carving. This abductive significance is absent when the same connections are used as evidence to exhibit to the Carnapian. Highlighting the well-connectedness of the structure- (or ground-, or reality-) notion will simply be evidence for the expediency or usefulness of the previously mentioned frameworks; questions of accurate representation, success-ful reference, or tracking won't even arise—or if they arise, they will do so 'internal' to the framework.

Thus, the serious ontologist should not expect that implementing this strategy will *convince* the Carnapian that *there is*, independently of the framework, such a thing as the world's structure, or reality, or grounding relations. The aim should rather be that of offering the kind of considerations that a Carnapian would find 'kosher'. In order to be kosher by Carnapian lights, I take it that a justification offered for a framework should: (a) *not directly employ* metaphysically charged terms, but rather mention them; this is to avoid using the terms outside of the framework that is being built, thus risking a slip into nonsense; and (b) not go beyond advocating the practical expediency of such terms. I believe that the argu-ments employed by, for example, Sider in *Writing the Book of the World* in order to support his realism about structure could be borrowed—or perhaps less politely, parasitically repurposed—in order to pursue exactly this aim.

Also, the serious ontologist should aspire to nothing more than providing the Carnapian with reasons that support at least the *provisional adoption* of the framework she wishes to set up. After all, the Carnapian is typically also a plural-ist; that is, somebody who is open to there being many linguistic frameworks suited to a variety of different purposes. In this pluralist spirit, the Carnapian may allow that, as long as some 'kosher' justificatory considerations are given for introducing a certain framework, its supporters should be allowed to use it. The Carnapian will defer to science the final verdict as to the ultimate effectiveness of the proposed framework, trusting that 'the work in the field will sooner or later lead to the elimination of those forms which have no useful function' (1950, p. 40).

However, not all Carnapians need be pluralists in the sense just hinted at. A case in point is provided by Amie Thomasson, who resists the idea of a plurality of meanings for the existential quantifier and, hence, a plurality of frameworks based on such meanings. Thomasson opposes Sider's idea of a joint-carving exist-ential quantifier by arguing that the existential quantifier has a single meaning, which is captured by its inferential role. Contending that there is a meaning for the existential quantifier that goes beyond these formal features, for example by performing a joint-carving function, is akin to a category mistake whereby we illicitly lump quantifiers together with predicates:

> Thinking of the quantifier as a would-be joint carving term seems to arise from the attempt to assimilate other parts of speech to the structure-tracking function of many of the predicates of natural science.   (2015, p. 315)

Thomasson does not defend at length the idea that existential quantification is formal and therefore not joint-carving. Yet, since this idea is undeniably the dominant one, she claims the burden of proof is on Sider to adequately motivate departure from the received view. Sider could reply (as he does in his 2009, pp. 404–407) that there are ways of treating quantifiers as properties of properties, or even ways of treating the naturalness of quantifiers nominalistically, without reifying their meanings. Plus, he could motivate his proposal by showing how the idea of joint-carving quantification is in many ways either already familiar (to some extent) or theoretically advantageous, again appealing to the putative connections it bears to already well-established notions. This would provide the Siderean project with a motivation that could at least be approved by the Carnapian, with no need for them to draw further heavyweight metaphysical conclusions from it. Once these motivations have been provided, the burden would shift back on the opponent, who would have to show that they are defective and not even provisionally acceptable.

So, there is a way for the serious ontologist to address specific qualms like those expressed by Thomasson; the strategy aims at providing the Carnapian with considerations that suffice to keep the serious ontologist's framework as a *live option*, thus forcing the Carnapian into a position of at least 'provisional' pluralism.

I have held so far that the Carnapian will accept, or at least will be cornered into provisionally accepting, the considerations provided by the serious ontologist aimed at establishing expediency and fruitfulness. This may not happen, though. The Carnapian might contend that these considerations are not kosher after all, for instance because a number of metaphysically charged notions are still being *used* by the serious ontologist, instead of being mentioned. For instance, the Carnapian may contend that it is objectionable for Sider to say that the notion of 'structure' is useful to account for the fact that some disputes are substantive, or that reference magnetism obtains, because those of substantivity and of reference magnetism are metaphysically loaded notions that the serious ontologist illicitly uses outside of a framework. The serious ontologist can fix this by turning all usages into mentions, thus stating that the notion of 'structure' helps us shed light on the notions of 'substantiveness' and 'reference magnetism', where 'substantiveness' and 'reference magnetism' are intended as terms internal to an as yet not fully specified framework, which is precisely *being introduced*, somewhat *holistically*, by the serious ontologist with the act of establishing a number of connections. The Carnapian could insist that introducing the framework 'in bulk', as it were, is not good enough if the nodes that compose the framework are too foreign to concepts we already use and deem convenient. It would then be up to the serious ontologist to show either that (i) these notions are at least already implicitly present and fruitfully used in other regions of our discourse; or (ii) closeness to other more familiar and well-established notions makes up for this flaw.

Also, the Carnapian may object that the serious ontologist will not think of her framework as just one framework among the others, but as being *privileged*. This conviction is, however, unacceptable for the Carnapian, whose view is that the point of ontology is to build useful and explanatory fruitful frameworks, where *more than one framework could be equally fit* for the task.

Of course, there may remain an unbridgeable gap between the Carnapian and the serious ontologist as regards the putative objective superiority of the proposed framework. For the former will think the framework has (if anything) just a practical import, which may be paralleled by the practical import of other frameworks, while the latter will think that there has to be more to their own framework besides its practical benefits—namely, a genuine, ultimate metaphysical 'fit' with the world. This contrast, however, need not interfere with the dialectic just described, where the serious ontologist furnishes 'kosher' considerations and the Carnapian judges them sufficient for a provisional admission of the framework. We could think of this contrast as a separate, 'bedrock disagreement', where the disputants simply have to 'agree to disagree'. The only way in which a conversation between the two can start is (as I have been at pains to show) if the party with the greater ontological commitments provides the opposite party with considerations that are independent of such commitments, and that can in principle be accepted by them.

A strictly related worry is that, by turning the language of ontology into a Carnapian framework, the serious ontologist will have to accept the Carnapian pluralistic tenet that all frameworks are (more or less) *equally good* ways of describing reality. This would seem to directly contradict the idea that one language is privileged. But again, the controversy over the equal validity of frameworks can be regarded as a separate, 'bedrock' disagreement that plays no relevant part in the dialectic so far described. The serious ontologist can be Carnapian up to the point of accepting that ontological questions are true within a framework, to the extent that this helps with her case for their meaningfulness. Since the privilege of one framework over the others is simply not the focus of the present dialectic, the serious ontologist should be under no pressure to go pluralist, if she has contrary assumptions.

2.3.3 A Challenge about Understanding

So far, we have seen how certain sentences that are of importance for the serious ontologist can be given truth-conditions. The key move consists in translating these sentences into some suitable language introduced for the purpose of doing ontology or metaphysics. Yet, if we focus on this newly introduced language, we seem to be exposed to a further challenge that an overall sceptic of the enterprise—and at this point, not necessarily a Carnapian one—may pose.

The challenge has it that by means of this strategy we do not greatly advance our *understanding* of what ontologists mean when they employ a sentence in their technical language. For, the critic might urge, even if we accept the biconditionals formulated along the lines surveyed in section 2.3.1, repeated below in schematic form:

'There are Fs' is true iff $\mathscr{S}$ (There are Fs).
'There (really) are Fs' is true iff there are features φ such that
    it is part of reality that Fs have φ.
'There are Fs' is true iff Fs are substances or grounded in a
    substance.

we do not seem to grasp well enough what the truth-conditions offered on the right-hand side are, where this casts a shadow on the meaningfulness of the employed sentences. So, for instance, what would it be for the sentence 'There are Fs' to be *structural*? Or what would it be for it to be part of *reality* that Fs have feature φ? Or for them to be *grounded* in a *substance*? I will interpret this kind of discomfort as a request to elaborate what it is for these truth-conditions to obtain *in more familiar terms*: for instance, by using ordinary language or the linguistic resources of the empirical sciences. Allaying this discomfort depends on whether the serious ontologist accepts that there are more familiar terms available.

For some theorists, we might have a chance to elucidate the right-hand sides of at least some instances of the biconditionals above in terms of the language of the sciences. For example, we might have a chance to elucidate structure-talk in certain instances of the first biconditional, or ground-talk in certain instances of the third biconditional, in terms of fundamental physics. The problem is, we may not be in a position to do so *right now*, because we may not (yet) know all of the facts, such as about fundamental physics, that would be needed to perform such spelling-out. A partial fix to this situation (inspired by remarks due to Sider 2011, p. 117) would be that of providing an elucidation of the relevant instances of the biconditional's right-hand side in terms of 'toy truth-conditions' for the right-hand sides themselves. These would be conditions that approximate the (hopefully forthcoming) perfectly fundamental conditions which would allow a joint-carving elucidation. The point of these toy truth-conditions is 'to convince us that real, non-toy metaphysical truth-conditions exist' (Sider 2011, p. 117). So, the serious ontologist who is on board with a naturalistic elucidation of (at least some of) her statements may at least begin to meet the sceptic's challenge by invoking 'toy' truth-conditions for relevant instances of the biconditional's right-hand side, which ought to be accepted as being en route to 'non-toy' truth-conditions.

Yet, how should this challenge be received by theorists (like Kit Fine) who are not interested in naturalistic elucidations, for instance because they do not embrace the primacy of the physical and instead contend that there are metaphysically special facts which go beyond the facts ascertained by science? Here it seems that spelling out what is expressed on the right-hand side of the second biconditional (formulated by using Fine's reality operator) in more familiar terms would be significantly harder, for lack of further linguistic resources. Fine also acknowledges: 'the metaphysical circle of ideas to which [the notion of reality] belongs is one from which there appears to be no escape' (2009, p. 175). Note that an analogue of the less ambitious strategy adopted by Sider won't work here. If we settle for an elucidation of the right-hand side in the language of, say, fundamental physics, this in itself is not going to persuade the opponent that we are en route to a purely metaphysical elucidation. So the strategy needs to change.

One possible reply available to the serious practitioner is that of conceding that understanding is not incredibly enhanced by the provision of the biconditionals specified above, *if* what we expect from understanding is exclusively something akin to 'being capable to say the same thing in other terms'. Yet, understanding may not exclusively have to do with the capability to rephrase. Understanding may also be connected with phenomena like the *prima facie* intelligibility of a sentence or notion: 'the fact that a notion appears to make sense is strong *prima facie* evidence that it does make sense' (Fine 2001, p. 13); or the *integration* of that sentence or notion within a number of relevant linguistic practices. Speaking of the metaphysically charged notion of fact, Fine argues that, since this notion is indispensable to understand the—supposedly intelligible—positions held by A-theorists ('There are tensed facts') and B-theorists ('There are no tensed facts'), it is almost impossible to deny its intelligibility (Fine 2001, p. 13). Similarly, regarding the metaphysical notion of reality, he argues that if one understands— as it seems anyone would do—a position like that endorsed by Democritus, to the effect that there is nothing more to the world than atoms in the void, then if one is 'willing to go along with me so far, [they] will thereby have endorsed a metaphysical conception of reality' (Fine 2009, p. 175). Similarly, we seem to have a grasp of how to discuss and in principle settle questions pertaining to reality and ground (Fine 2009, p. 176); but if we do, it becomes increasingly difficult to impute unintelligibility to these notions. These phenomena may be therefore stressed by the serious ontologist in order to show the sceptic that, despite our reduced capability to elucidate the conditions on the right-hand side in more familiar and less metaphysically loaded terms, an *active use* of these terms (cf. also Rosen 2010, p. 134; Schaffer 2009, p. 376), in which even the sceptic herself might happen to engage, is a sign that we *do* have an understanding—albeit one where we cannot evade the small circle of metaphysical words—of what these truth-conditions consist in. This in turn may invite toning down allegations of meaninglessness based on lack of understanding.

2.3.4 Serious Ontology and Analyticity

The attempt run so far may also be opposed with the following objection, again not to be necessarily raised by a Carnapian: if one introduces Ontologese as a Carnapian framework, one has to commit to the thesis that existence sentences are typically *analytic*; that is, knowable in virtue of the obtaining of certain semantic or logical connections that are sanctioned by a framework. However, serious ontologists differ from critics of ontology precisely in their holding that existence questions are not analytic! This contrast is reflected, for instance, in Dorr's (2005) portrayal of the dialectic between serious ontologists and holders of the deflationary, Carnapian view. In Dorr's view, the Carnapian is a supporter of 'the view that ontological claims are typically analytic when true. Conversely, those who take ontological disagreement seriously have tended to find it obvious that controversial ontological claims [...] are synthetic' (2005, pp. 257–258). It would therefore seem wildly unfair to how serious ontologists conceive of their work to make a proposal which leads to an analytic conception of ontological questions.

Certainly it would seem to be a cost for the serious ontologist if she had to admit that existence statements are analytic. Yet, there seems to be at least a way of making this cost more bearable. The serious ontologist may accept the analyticity of existence statements if there were reasons (for her) to think that this analyticity *appropriately depends* (in a way to be better specified) on certain non-semantic facts.

A recent proposal advanced by Carrie Jenkins becomes relevant at this point. Jenkins (2005, 2008) argues that the analyticity of arithmetical concepts can be 'grounded in' (or mirror, or be sensitive to) reality. This option can be applied to the analyticity of existence sentences as well, if one admits that there are reasons to think that the analytic truths that obtain in the Carnapian framework are appropriately grounded in facts that are relevant to the serious ontologist (see Jenkins 2015). Thus, for a Quinean serious ontologist like Sider, it seems possible to hold that even if the introduction of Ontologese as a Carnapian framework meant that certain key statements are analytic, this analyticity could be considered harmless as long as there are reasons Sider can point at, mainly concerning certain conceptual connections and broadly abductive considerations, which suggest—*at least to him or whoever is sympathetic to his project*—that these analytic truths relevantly depend on, for example, the facts described by an empirical science like fundamental physics. Similar remarks would seem to hold (mutatis mutandis) for non-naturalists like Fine: they may ultimately consider analyticity a tolerable price to be paid if there were reasons proceeding from, for example, a priori methods or broad abductive considerations indicating—*to them or to their sympathizers*—that the analytic truths in questions are relevantly dependent on the real.

Note that the manoeuvre just described is intended to make the idea of analyticity acceptable to the serious ontologists, who are free to believe that the analytic truths they defend are grounded in certain facts. The Carnapian reaction to a sentence like 'Analytic truths are grounded in empirical facts' should not be relevant here.[6] My point in this section was merely that the serious ontologist does

---

[6] The Carnapian could question the semantic import of this statement understood as *external* to a framework. At this point, the serious ontologist would have to show that this statement is (i) internal and (ii) worthy of being used for the purposes of inquiry.

not have to capitulate to analyticity tout court, but has the means to *make analyticity more agreeable* and in accordance with her project.

2.4 Two Ways of Overcoming a Stalemate

A consequence of the present vindication of the meaningfulness of ontological questions is that a proposal is made as to how to bring the serious ontologist and the Carnapian theorist closer to each other, as engaged in the same task of introducing and developing linguistic frameworks. A similar objective is pursued by Dorr (2005), who wishes to overcome the dialectical stalemate between the serious ontologist and the Carnapian deflationist. As he reconstructs it, the stalemate is as follows: on the one hand, the serious ontologist purports to cast her questions in Ontologese, a language whose quantifiers are apt to capture certain fundamental ontological truths; on the other hand, the Carnapian denies that there is any special meaning to the quantifiers or claims not even to understand them. Dorr wishes to overcome the stalemate by 'initiating' the Carnapian deflationist to the ontology debate. This initiation consists in (1) having her accept that there is a language of ontology modelled along lines acceptable by Carnapian standards; and (2) having her accept that she is indeed speaking that language. In other words, resolving the stalemate implies showing that the Carnapian *had been a party to the debate all along.*

Importantly, no such objective is pursued in the present chapter. My objective is, as stated, to show that the meaningfulness of ontological questions as cast in serious-ontology terminology can be defended in terms acceptable to the Carnapian herself. This involves setting Ontologese forward as a Carnapian framework. However, this does not require the Carnapian to *endorse* the framework, let alone for her to acknowledge she had been using any other framework all along. My goal here was much more modest; namely, have the Carnapian at least *provisionally accept or tolerate* Ontologese as meaningful. This has the result of making it possible for the serious ontologist and the Carnapian to see each other as peers who are both engaged in proposing and exploring certain linguistic frameworks, motivated by broadly pragmatic considerations.

This result should not, however, obscure the main purpose I have been pursuing so far; namely, arguing that being able to vindicate the meaningfulness of ontological questions *reduces the threatening impact* of the Carnapian critique in terms of meaninglessness. The moral that can be drawn from all this should be mainly that that lack of meaning is not the number-one problem for serious ontology, for there are ways in which such meaningfulness can be relevantly vindicated. The following section deals with the question of what other problems serious ontology might still be left with, once the semantic one has been 'deflated'.

2.5 Serious Ontology Vindicated? Not So Fast...

I have argued that it is possible to defend the meaningfulness of serious onto-logical questions in terms acceptable to a modern-day (hence non-verificationist) Carnapian. This, however, might not be enough to defend the respectability of ontology, for although meaninglessness need not be the number-one problem, this field of inquiry may be beset by other difficulties.

For example, it might be argued that the main problem for serious ontology is not so much a semantic one, but an *epistemic* one. There are at least two ways to shed light on this problem. According to the first way, the methods serious ontologists employ fail to ensure that we do *not* believe true propositions about what there is (or what is real, or what grounds what) *by sheer luck* (Warren 2016b). What is problematic is that we seem to lack an explanation of how we happen to be reliable believers, if we are such (cf. Field 1988). That we are reliable believers in matters of metaphysics despite the epistemic limitations we suffer from in this field of inquiry—such as lack of causal access to certain objects—is a striking phenomenon. As Joshua Schechter explains, '[a]t least *ceteris paribus*, a theory that provides an explanation of a striking phenomenon is better than one that treats it as merely accidental' (MS, p. 6) (cf. also Korman 2014, p. 2). However, since no explanation seems forthcoming in the case of metaphysics, the theory appears doomed to treat the phenomenon as accidental or lucky, thus incurring a cost. So, in this specific case, the trouble lies not so much in our lack of true beliefs, but rather in explanatory deficiencies associated with the epistemology of metaphysics.

According to the second way of advancing an epistemic challenge, the problem is one of underdetermination of theory by evidence. At least with respect to some ontological debates, it may be contended that all the competing options in the debate are equivalently well positioned to explain the key data and to do so with comparable degrees of simplicity, parsimony, and other theoretical virtues. It then becomes difficult to decide which theory is favoured by both the available data and by abductive considerations. This ultimately implies that there is insufficient justification to endorse a single theory over the others (Bennett 2009; cf. also Willard 2013; Kriegel 2011; Wilson 2011; Bradley 2018), something which in turn seems to prejudge our claim to knowledge in this field of inquiry.

These challenges do not have straightforward answers, and it is improbable that any satisfactory solutions will emerge in the future. It is therefore possible that, even though the serious ontologist manages to dodge the meaninglessness problem, she will be left with a much more insidious difficulty, namely the epi-stemic challenge as sketched in the two ways above. Vindicating the meaningful-ness of ontological questions is therefore not yet a way of conclusively rescuing serious ontology.

Let me also add a second and final point: showing that the meaninglessness critique can be resisted is also a way of providing *a critique of this critique*. The idea that metaphysical questions are just sheer 'nonsense' has been a very influential one, and still has several supporters among the critics of ontology and metaphysics (Price 2009; Thomasson 2015, 2016; Chalmers 2009; Hofweber 2009, etc.). If the considerations offered in section 2.3 are on the right track, the critique—or at least one influential version of it—does not have as much traction as its proponents would expect, and its role in an overall critical assessment of ontology should therefore be downplayed (see again Wilson 2011). Plus, more energy should be spent in articulating and exploring the epistemic challenges mentioned above, as well as possible ways of facing these challenges.

2.6 Conclusion

Ontology has long been criticized on account of the alleged lack of meaning of its questions and central tenets; to this day, this semantic critique—aptly purged of residual verificationist traces—seems to be alive and well. In contrast with it, it is possible to argue that existence questions and claims are not meaningless by adducing considerations that a Carnapian deflationist could accept. This, however, does not mean that ontology is conclusively vindicated. Ontology may have much bigger problems than semantic defectiveness: for example, epistemic defectiveness. But this is another story.[7]

References

Bennett, K. 2009. 'Composition, Colocation, and Metaontology'. In D. J. Chalmers, David Manley, and Ryan Wasserman (eds.), *Meta-Metaphysics: New Essays on the Foundations of Ontology*, 38–76. New York: Oxford University Press.

Bradley, D. 2018. 'Carnap's Epistemological Critique of Metaphysics', *Synthese*, 195(5): 2247–2265.

Carnap, R. 1928. *Pseudoproblems in Philosophy*, transl. by R. A. George. Berkeley/Los Angeles, CA: University of California Press.

[7] This chapter was presented at Trinity College, Dublin, during the conference The Language of Ontology, in September 2017. I am grateful to Vera Flocke, Thomas Hofweber, Jonathan Schaffer, and Richard Woodward for helpful feedback during the conference. Special thanks to David Kovacs and Raffael Krismer for reading and commenting on this chapter during the writing process. Work on the ideas that inspired this chapter was funded by the Humboldt Foundation, whose fellowship allowed me to collaborate with the DFG Emmy Noether Research Group 'Ontology After Quine' (WO-1896/1-1) led by Richard Woodward at the University of Hamburg.

Carnap, R. 1950. 'Empiricism, Semantics and Ontology', *Revue Internationale de Philosophie*, 4 (1950): 20–40.

Chalmers, D. J. 2009. 'Ontological Anti-Realism'. In D. J. Chalmers, David Manley, and Ryan Wasserman (eds.), *Meta-Metaphysics: New Essays on the Foundations of Ontology*, 77–129. New York: Oxford University Press.

Chalmers, D. J., Manley, D., and Wasserman, R. (eds.). 2009. *Meta-Metaphysics: New Essays on the Foundations of Ontology*. New York: Oxford University Press.

Dorr, C. 2005. 'What We Disagree about When We Disagree about Ontology'. In Mark Eli Kalderon (ed.), *Fictionalism in Metaphysics*, 234–286. Oxford: Oxford University Press.

Eklund, M. 2009. 'Carnap and Ontological Pluralism'. In D. J. Chalmers, David Manley, and Ryan Wasserman (eds.), *Meta-Metaphysics: New Essays on the Foundations of Ontology*, 130–156. New York: Oxford University Press.

Field, H. 1988. 'Realism, Mathematics and Modality', *Philosophical Topics*, 16(1): 57–107.

Fine, K. 2001. 'The Question of Realism', *Philosophers' Imprint*, 1(1): 1–30.

Fine, K. 2009. 'The Question of Ontology'. In D. J. Chalmers, David Manley, and Ryan Wasserman (eds.), *Meta-Metaphysics: New Essays on the Foundations of Ontology*, 157–177. New York: Oxford University Press.

Hofweber, T. 2009. 'Ambitious, Yet Modest, Metaphysics'. In D. J. Chalmers, David Manley, and Ryan Wasserman (eds.), *Meta-Metaphysics: New Essays on the Foundations of Ontology*, 260–289. New York: Oxford University Press.

Jenkins, C. S. I. 2005. 'Knowledge of Arithmetic', *British Journal for the Philosophy of Science*, 56(4): 727–747.

Jenkins, C. S. I. 2008. *Grounding Concepts: An Empirical Basis for Arithmetical Knowledge*. Oxford: Oxford University Press.

Jenkins, C. S. I. 2015. 'Serious Verbal Disputes: Ontology, Metaontology, and Analyticity', *Journal of Philosophy*, 111(9–10): 454–469.

Kitsik, E. 2020. 'Explication as a Strategy for Revisionary Philosophy', *Synthese*, 197: 1035–1056. doi: https://doi.org/10.1007/s11229-018-1774-z.

Korman, D. Z. 2014. 'Debunking Perceptual Beliefs about Ordinary Objects', *Philosophers' Imprint*, 14(13): 1–21.

Kriegel, U. 2011. 'Two Defenses of Common-Sense Ontology', *Dialectica*, 65(2): 177–204.

Price, H. 2009. 'Metaphysics after Carnap: The Ghost Who Walks?'. In D. J. Chalmers, David Manley, and Ryan Wasserman (eds.), *Meta-Metaphysics: New Essays on the Foundations of Ontology*, 320–346. New York: Oxford University Press.

Putnam, H. 1987. *The Many Faces of Realism*. La Salle, IL: Open Court.

Quine, W. V. O. 1960. *Word and Object*. Cambridge, MA: MIT Press.

Quine, W. V. O. 1981. *Theories and Things*. Cambridge, MA: Harvard University Press.

Rosen, G. 2010. 'Metaphysical Dependence: Grounding and Reduction'. In B. Hale and A. Hoffmann (eds.), *Modality: Metaphysics, Logic, and Epistemology*, 109–136. Oxford: Oxford University Press.

Schaffer, J. 2009. 'On What Grounds What'. In D. J. Chalmers, David Manley, and Ryan Wasserman (eds.), *Meta-Metaphysics: New Essays on the Foundations of Ontology*, 347–383. New York: Oxford University Press.

Schechter, J. MS. 'Luck, Rationality, and Explanation: A Reply to Elga's "Lucky to Be Rational"', unpublished manuscript.

Sider, T. 2009. 'Ontological Realism'. In D. J. Chalmers, David Manley, and Ryan Wasserman (eds.), *Meta-Metaphysics: New Essays on the Foundations of Ontology*, 384–423. New York: Oxford University Press.

Sider, T. 2011. *Writing the Book of the World*. New York: Oxford University Press.

Thomasson, A. L. 2009. 'Answerable and Unanswerable Questions'. In D. J. Chalmers, David Manley, and Ryan Wasserman (eds.), *Meta-Metaphysics: New Essays on the Foundations of Ontology*, 444–471. New York: Oxford University Press.

Thomasson, A. L. 2015. *Ontology Made Easy*. New York: Oxford University Press.

Thomasson, A. L. 2016. 'Carnap and the Prospects for Easy Ontology'. In S. Blatti and S. Lapointe (eds.), *Ontology after Carnap*, 122–144. New York: Oxford University Press.

Warren, J. 2016a. 'Internal and External Questions Revisited', *Journal of Philosophy*, 113(4): 177–209.

Warren, J. 2016b. 'Sider on the Epistemology of Structure', *Philosophical Studies*, 173(9): 2417–2435.

Willard, M. B. 2013. 'Game Called on Account of Fog: Metametaphysics and Epistemic Dismissivism', *Philosophical Studies*, 164(1): 1–14.

Wilson, J. M. 2011. 'Much Ado about "Something"', *Analysis*, 71(1): 172–188.

3

Collapse and the Varieties of Quantifier Variance

Matti Eklund

3.1 Introduction

Quantifier variance—a much-discussed thesis in recent discussions of ontology—will be my focus here. The thesis has been characterized in many not obviously equivalent ways. Eventually, the differences between the characterizations will be a theme. Quantifier variance was introduced into the literature, under that name, by Eli Hirsch in a series of articles from the early 2000s onwards, collected in his (2011), but the general idea has since Hirsch's important work taken on a life of its own (and Hirsch himself credits Putnam with the basic idea). In his recent (2015)—which will be the focus of some of the present discussion—Jared Warren operates with this characterization:

> there are distinct and inequivalent quantifier meanings such that the different parties in various ontological disputes can be interpreted as using different unrestricted existential quantifiers.[1]

In his seminal (2011) book, Ted Sider characterizes quantifier variance as follows:

> ontological deflationists cannot accept that quantifiers carve at the joints. In my view they should go further and uphold *quantifier variance*, to use Hirsch's term: the claim that there are multiple candidates to be meant by quantifiers, none of which carve perfectly at the joints, but none of which are exceeded in joint-carving by any other quantifier candidate.[2]

This at least provides a general idea of what quantifier variance is about, even if, as we will see, there are importantly different formulations of the thesis.

Quantifier variance is often held to be significant for broader issues regarding ontology. Here is what Warren says about the matter:

---

[1] Warren (2015), p. 241. [2] Sider (2011), p. 175.

Matti Eklund, *Collapse and the Varieties of Quantifier Variance* In: *The Language of Ontology*. Edited by: J. T. M. Miller, Oxford University Press (2021). © Oxford University Press. DOI: 10.1093/oso/9780192895332.003.0004

So, when a compositional nihilist says "there are no chairs!" and a compositional universalist replies "there are so chairs!", they need not be really and truly disagreeing, since each might be speaking the truth in their own language with their own quantifier. Quantifier variance has been championed by Hilary Putnam and Eli Hirsch, but it has come under heavy fire from ontological realists in every camp.[3]

Sider takes quantifier variance to entail what he calls "ontological deflationism", characterized as follows:

> According to this view, the philosopher's question of whether holes exist is confused, because the extraordinary, philosophical sense of the existence of a hole has not been, and cannot be, clearly specified. The only coherent question is the more mundane one of what exists according to ordinary standards. And this mundane question can be settled by a conceptual analysis of ordinary standards; there is no need to resort to the Quinean methodology. Likewise for the other questions of philosophical ontology—questions about the existence of numbers, propositions, events, past and future objects, tables and chairs, and so on.[4]

Somehow, quantifier variance is supposed to have a deflationary upshot for ontology. It is something to be opposed by "ontological realists". Note that it is not obvious how quantifier variance could have any such upshot. Take Warren's characterization of quantifier variance. It says only that there are different quantifier meanings, whence ontological disputants can find themselves having a merely verbal dispute. But why should this be thought to be in conflict with any kind of "realism"? Is it not a philosophically fairly boring fact that disputants can happen to speak past each other?

What I will do here is to discuss how quantifier variance is best understood, and how to think about its purported broader significance for ontology. I will do this through discussing two arguments that have prominently been used against the thesis of quantifier variance: the collapse argument and the so-called Eklund-Hawthorne argument.[5] The upshot of the discussion will be that there are different kinds of quantifier variance theses, with different sorts of implications for ontology and not all equally vulnerable to the counterarguments proposed. Thus put, the project of the chapter may sound bland. But I believe that distinguishing between the different quantifier variance theses both helps sort out significant confusions in the literature and helps put the spotlight on importantly different ways in which one might be an ontological deflationist.

---

[3] Warren (2015), p. 241.   [4] Sider (2011), p. 167.
[5] I have elsewhere used labels such as "the Tarskian argument" (Eklund 2008) and "the semantic argument" (Eklund 2009) for the latter.

In the background of the discussion of quantifier variance is the ("Quinean") assumption that existence is adequately expressed using so-called existential quantification. I too will take this assumption for granted.[6] For someone who rejects the assumption, seeing existential quantification as ontologically innocent and seeing existence as better expressed using an existence predicate, things will look different. In her setting, the relevant variance thesis is not quantifier variance but a corresponding thesis about what different existence predicates there are. In occasional footnotes, I will remark on how differently things look from that perspective.

3.2 The Collapse Argument

Warren's formulation of quantifier variance invites the question what it is for there to be different unrestricted existential quantifiers. Warren addresses this:

> according to quantifier variance, an expression in any given language is an existential quantifier expression just in case it plays the inferential role of the existential quantifier, i.e., if it obeys the standard introduction and elimination rules for the existential quantifier.[7]

Quantifier variance as Warren states it then involves the claim that there are non-coextensive expressions which all play the inferential role standardly associated with the existential quantifier.[8]

This thesis is disproven if it can be shown that any two expressions with this inferential role must be equivalent. This is what the so-called *collapse argument* seeks to show. The collapse argument goes back to work by Harris (1982), and has been used by, for example, Hale and Wright (2009) in attempts to refute quantifier variance.

Warren uses the dispute between (mereological) universalists and (mereological) nihilists in metaphysics to illustrate quantifier variance. (Mereological nihilism is the thesis that no matter what some objects are, those objects do not have a sum. Mereological universalism is the thesis that no matter what some objects are, those objects do have a sum.) Quantifier variance, as applied to this dispute, says that there is a language, Universalese, where the universalist's utterances come out true, and a language, Nihilese, where the nihilist's utterances come out true; and these languages employ different existential quantifier

---

[6] For some discussion of the reasonableness of such an assumption, see Eklund (2014).

[7] Warren (2015), p. 242.

[8] In a non-Quinean setting things would look very different. What would be the inferential role associated with an existence predicate of the kind the non-Quinean uses?

expressions, in the sense characterized. While it may be useful to have a concrete example like universalism/nihilism in mind, I will speak instead of "Biglish" and "Smallish", where Biglish corresponds to a more liberal ontological view and Smallish corresponds to a more restrictive one; and I will reformulate examples accordingly.[9]

Working with this example, here is the collapse argument as Warren presents it, in broadest outline. I use "$\exists_B$" for the Biglish quantifier and "$\exists_S$" for the Smallish quantifier. Suppose

$$\exists_B x\ \text{chair}(x) \tag{1}$$

Then let "α" be a name of an object witnessing the truth of (1). We then have, by the standard elimination rule for the quantifier,

$$\text{chair}(\alpha) \tag{2}$$

If the Smallish quantifier is indeed an existential quantifier, then, the argument runs, it obeys the standard introduction rule for an existential quantifier. But then from (2) we can infer

$$\exists_S x\ \text{chair}(x) \tag{3}$$

But then, Warren says, stating the upshot of the argument, "We've established, in [Smallish]... that '[$\exists_S$]x chair(x)' is true. But this is a disaster, since, by stipulation, '[$\exists_S$]x chair(x)' is false in [Smallish]".[10]

Warren notes that as presented, the collapse argument is based on a non sequitur: sentence (1) is a sentence only of Biglish and (3) a sentence only of Smallish— so in which language were we supposed to carry out the argument?

There is no doubt that there is a problem. But can the argument be repaired? One obvious strategy for the friend of the collapse argument is to say that if indeed there are such languages as Smallish and Biglish, one should be able to *combine* the two languages, and then in the combined language argue that the two supposedly inequivalent quantifiers are equivalent.

Warren considers simply adding sentences like (1) to Smallish and says about this:

---

[9] I here follow Sider (2011); see p. 181.
[10] Warren (2015), p. 243. Warren's own exposition is considerably more careful and elaborate. I have tried to distil the argument down to bare essentials.

we could add this sentence to [Smallish], but then we'd also need to add the [Biglish] quantifier rules to complete the collapse argument and this would alter the language and thereby block the *reductio* of quantifier variance.[11]

This may be somewhat quick. Warren notes that just because the collapse argument goes through in the combined language Smallish∪Biglish does not immediately mean that there cannot be a language Smallish as envisaged. That is surely correct. But the needed extra premise—if there is a language Smallish as envisaged, then there must also be a language Smallish∪Biglish with two different existential quantifiers—is, although far from obviously true, rather natural to accept. If there are such-and-such meanings for expressions to have, why can't expressions with these different meanings cohabit—exist in the same language? (There may be good reasons not to accept the general principle that in any case where there are expressions with different meanings, they can cohabit. The semantic paradoxes present problems. But in the present case we would be dealing with paradox-independent restrictions on the general principle.)

Whatever in the end to say about Warren's objection, Warren's own preferred suggestion is that a sentence like (1) of Biglish be translated non-homophonically into Smallish, using "the plural quantifiers and predicates of [Smallish] to stand proxy for the singular quantifiers and predicates of [Biglish]".[12] The reason this is supposed to help is that if we replace the sentence of Biglish in the above argument with its non-homophonic translation into Smallish, then the reasoning of the argument does not go through.

When assessing this suggestion, let us distinguish between two theses the friend of quantifier variance might maintain regarding what languages there are. The *weak thesis* is that there are languages like Biglish and Smallish as envisaged, in the sense that there are two languages like ordinary language except that the "biggist's" (e.g. the universalist's) characteristic utterances are true in the one but the smallist's (e.g. the nihilist's) characteristic utterances are true in the other. The *strong thesis* says that there can be such languages, while both languages employ what can be regarded as, in some sense, *different unrestricted existential first-order quantifiers*, expressions whose meanings are *unrestricted existential quantifier meanings*.[13]

The difference between the thesis is that the weak thesis does not say anything about what kinds of meanings the relevant expressions have. The friend of the weak thesis will have to say something also of utterances of sentences that on the surface involve unrestricted existential quantification, but there is nothing in

---

[11] Warren (2015), p. 246.   [12] Warren (2015), p. 246f.

[13] In the non-Quinean setting, the strong thesis would be the claim—however it is to be cashed out—that different languages can contain co-extensive predicates which all count as existence predicates.

the thesis that commits her in any way regarding what kinds of meanings these sentences and the expressions they contain actually have.

It can of course be questioned what the strong thesis even means. What does it even mean to say that there are these different meanings? But whatever exactly the strong thesis amounts to, the supposed difference between the two theses should be plain. The weak thesis in no way commits to there being different unrestricted existential first-order quantifiers. The weak thesis could be true, for example, because one of the parties does not use "there are" to express a quantifier meaning. The friend of the weak thesis can even completely dismiss the question of which expressions have quantifier meanings; for the friend of the strong thesis, by contrast, that issue is central.

Warren's translation suggestion illustrates the distinction between the weak and strong theses. Assuming the plural translation suggested by Warren to be otherwise workable, the weak thesis may well be vindicated. But the plural translation is not helpful when it comes to vindicating the strong thesis. If we speak Smallish, then we understand the speaker of Biglish not as using a different unrestricted existential first-order quantifier but as employing different linguistic means.

Recall Warren's own statement of quantifier variance: "Quantifier variance is a meta-ontological view according to which there are distinct and inequivalent quantifier meanings such that the different parties in various ontological disputes can be interpreted as *using different unrestricted existential quantifiers*". Taken at face value, the formulation suggests that Warren is concerned with the strong thesis: quantifier variance as he presents it requires that the parties use different unrestricted existential quantifiers. The mere fact that the disputants speak different languages, and mean different things by locutions like "there are",[14] does not mean that they use different unrestricted quantifiers: for it may be that at least one of the disputants does not use an unrestricted quantifier at all. And to stress, if Warren is concerned with the strong thesis, what he says about translation is problematic. What language is the quantifier variantist herself supposed to speak? If she speaks Smallish, then given Warren's suggestion about translation, she can't say of speakers of Biglish that they "use a different unrestricted existential quantifier". (If she speaks Biglish, a different concern arises: must she not interpret the speaker of Smallish as using a restricted existential quantifier?)

Warren's explicit formulation of quantifier variance suggests that he is concerned with the strong thesis, but his own reasoning reveals that he is concerned with the weak thesis.

---

[14] I will throughout follow established custom in philosophical discussions of ontology and treat "there are" as itself a quantifier expression. This isn't true to the linguistic facts, but it doesn't matter. The important thing is just to speak of some natural language expression which is a quantifier, and "there are" is the standard example used.

3.3 Free Logic

In a different context, Jason Turner suggests responding to the collapse argument by adopting the quantifier rules of a version of free logic instead of classical logic. Turner's proposal is that, using the appropriate logic, one cannot infer something of the form "∃xF(x)" simply from "F(t)"; one also needs "∃x(x=t)".[15] This blocks the collapse argument: we cannot infer

$$\exists_s x \ chair(x) \tag{3}$$

from

$$chair(\alpha), \tag{2}$$

unless we have

$$\exists_s x \ (x=\alpha).$$

In Turner's context, this seems clearly to be the right response. He is concerned to defend a version of what has come to be called *ontological pluralism*—the thesis that there are different modes of being. As Turner and Kris McDaniel develop the thesis, it amounts to claiming that there are different natural quantifiers: for each mode of being, there is a natural quantifier ranging over exactly what enjoys that mode of being.[16] Then one can reason that even if something is in the range over the quantifier ranging over (say) all abstracta, it is not in the range of a quantifier ranging over all concreta—and adopting free logic the way Turner does reflects this.

The quantifier variance setting is different. In the case of quantifier variance, the hypothesis is that there are—at least in *some* sense, recall the weak/strong distinction—different *unrestricted* quantifiers. This does not mean that Turner's strategy cannot be used. I will return to it. What it does mean is that Turner's strategy is more problematic in that case.

3.4 Quantifier Variance Theses

It is worth comparing some different characterizations of quantifier variance found in the literature in light of the distinction between the weak and the strong

---

[15] Turner (2010), p. 25f.   [16] See, for example, McDaniel (2017) and Turner (2010, 2012).

theses. In section 3.5 I will turn to the question of what sort of quantifier variance thesis is more philosophically significant.

Hirsch's own formulations consistently suggest the weak thesis. In the introduction to his (2011), he states, "Quantifier variantism says that there is no uniquely best ontological language with which to describe the world. I take this to imply that (i) there are a number of possible truth-conditionally equivalent ontological languages, and (ii) these languages are of equal metaphysical merit".[17] In his (2002), one of his earliest papers defending quantifier variance, he characterizes quantifier variance by saying,

> Putnam's doctrine of quantifier variance implies that the expression "there exists something" can be interpreted in a way that makes the sentence true or in a way that makes the sentence false. Since both interpretations are available to us, we have a choice between operating with a concept of "the existence of something" that satisfies the mereologist or operating with a different concept that satisfies the anti-mereologist.[18]

In a (2009) paper, the characterization is that quantifier variance demands that it is possible "that quantifier-like expressions in different languages may have different semantic functions; they may contribute differently to the characters of sentences".[19] Nowhere do we see the characteristic demand of the strong thesis: that the quantifier-like expressions of the different expressions really have quantifier meanings.

Here is the formulation of quantifier variance that Hirsch and Warren operate with in their joint (2019):

> A modest form of quantifier variance says that, in many ontological disputes, if you are on one side of the dispute, you can conceive of a possible language whose sentences are true just in case philosophers on the other side of the dispute would be willing to assert them. More explicitly, this means that, if your opponents hold the X-position you can conceive of a possible X-language such that…in any context of utterance, [a] speaker of the X-language can both reasonably and truthfully assert the same (phonetically individuated) sentences (with respect to a possible world) that the X-philosophers assert.[20]

I am actually not sure what Hirsch and Warren have in mind when they call this form of quantifier variance "modest", but their statement does correspond to what I earlier called the weak thesis.

Ted Sider (2007) characterizes "Neo-Carnapian quantifier variance" as follows:

---

[17] Hirsch (2011), p. xiv.   [18] Hirsch (2002), p. 69.   [19] Hirsch (2009), p. 239.
[20] Hirsch and Warren (2019), p. 592.

There is a class, C, containing *equally* and *maximally* natural candidate meanings for quantifier expressions, in that: (i) no member of C is more natural than any other member of C, and (ii) no candidate meaning for quantifier expressions that is not in C is as natural as any member of C. Each position in the debate over the ontology of composite material objects comes out true under some member of C.[21]

Sider here crucially speaks of "meanings for quantifier expressions", and seamlessly goes on to discuss these as "quantifier meanings". For quantifier variance as Sider conceives of it to be true, there must be different kinds of quantifier meanings as described—and Sider (2007) is then largely devoted to a discussion of what this might mean. In that work, Sider then focuses on the strong thesis.

In his later (2011) book, however, Sider explicitly distances himself from the strong thesis. The official characterization of quantifier variance, quoted above, is that it is "the claim that there are multiple candidates to be meant by quantifiers, none of which carve perfectly at the joints, but none of which are exceeded in joint-carving by any other quantifier candidate". This does not clearly indicate whether it is the strong or the weak thesis Sider has in mind. But Sider goes on to reflect that what friends of quantifier variance "really care about is vindicated simply by the claims that: i) there are multiple possible languages of this sort; ii) quantificational claims can have different truth-values in the different languages; and iii) none of the languages are more joint-carving than the rest".[22] Hence, it need not bother quantifier variantists—in Sider's (2011) sense—if what is superficially a quantifier expression in another language gets interpreted in such a way as not to have a quantifier meaning.

My remarks here have focused on relating the different formulations to the weak and strong theses characterized. But there are obviously other salient differences as well. Some characterizations—the one from the introduction to Hirsch's (2011) and Sider's two characterizations—explicitly mention something about being best, or most natural or most joint-carving. Other characterizations—Hirsch's other characterizations and the one from Hirsch and Warren's joint paper—do not mention anything of the kind.

3.5 Philosophical Significance

Is the weak thesis or the strong thesis more philosophically significant? Or, better, since the strong thesis entails the weak one: what, if anything, of philosophical significance does the strong thesis add to what the weak thesis already provides?

---

[21] Sider (2007), p. 209.　　[22] Sider (2011), p. 176.

The answer may depend on ulterior philosophical motives. Let me in what follows describe some different outlooks on ontology, all in some way related to the broad theme of quantifier variance, and how they relate to the weak and strong theses.

Suppose that philosopher X sets out to show that some ontological disputes are verbal, in the sense that the propositions the disputants affirm actually are consistent with each other, contrary to appearances. Let me call the thesis that X defends *verbalism*. On her view, some or many ontologists speak past each other, speaking somewhat different languages and not noticing that they do so. Notice that this verbalism is compatible with taking ontology very seriously. Consider a view like Ted Sider's ontological realism, according to which there is a privileged quantifier and the proper way to do ontology is to consider what exists in the sense of the privileged quantifier. An ontological realist can take in her stride the point that ontologists tend to speak past each other. That descriptive point about how ontology tends to be practised is consistent with the significance and feasibility of her envisaged project of investigating what exists in the sense of the privileged quantifier. (It would be different if it were *plainly impossible* to have an ontological dispute which is non-verbal: but such a strong verbalist claim—much stronger than a claim to the effect that ontological disputes tend to be verbal— falls on its own implausibility.[23])

For X's purposes, it does not *immediately* matter whether it can be said that these philosophers use different unrestricted existential quantifiers. All that matters is that they use "there are" and similar expressions with different meanings. Perhaps not more than one of these meanings is a meaning of an unrestricted quantifier—but why should that be a concern? Only the weak thesis is immediately relevant. X is in no way committed to the strong thesis. What she says is compatible with the strong thesis, and there could be independent reasons to believe the strong thesis, but that is another matter.

Compare now philosopher Y, seeking to defend a more principled deflationary view. On Y's view, there is no metaphysically privileged quantifier meaning, but there simply are different languages, with different quantifiers, all equally apt for the task of describing the world. No language, and no quantifier, is metaphysically privileged over all others. Y's view deflates ontology in the following sense. While ontology might have seemed deep when it was thought that questions about what exists had some special metaphysical standing, one can, given Y's view, see that they don't (a language using "exists" could without loss be replaced by one of the alternative languages), and no other notion of existence has that special metaphysical standing either. Notice that Y's view has nothing to do with verbalism. It is perfectly consistent with Y's

---

[23] On this issue regarding verbalism, see further my (2016).

view that disputing ontologists seldom or never are talking past each other but instead typically use expressions with the same meanings.

I remarked above on the fact that some but not all of the characterizations of quantifier variance include a clause about a best, or most natural, or most joint-carving quantifier meaning. Any such clause would be beside the point for X's purposes; but such clauses go straight to the heart of what Y is after.

Recall too Sider's saying that according to ontological deflationism, "the extraordinary, philosophical sense" of "exists" simply "cannot be" clearly specified, and the only coherent question in the vicinity "is the more mundane one of what exists according to ordinary standards". Ontological deflationism in this sense can be vindicated by Y's view. Y is naturally understood as saying that there are different mundane existence concepts but no "extraordinary" one. X's view, by contrast, is of no help in vindicating it, since X's view doesn't immediately do anything to cast doubt on there being a special philosophical sense of "exists".

When it comes to Y's view it is clearly the strong thesis which is relevant, for Y's view, as stated, is centrally concerned with what quantifier meanings there are. Moreover, Y's thesis seems more philosophically significant than X's, since Y's thesis is of greater principled significance for ontology.

Recall here Turner's appeal to free logic. How to evaluate this appeal depends crucially on whether it is X's or Y's view that is at issue. If it is X's verbalism that is at issue, then the question is whether the disputants' respective quantifiers are governed by the rules of free logic—or better, whether when the disputants state in their respective languages what the rules are, they say things that sound free logic-y. If it is Y's thesis that is at issue, the question is what sorts of rules the "best" quantifiers are governed by—classical rules or free logic rules.

The theoretical map can be made more complicated. There is a view in the ballpark of Y's but relevantly different that deserves bringing up. Why focus on Y's view *as stated*—which centrally concerns what quantifier meanings there are—instead of a view in the same ballpark? This other view would rather say,

> A language which employs our existence concept is just one among many possible languages there are, languages that instead use other kinds of representational means describe the world equally well, and no kind of possible language is metaphysically privileged over all others.

Call this Z's view. Z's view is of the same general kind as Y's. Z, like Y, presents a thesis about what possible languages there are and how they relate; contrast X, who makes a claim about how actual debates are prosecuted. The difference with Y's view is that Z's view does not commit itself to the other languages employing expressions with quantifier meanings. The other languages need not employ anything like a counterpart of the quantifier we employ.

Note that there are importantly different kinds of views of Z's kind. On one type of view of that kind, there are possible languages as good as ours that employ nothing like ordinary quantification. On another type of view of Z's kind, it is only said that there are possible languages as good as ours where the counterpart of the existential quantifier is only somewhat unlike the ordinary existential quantifier—maybe it only obeys slightly different inference rules. A reason for emphasizing the possibility of the latter kind of view is that already slight differences in what inferences rules are obeyed affect the applicability of the collapse argument.

Z's view appears to pack the same deflationary punch as Y's view: it deflates ontology in the same way. What is so special about questions about what *exists*, if we can equally well state our theory of the world in, so to speak, existence-free terms?[24] But Z's view, like X's, needs only the weak thesis—despite the other differences there are between X and Z.

Could Y's view possibly have a significance which Z's view lacks? Perhaps like this. Z's view alone does not preclude that there is only one way—or one best way—to describe the world in quantificational terms. One can then say, even given Z's view, that if the world is to be described in quantificational terms at all, then it is a given how that is to be done. Y's view does preclude this. To the extent that this is an important difference, Y's view does have significance which Z's view lacks.

Whatever in the end to say about the differences between the views of Y and Z, there is a significant distinction between the view of X on the one hand and the views of Y and Z on the other. X's claim concerns what languages are actually spoken by some theorists; Y's and Z's claims concern possible languages and the relation between them. X's claim in no way involves judgements about which languages are in some sense better than others; Y's and Z's claims are centrally concerned with such judgements. While all three envisaged theorists focus on language and approach questions of ontology via language, they do so in fundamentally different ways.

3.6 Dorr's Template

I have used the views of philosophers X–Z to illustrate the difference between the weak and the strong theses, the relationship between these theses, and what

---

[24] If, in order to express existence, a quantifier must be governed by some definite set of rules, then a position like Z's should seem still more reasonable. Suppose it is held, for whatever reason, that the inference rules a quantifier must obey to express existence are familiar from classical logic. Then what of a language whose quantifier obeys instead, for example, the rules that Turner discusses? Such a quantifier does not express existence, given the assumption. But it is very much a further question whether this means that the language thereby describes the world less well.

significance different theses in the vicinity of "quantifier variance" can be said to have. The collapse argument itself has temporarily disappeared from view; let me now return to that argument.

Cian Dorr (2014) presents the following general strategy behind using a collapse argument against quantifier variance.

Interpretation premise: "∃" has the "∃-Intro" and "∃-Elim" properties in the languages of each of $L_1, \ldots, L_n$.

Theorem: If $\exists_1$ has these properties in L_1 and $\exists_2$ has them in L_2, and (...possible further conditions on L_1 and L_2...), then $\exists_1$ in L_1 is "equivalent" to $\exists_2$ in L_2.

Conclusion: The meanings of "∃" in the languages of $L_1, \ldots, L_n$ are all "equivalent" (...provided that these languages pairwise satisfy the relevant further conditions).[25]

There are, as Dorr emphasizes, importantly different formulations of the "∃-Intro" and "∃-Elim" rules, and one gets different versions of the argument depending on what rules one focuses on (and perhaps different versions of quantifier variance depending on what rules one takes as characterizing an existential quantifier). Each version must be evaluated separately.

Using Dorr's template, let me revisit the weak and strong theses. Dorr's template involves certain placeholders, like the talk of satisfying "relevant further conditions". But even without getting into what the further conditions might be, we can make some remarks. Given the strong thesis, we have a natural motivation for the interpretation premise. It is natural to think that for two expressions to express unrestricted existential quantifier meanings is for them both to satisfy such-and-such introduction and elimination rules. Given the weak thesis, there is not the same immediate reason to suppose that the expressions in question satisfy the same inference rules. Insofar as there is reason to accept the interpretation premise, it comes from a different source: direct attention to how the specific languages are actually used.

One complication for the friend of the collapse argument is that it is not sufficient for her purposes that in the different languages same-sounding statements of the rules come out true: for such a statement might include an expression, like "singular term", which itself varies in meaning across languages. Expressions that fall under "singular term" of one language might fail to fall under "singular term" of another. The speaker of Biglish will talk of her "singular terms referring to tables", but a speaker of Smallish employing Warren's plural translation will describe these same terms not as "singular terms" but as "plural terms".

---

[25] Adapted from Dorr (2014), p. 508f. Dorr presents the strategy in the case of a simpler example, disjunction. I have reformulated in terms of existential quantification.

To illustrate, consider an argument that Michaela McSweeney (2017) offers regarding quantifier variance. McSweeney's overall aim is to provide a criterion for when we are justified in holding two theories to be metaphysically equivalent. The details of McSweeney's positive proposal do not matter for present purposes, but briefly, her proposal centres on there being a common definitional extension of these theories.[26]

Regarding quantifier variance, she says,

> The quantifiers occupy the exact same proof-theoretic role for the universalist and the nihilist. Both the nihilist and the universalist will themselves *say* that they are using our regular old semantics and inference rules for the quantifiers. And if they are right that they are doing so, then there is a very quick argument that there can be no [common definitional extension] of universalism and nihilism. Let's call universalism T_u and nihilism T_n. The quantifiers, exists$_u$ in L_u and exists$_n$ in L_n, have the same inference rules. When we move to L+, we cannot change these inference rules, for [that would violate] the requirement that L+ be a superset of L_u (and of L_n).[27]

And then, McSweeney concludes, exists$_u$-sentences and exists$_n$-sentences will be interderivable in L+, which contradicts the quantifier variantist claim. But consider the crucial claim that "the nihilist and the universalist will themselves *say* that they are using our regular old semantics and inference rules for the quantifiers". A quantifier variantist could in principle respond that more care is needed: while these theorists will utter same-sounding sentences of their respective languages when stating how their quantifiers work, we cannot conclude from this that the rules are the same, for some expressions employed in these statements may well differ in meaning.

Above I distinguished between the views of philosophers X, Y, and Z. Perhaps unsurprisingly, this distinction does not always map neatly onto the views of actual philosophers, even though I think the views of X, Y, and Z are the natural views in the vicinity. Consider, for example, Dorr (2014) and John Hawthorne (2006). These discussions both target the same sort of view, which, following Dorr, I will call "conciliationism". Dorr and Hawthorne characterize certain idealized communities, such that these communities use certain expressions and sentences differently from each other, and the conciliationist view is that all the communities express truths using these sentences. Neither Dorr nor Hawthorne demand that the communities employ different quantifier meanings (as opposed to merely using expressions like "something" or "there are" to mean different

---

[26] To be a bit more precise, McSweeney uses a tweaked notion of common definitional extension (see 2017, p. 279f), but these details do not matter for present purposes.

[27] McSweeney (2017), p. 282f.

things). Dorr's article is an extended discussion of the collapse argument. He discusses, roughly, under what conditions it is plausible that these communities mean such things by their quantifier expressions that a version of the collapse argument can be employed to show that their quantifier expressions are coextensive. He focuses on different statements of the rules of inference governing the quantifier expressions, and on the conceptual resources used in characterizing them. Hawthorne's discussion touches upon many different things, but among other things, he presents a version of the argument against quantifier variance to be presented in section 3.7.

Neither Dorr nor Hawthorne is concerned with the question that theorists Y and Z are concerned with—about what kind of language, if any, is in a certain sense best. Dorr even explicitly disavows talk of metaphysical merit, on the ground that he does not see a distinction between metaphysical and pragmatic grounds for preferring a language. The best understanding is that they instead are concerned with what X is concerned with. But their discussions are conducted as regarding certain idealized communities, so it is not entirely straightforward to apply the supposed lessons of their discussions to actual disputes, and thus to establish the sort of verbalist thesis that X is interested in.

It may be suggested that their aim is different from those of X–Z, but what could the alternative aim reasonably be? They are not making claims about actual theorists and their languages, and they are not evaluating the merits of the merely possible languages they discuss.

3.7 The Eklund-Hawthorne Argument

Thus far I have focused on the so-called collapse argument, which seeks to use the basic argumentative technique of Harris (1982) to show that two quantifiers obeying the standard inference rules are equivalent, in a way that disproves the doctrine of quantifier variance. I will now turn to another argument which has been used against quantifier variance: the so-called *Eklund-Hawthorne argument*. I will show that the very same issues arise with respect to this argument.

Here is the Eklund-Hawthorne argument as set out by Sider:

> Consider two characters, Big and Small. Big speaks an "expansive" language, Biglish, in which speakers freely quantify over tables. Big introduces a name, "a", for a table, and thus accepts "Table(a)". Small speaks a "smaller" language, Smallish, in which speakers refuse to quantify over tables. But Small is a quantifier variantist, and thinks that he does not genuinely disagree with Big. So Small says to himself, speaking in Smallish: "Even though there are no tables, the sentence 'Table(a)' is true in Biglish". But this commits Small—and all quantifier

variantists, who must accept the scenario as described—to rejecting familiar Tarskian ideas about semantics…In order for "'Table(a)' is true in Biglish" to be true in Smallish, "There is something that 'a' denotes in Biglish" must be true in Smallish. But what would this object—in the Smallish sense of "object"—be, if not a table?[28]

I prefer to use Sider's formulation to work with over, for example, one of my own for a number of reasons. It is a nice formulation. Those who discuss the argument frequently turn to this formulation. And if I worked with one of my own formulations, I would have a harder time resisting a temptation to get bogged down in, and try to defend, details regarding the formulation.[29]

The argument purports to present a certain problem for the quantifier variantist. But exactly what is the problem?

In a joint paper critically discussing the Eklund-Hawthorne argument, Hirsch and Warren (2019) present the argument as follows (they speak of universalism and nihilism—as elsewhere, I have replaced such talk with generic talk of "big" and "small"):

1. We are in the position to acknowledge the possibility of there being a language Biglish corresponding to the standpoint of the Biggists.
2. If it is impossible in one language to formulate a Tarskian semantics for another language, then speakers of the first language are in no position to acknowledge the possibility of the second language.
3. It is impossible to formulate in Smallish a Tarskian semantics for Biglish.
4. Therefore, our language cannot be Smallish.
5. Therefore, Smallism is not true.[30]

As stated in Hirsch and Warren's numbered argument, the conclusion is just that nihilism is not true. And the mere fact that nihilism is untrue is compatible with quantifier variance. Quantifier variance, however exactly it is to be characterized, just says that there are different languages where different ontological sentences come out true. This is perfectly compatible with there being a fact of the matter regarding what sentences come out true in our language and hence which theses are true. But they go on to reflect, separately,

---

[28] Sider (2011), p. 181. My own presentations of the argument are found in, for example, (2008) and (2009), and Hawthorne's presentation is in his (2006).

[29] Turner's move is as relevant here as in the case of the original collapse argument. In a free logic setting, I cannot even reason from the truth of an atomic sentence in my own language to the conclusion that a singular term in the sentence refers to something.

[30] Hirsch and Warren (2019), p. 593.

If the argument succeeds it will generalize to show that our own language must be, in a sense, as "big" as any language that we can make intelligible to ourselves.... [This] certainly means that we cannot view another possible language's ontology as being "bigger" than our own, as modest variantism often requires.[31]

We can state this as a new conclusion:

6. Therefore, we cannot view another possible language's ontology as being "bigger" than our own, as modest variantism often requires.

They turn to challenge the argument by challenging premise 3, and they do so by formulating a "Tarskian semantics", where a semantics is "Tarskian" in the sense at issue "just in case it generates truth conditions for sentences compositionally in the familiar fashion by mapping items from each syntactic category to objects of the appropriate type—names map (singularly) to objects, monadic predicates map (dividedly) to the objects they are true of, and so on and so forth".[32]

The specific way that they construct a Tarskian semantics involves finding entities quantified over in N such that the singular terms of U occurring in true atomic sentences refer to such entities. But to rely on this strategy is to overlook a central element of the Eklund-Hawthorne argument. Consider again the bit that comes after conclusion 5. To repeat: Hirsch and Warren agree that the upshot of the argument is "that we cannot view another possible language's ontology as being 'bigger' than our own, as modest variantism often requires". But if one makes sense of the supposedly bigger language U by interpreting its referring terms as referring to entities quantified over in one's own language, one makes *sense* of it, but only at the expense of treating it as not in fact *bigger*.

This immediately raises a further question: in what sense can one regard "another possible language's ontology as being 'bigger'" to begin with? The most straightforward sense in which another language's ontology can be bigger is if there are things that are in the range of that language's quantifiers that aren't in the range of the quantifiers in one's own language. But thus understood, the claim that another language's ontology is bigger is obviously self-refuting: one quantifies over the entities supposedly only quantified over in the other languages. Hirsch and Warren might then say that the only reasonable sense that can be made of the claim is something like: one language is in the relevant sense "bigger" than another if what *superficially* are quantifiers and singular terms in both are such that *superficially* the domain of

---

[31] Hirsch and Warren (2019), p. 593.   [32] Hirsch and Warren (2019), p. 594.

quantification of the former contains more than the domain of quantification of the latter, regardless of what deeper semantic differences there are beneath the surface appearances. A different view, however, would be that one need not and should not focus merely on superficial features, but one can focus on deeper similarities regarding the meanings of the expressions, for example similarities in what rules they obey.

Having rejected premise 3 in their original formulation of the Eklund-Hawthorne argument, Hirsch and Warren go on to consider the possibility that the demand is not just for some Tarskian semantics or other, but for a Tarskian semantics that satisfies some further condition.

One possible demand is that a semantics for a language should provide synonyms for the expressions of the object language. Hirsch and Warren reject this demand as implausibly strong. They then consider the demand that the semantics should be especially natural or simple, and note, among other things, that it is not out of the question that the only semantics that can be given in one language for another language is quite unnatural and complex.[33] A third possibility they consider is that the semantics offered should in some sense "explain" reference. They consider two versions of this, where the most relevant for present purposes is the version they spend the most time on, according to which the demand is that "the mapping used in the semantics be identical to the unique (privileged) reference relation". They call a semantics satisfying this condition a *Reference Semantics*. They reject the demand for a Reference Semantics, saying in essence that if the languages at issue employ different concepts of existence, then they will relatedly employ different concepts of reference. Let me quote what they say:

> The semantic shape of an alien language need not fit easily against the shape of our language. All that matters, for variantists, is that we can understand the coarse-grained truth conditions of their sentences. Their concept of the existence of something does not match ours, and as goes existence so goes reference. It is okay that we cannot provide a semantics for their language in terms of our concept of reference, though of course in terms of their concepts it is trivially true to say "The word 'table' refers to tables". The basic upshot is that the truth conditions of the sentences of an alien language need not depend on reference in our sense of "reference".[34]

This may seem obviously right. As goes existence, so goes reference—and hence, it may be thought, to the extent that an argument against quantifier variance relies on

[33] Hirsch and Warren (2019), p. 601.   [34] Hirsch and Warren (2019), p. 604.

the demand for a Reference Semantics, it begs the question. However, there are complications. For example, Hirsch and Warren's own characterization of quantifier variance is neutral on the issue of whether some existence concept is privileged. So even if what they argue is correct and there are, in some sense, different reference relations to employ, one could be privileged. But I will focus on other difficulties regarding what Warren and Hirsch say about the Eklund-Hawthorne argument, and I now turn to them.

A first item of business is to relate this argument back to the collapse argument. Recall Warren's complaint regarding the collapse argument as initially formulated: the sentence

$$\exists_B x\ chair(x) \tag{1}$$

and the sentence

$$\exists_S x\ chair(x) \tag{3}$$

belong to different languages, so how can one and the same argument have (1) as a premise and (3) as a conclusion? But one way of repairing the argument, distinct from the ones discussed above, is to reason first in Biglish, and there conclude

$$chair(\alpha), \tag{2}$$

and then turn to Smallish and there reason that "chair(α)" of Biglish is true, and from there conclude, in Smallish, that there exists something which satisfies "chair(x)" of Biglish. Assuming we can disquote, (3) follows. The question will be whether such moves are justified.

Enter the distinctions drawn earlier, between the strong and the weak theses, and between the views of philosophers X, Y, and Z. X is a verbalist and defends only the weak thesis. For X it will be a kind of empirical claim whether one can take a true putative subject-predicate sentence of the language of another disputant and assume that there is something to which the subject term refers; it will likewise be a kind of empirical claim whether predicates like "chair(x)" plausibly have the same meaning in the languages of the different disputants. Y's and Z's claims, by contrast, concern what possible languages there are, and how these languages compare. In that setting the relevant claim to investigate will concern, for example, whether a language in which we cannot perform the relevant disquotation will be expressively deficient.

I will not here attempt to assess these different kinds of assumptions. My only point here is that the different claims rely on quite different assumptions, and proper assessment would look very different depending on what claims and assumptions we are focusing on.

3.8 Concluding Remarks

Here is what I hope to have accomplished here. I have distinguished and discussed some different theses that go under the name quantifier variance. I have distinguished and discussed some different claims that can be made about the significance of quantifier variance. I have discussed some prominent arguments against quantifier variance, the collapse argument and the Eklund-Hawthorne argument, in light of these distinctions. One thing I have not done is to try to render categorical judgements about what we should say. I am, as indicated above, sceptical of the significance of X's verbalism. That leaves the views of Y and Z. I used to think that Y's position best captured the significance of quantifier variance. But I now incline towards Z's view, and hence towards thinking that it does not really matter whether the languages concerned contain expressions with quantifier meanings.

References

Chalmers, David, Manley, David, and Wasserman, Ryan (eds.) 2009. *Metametaphysics*. Oxford: Oxford University Press.

Dorr, Cian. 2014. 'Quantifier Variance and the Collapse Theorems', *The Monist*, 9: 503–570.

Eklund, Matti. 2008. 'The Picture of Reality as an Amorphous Lump'. In Theodore Sider, John Hawthorne, and Dean Zimmerman (eds.), *Contemporary Debates in Metaphysics*. Oxford: Blackwell.

Eklund, Matti. 2009. 'Carnap and Ontological Pluralism'. In David Chalmers, David Manley, and Ryan Wasserman (eds.), *Metametaphysics*. Oxford: Oxford University Press.

Eklund, Matti. 2014. 'On Quantification and Ontology'. In *Oxford Handbooks Online*, www.oxfordhandbooks.com.

Eklund, Matti. 2016. 'Carnap's Legacy for the Contemporary Metaontological Debate'. In Stephan Blatti and Sandra Lapointe (eds.), *Ontology after Carnap*. Oxford: Oxford University Press.

Hale, Bob and Wright, Crispin. 2009. 'The Metaontology of Abstraction'. In David Chalmers, David Manley, and Ryan Wasserman (eds.), *Metametaphysics*, 178–212. Oxford: Oxford University Press.

Harris, J. H. 1982. 'What Is So Logical about the "Logical" Axioms?', *Studia Logica*, 41: 159–171.

Hawthorne, John. 2006. 'Plenitude, Convention, and Ontology'. In *Metaphysical Essays*. Oxford: Oxford University Press.

Hirsch, Eli. 2002. 'Quantifier Variance and Realism', *Philosophical Issues*, 12: 51–73.

Hirsch, Eli. 2009. 'Ontology and Alternative Languages'. In David Chalmers, David Manley, and Ryan Wasserman (eds.), *Metametaphysics*, 231–258. Oxford: Oxford University Press.

Hirsch, Eli. 2011. *Quantifier Variance and Realism*. New York: Oxford University Press.

Hirsch, Eli and Warren, Jared. 2019. 'Quantifier Variance and the Demand for a Semantics', *Philosophy and Phenomenological Research*, 98: 592–605.

McDaniel, Kris. 2017. *The Fragmentation of Being*. Oxford: Oxford University Press.

McSweeney, Michaela. 2017. 'An Epistemic Account of Metaphysical Equivalence', *Philosophical Perspectives*, 30: 270–293.

Sider, Theodore. 2007. 'Neo-Fregeanism and Quantifier Variance', *Proceedings of the Aristotelian Society*, Suppl. Vol. 81: 201–232.

Sider, Theodore. 2011. *Writing the Book of the World*. Oxford: Oxford University Press.

Turner, Jason. 2010. 'Ontological Pluralism', *Journal of Philosophy*, 107: 5–34.

Turner, Jason. 2012. 'Logic and Ontological Pluralism', *Journal of Philosophical Logic*, 41: 419–448.

Warren, Jared. 2015. 'Quantifier Variance and the Collapse Argument', *Philosophical Quarterly*, 65: 241–253.

4

Ontological Expressivism

Vera Flocke

4.1 Introduction

The basic question of ontology concerns *what exists*. For example, do composite objects (objects with parts) exist? Realists say *yes*, and anti-realists say *no*. For example, universalism is a form of realism according to which any two objects compose another thing (see Sider 2001); and nihilism is a form of anti-realism according to which no two things ever compose another thing (see Sider 2013). Answers intermediate between these two extremes are possible. For example, van Inwagen (1995) argues that only living beings have parts; and Markosian (1998) argues that, as a matter of *brute*, not further explicable fact, some pluralities compose another thing, and others do not.

The basic question of meta-ontology concerns whether there are determinate, mind-independent ontological facts. For example, is there a determinate, mind-independent fact with regard to the existence of composite objects? Realists say *yes*, and anti-realists say *no*. Recent debates in meta-ontology usually are in-house debates between realists of different stripes. *Heavyweight realists*, such as Sider (2011), think that ontological debates are deep, and answering ontological questions requires philosophical work. But *lightweight realists*, such as Hirsch (2011) and Thomasson (2015), think that ontological debates are misguided, and the answers to ontological questions obvious. Here is a table, so some things are composite. 5 is a number, so there are numbers. And so on.

In this chapter, I provide an anti-realist alternative, and develop a version of *ontological expressivism*. Ethical expressivism is the view that utterances of normative sentences express noncognitive mental states. Analogously, ontological expressivism is the view that ontological existence claims express noncognitive mental states. An "ontological existence claim" is the utterance of a quantified sentence in the context of an ontological debate. The specific version of ontological expressivism that I will develop draws a distinction between *ontological* and *ordinary* existence claims. Ordinary existence claims are utterances of quantified sentences in non-philosophical contexts, and they express beliefs.

Lightweight realism is often motivated by the impression that something is going wrong in ontological debates. For example, Hirsch (2011 (2008, p. 178)) says that he has an "immediate intuitive feeling that [certain ontological disputes

Vera Flocke, *Ontological Expressivism* In: *The Language of Ontology*. Edited by: J. T. M. Miller, Oxford University Press (2021). © Oxford University Press. DOI: 10.1093/oso/9780192895332.003.0005

are] not substantive, that [they are] in some sense merely verbal".[1] Thomasson (2015, pp. 1–2) says in a similar spirit that, on the view of most philosophers throughout history, "many of the currently contested ontological questions, e.g. 'Do tables, chairs, and persons exist?' would have been thought far too obvious to be worth contesting".

Ontological expressivists agree that something is going wrong in ontological disagreements. However, they do not jump to the conclusion that ontological disagreements are pointless. They think that we need to reconsider what the point of these disagreements really is. According to ontological expressivists, ontological disagreements do not help us to figure out some determinate, mind-independent fact; but they help speakers to coordinate on a commonly accepted ontology.

I will in what follows focus on explaining a specific version of ontological expressivism. My strategy will be analogous to Gibbard's strategy in *Thinking How to Live*, as he describes it in the following passage:

> By sheer stipulation [. . .] the meaning of this phrase 'the thing to do' is explained expressivistically: If I assert 'Fleeing is the thing to do', I thereby express a state of mind, deciding to flee. I then proceed to ask how language like this would work. In the back of my mind, of course, is the hypothesis that important parts of our actual language do work this way. Mostly, though, I don't argue for this hypothesis; rather I ask whether the hypothesis is coherent and what its upshots would be.   (Gibbard 2003, p. 8)

Gibbard wants to show that normative discourse *can* be analyzed along expressivist lines. To show how this analysis goes, he stipulates an expressivist-friendly meaning for the phrase 'the thing to do'. Like Gibbard, I want to show that ontological disagreements *can* be analyzed along expressivist lines. To show how this analysis goes, I will stipulate an expressivist-friendly meaning for the sentence 'some things are composite', and draw out the upshots of this hypothesis.

My discussion will be organized as follows. I will develop a specific version of ontological expressivism that is modeled after Gibbard's (2003) norm-expressivism. I begin by explaining the norm-expressivist template (§4.2), and the difficulties that a transfer of the norm-expressivist template to ontology poses (§4.3). I then develop ontological expressivism by discussing what the semantic contents of quantified sentences are (§4.4), which mental states utterances of quantified sentences express in the context of ontological disagreements (§4.5), and what the difference between ontological and ordinary existence claims is (§4.6). I then discuss the content and function of ontological disagreements (§4.7), explain the

---

[1] I take this quotation from a passage where Hirsch discusses a particular disagreement between Locke and Butler about the identity of a tree. But Hirsch is clear that he means his view to generalize to many other ontological debates.

roots of ontological expressivism in the views of Carnap (§4.8), and conclude with a summary (§4.9).

Before I get started, I want to clarify some notational conventions: p is a proposition, 'p' (in single quotation marks) is a sentence (whose semantic value is p), and "p" (in double quotation marks) is an utterance of the sentence 'p' in a context.

4.2 The Norm-Expressivist Template

There are many versions of meta-ethical expressivism. Some expressivists, such as Ayer (1971 (1936)), think that utterances of normative sentences do not express propositions but instead express noncognitive mental states. On this view, normative sentences are distinguished by their lack of propositional content.[2] However, proponents of such an approach are under pressure to provide a compositional semantics that explains which mental state a complex sentence expresses as a function of the mental states that its component parts express. Beginning with Geach (1965), many philosophers have doubted that this semantic program can be successfully executed. In particular, if the semantic values of normative terms are noncognitive mental states, then it appears impossible to provide a *unified* semantics for languages that mix normative and descriptive terms.[3]

Norm-expressivists think that normative sentences do express propositional contents. They think of the expression of a mental state as an illocutionary act; something that we do when we utter sentences. They then argue that utterances of normative sentences perform a particular illocutionary act, which is the expression of a noncognitive mental state. This approach has no problem with providing a unified semantics for both descriptive and normative language, since both descriptive and normative sentences express propositional contents.[4] That's why I will use norm-expressivism as the template for ontological expressivism.

In more detail, Gibbard (2003, p. 57) argues that the semantic contents of declarative sentences are not ordinary propositions but sets of fact-plan worlds. A fact-plan world is an ordered pair $<w, p>$, where w is a world and p is a hyperplan.[5]

---

[2] In the words of Ayer (1971 (1936, p. 110)): "if I say to someone, 'You acted wrongly in stealing that money', I am not stating anything more than if I had simply said, 'You stole that money'. In adding that this action is wrong I am not making any further statement about it. I am simply evincing my moral disapproval of it".

[3] See Schroeder (2009) for an evaluation of the semantic program of expressivism.

[4] Yalcin (2018) provides a more detailed discussion of the difference between these two types of expressivism. Yalcin's expressivism is different from the view I develop here, however, since Yalcin's semantics brings in a new non-standard parameter, while my view brings in a new non-standard modality; see §4.7.

[5] I.e., p is a function that maps each occasion for action in w to a set of actions that are permitted on that occasion.

A *hyperplan* is a function from "occasions for action" to sets of actions. An "occasion for action" is a possible situation in which one has a choice between various actions that one could perform, and can be modeled as a world that is centered on an agent x and a time t ($<w, x, t>$) (Gibbard 2003, p. 57). Given an occasion for action, a hyperplan returns a non-empty subset of the actions that are permitted on that occasion. Sets of fact-plan worlds can equivalently be represented as functions from ordered pairs $<w, p>$ to truth-values.

According to Gibbard, the semantic content of *any* declarative sentence is a set of fact-plan worlds. There is a difference between normative and descriptive sentences, however. The semantic contents of descriptive sentences are functions from ordered pairs $<w, p>$ to truth-values where the hyperplan parameter does not matter; it is idle. But for normative sentences the hyperplan parameter does make a difference. Normative sentences express semantic contents whose truth-value depends on the non-standard hyperplan parameter.[6]

Gibbard goes on to argue that, because of the difference in the semantic contents of descriptive and of normative sentences, utterances of descriptive sentences express beliefs, but utterances of normative sentences express noncognitive mental states. Specifically, on Gibbard's view, "murder is wrong" expresses the acceptance of a norm that prohibits murder. The attitude of *norm-acceptance* can be explained in more detail as follows. The semantic contents of normative sentences are sets of fact-plan worlds $\{<w_n, p_m>, \ldots\}$ and are true or false only relative to specific values of the hyperplan parameter p. Specifically, if $w_@$ is the actual world, then $\{<w_n, p_m>, \ldots\}$ is true relative to p_n if and only if $<w_@, p_n> \in \{<w_n, p_m>, \ldots\}$. In order to assign a truth-value to the set $\{<w_n, p_m>, \ldots\}$, it thus has to be assessed relative to a specific value of the hyperplan parameter (or relative to a certain range of values of this parameter that assign the same truth-value to the set $\{<w_n, p_m>, \ldots\}$). The acceptance of a norm n is a disposition to assess the semantic contents of normative sentences only relative to hyperplan parameters that model n. For example, someone who accepts a utilitarian norm, represented by hyperplan p_U, assesses the truth of sets of fact-plan worlds by considering whether they contain $<w_@, p_U>$ as element.

This explanation of the nature of norm-acceptance is not fully explicit in Gibbard's text. But some of what he says points in the direction of this account.

---

[6] The fact that some expressivist views are built on relativistic foundations raises a question. What, fundamentally, is the difference between relativism and expressivism? I think this is a difficult question that I cannot fully answer here. MacFarlane (2014, p. 173) suggests the following. Consider the following two utterances:
"He believes that murder is wrong."
"He believes that grass is green."
According to MacFarlane, a truth-relativist would say that (1) and (2) are ascriptions of the very same mental state, while a norm-expressivist would say that (1) and (2) are ascriptions of fundamentally very different attitudes. Believing that murder is wrong fundamentally involves a noncognitive attitude toward norms, i.e., norm-acceptance. Believing that grass is green involves no such attitude.

For example, Gibbard (2003, p. 91) says: "Hera accepts hyperplan p. She thus regards an act a as okay to do in a situation s if and only if her plan p permits a in s." The acceptance of a plan, in Gibbard's terminology, stands proxy for the acceptance of a norm. It is unclear, however, whether Gibbard intends this remark as a *definition* of norm-acceptance. Whether or not it was Gibbard's intention to define norm-acceptance in this way, it is in any case possible to construe the acceptance of a norm n as a disposition to assess the truth of semantic contents only relative to hyperplan parameters that model n.

This discussion of norm-expressivism gives us a template to match. Norm-expressivists think that both normative and descriptive sentences express propositional contents. However, normative sentences express contents that are in a sense standpoint-dependent; their truth depends on the value of a non-standard hyperplan parameter. Because of this difference, utterances of normative sentences express noncognitive mental states while utterances of descriptive sentences express beliefs. In §4.3, I will begin to discuss how this template can be transferred to ontology.

4.3 Transferring the Template

Norm-expressivism, as explained in §4.2, draws a distinction between two different kinds of speech acts: utterances that express beliefs and utterances that express noncognitive mental states. This distinction is furthermore reflected on the sentential level as a distinction between descriptive and normative sentences; and on the propositional level as a distinction between two kinds of propositions (those whose truth-value depends on the hyperplan parameter p and those whose truth-value is insensitive). This distinction is very important. Not all utterances express noncognitive mental states, and we need a systematic explanation for which utterances do and which ones don't.

Ontological expressivists need an analogous distinction. Consider the utterance, "Some prime number is greater than 7." In the context of a philosophical discussion, this utterance can be understood as the affirmation of a Platonist ontology. Let's call these kinds of utterances "ontological existence claims". Ontological expressivists think that ontological existence claims express noncognitive mental states. But in a mathematical context, the very same utterance can be understood as the description of a mathematical fact. Let's call these kinds of utterances "ordinary existence claims". Ordinary existence claims express a belief.

Many meta-ontologists draw a related distinction between two kinds of existence claims. For example, Fine (2009) distinguishes between "ontological" and "quantificational" questions; the former concern what's metaphysically real and are expressed using universal quantifiers; the latter merely concern what exists and are expressed using existential quantifiers. As a second example, Thomasson

(2015) (inspired by Carnap (1950)) distinguishes between "internal" and "external" existence claims; the former are made using an interpreted language, while the latter are not properly meaningful. So, it is not a distinctive feature of ontological expressivism that the view distinguishes between two kinds of existence claims. What's distinctive is how the distinction is drawn: ordinary existence claims express beliefs while ontological existence claims express noncognitive mental states.

Given that ontological expressivists distinguish between ontological and ordinary existence claims, they are confronted with a question. When does the utterance of a sentence express a noncognitive mental state, and when does it express a belief? What is the difference between the two kinds of existence claims? Unlike norm-expressivists, ontological expressivists cannot draw the distinction at the sentential level. As the above example illustrates, utterances of one and the same sentence ("Some prime number is greater than seven") can in some contexts express a belief and in other contexts express a noncognitive mental state. Furthermore, the kind of distinction that norm-expressivists draw at the propositional level is not easily replicated in the ontological case.

In more detail, Gibbard's distinction between worlds and hyperplans is an instance of a more general distinction between a perspective-independent or non-conventional "substratum" (in this case: a world) and a "carving" (in this case: a hyperplan) which in some way depends on a perspective or is conventional.[7] For example, in each world w, and at each occasion for action in w, a certain range of actions (which could be a unique action) maximize utility. This is how worlds provide a perspective-independent substratum. A hyperplan is a function that maps each world w and each occasion for action in w to a set of actions that can permissibly be performed on that occasion. For instance, a hyperplan that represents a utilitarian norm maps each world w and each occasion for action in w to the set of actions that maximize utility on that occasion. Hyperplans thereby carve a conventional, normative structure into the non-conventional substratum provided by the descriptive facts that hold at a world.

It appears impossible to reproduce an analogous distinction in the ontological case.[8] To see this point, it may be helpful to consider a proposal due to Chalmers (2009, §9). Chalmers suggests representing ontologies by means of "furnishing functions" that map worlds to domains of quantification. He then argues that the semantic contents of quantified sentences are sets of pairs $<w, f(w)>$, where w is a world and f is a furnishing function. If successful, one could then use this construction in order to transfer the norm-expressivist template to ontology.

---

[7] The terminology is due to Einheuser (2006).
[8] Thanks to Agustín Rayo for raising this point.

However, I am skeptical of this strategy. In particular, it is not clear what a world *minus* a domain of quantification is. Once one subtracts a domain from a world, there seems nothing left that is recognizably a world. It hence seems that the distinction between worlds and domains is not well defined, and it is therefore unclear what the parameter *f* is supposed to represent.

To illustrate the difficulty, it may help to consider the case of mereology. Mereological nihilists think that only simple objects exist, universalists think that any two things compose a third, and proponents of van Inwagen's (1995) "organicist" view think that a plurality of things *xx* compose some object *y* only if the plurality *xx* makes up a living being. It is tempting to think that simple objects provide a sort of substratum onto which the various mereological views impose different carvings. But this view amounts to saying that there really are only simples. Composite objects are not genuine constituents of reality but conventionally imposed. Rather than providing for a sense in which composition facts are perspective-dependent, this view amounts to a vindication of nihilism. Because of this difficulty, it is better to develop ontological expressivism without the distinction between a substratum and a carving.[9]

In sum, ontological expressivists need an explanation for why some utterances of quantified sentences express beliefs and others express noncognitive mental states, and it is hard to see how this explanation might go. In §4.4, I will propose a solution.

4.4 Objective and Non-Objective Propositions

Norm-expressivists think that normative propositions are standpoint-dependent, and descriptive propositions are not. Norm-expressivists then formally account for this sort of standpoint-dependence by arguing that the truth-value of normative propositions depends on the value of the hyperplan parameter. We can transfer the norm-expressivist template to ontology by formally accounting for standpoint-dependence, not as a sort of relative truth, but as a form of *modal contingency*.

In more detail, suppose that propositions are sets of worlds. The standard view is that a unique world is actual, and that a proposition is true iff the actual world is one of its elements. I think that ontological expressivists need to revise this standard conception, and instead say that multiple worlds are *candidates for being*

---

[9] A form of norm-expressivism can in principle be recovered as a special instance of ontological expressivism. On this approach, normative sentences express non-objective propositions; or candidate actual worlds differ with regard to the normative propositions that are true at them. This point shows that the distinction between worlds and hyperplan is in fact an inessential component of norm-expressivism.

actual.[10] We can then say that a proposition is *objective* iff it is true at all worlds that are candidates for being actual, and *non-objective* (or standpoint-dependent) iff it is true at only some of the worlds that are candidates for being actual. For example, applied to the case of composition, the view is this: multiple worlds are candidates for being actual, some of which contain composite objects and some of which do not. The proposition that some things have parts is therefore non-objective. However, the various candidate actual worlds also agree in many respects. For example, they all agree that Barack Obama was the 44*th* US president. If a proposition p is objective if and only if p is true at all worlds that are candidates for being actual, then we can use modal operators to reason about objectivity. Let $A = \{w_{@.1}, w_{@.2}, w_{@.3}, \ldots\}$ be the set of candidate actual worlds, and let the box '$\square$' express objectivity. Then '$\square p$' is true if and only if p is true at each world in the set A. Objectivity, on this view, is a form of necessity, and non-objectivity a form of modal contingency.

If multiple worlds are candidates for being actual, when is a proposition true? This question can be answered in two ways. On a relativist approach, propositions are fundamentally true or false only relative to a world. However, on an alternative, absolutist approach, truth fundamentally is a monadic property, and agents are *located at* a world depending on the kind of ontology that they accept. On the absolutist approach, speakers who accept different ontologies are like the inhabitants of different worlds. The proposition that some things are composite is "true for" a universalist and "false for" an absolutists; just as the proposition that Hillary Clinton is the 45*th* US president is false "for you" but "true for" your counterpart in a nearby possible world. But truth is absolute. My sympathies are with the absolutist approach, but nothing in what follows depends on this choice.[11]

How could multiple worlds be candidates for being actual? First, let's talk about what *worlds* are. According to modal realists, such as Lewis (1986), worlds are like physical universes. Arguing that multiple worlds are candidates for being actual then amounts to arguing that multiple physical universes are candidates for being actual. This is very implausible. However, according to abstractionist accounts, worlds are abstract objects that represent classically complete ways things might be. Three parts of this conception are important: worlds are *abstract* (and not concrete, as a modal realist would say). Second, worlds *represent* ways things might be. In particular, worlds represent ways the actual physical universe we live in might be. If a world represents how things actually are, then it is a candidate

---

[10] Barnes and Williams (2011) also suggest that there are multiple actualized worlds and use this notion to develop a theory of metaphysical indeterminacy.

[11] For more on the difference between absolutism and relativism, see Cappelen and Hawthorne (2009).

actual world. Third, worlds are *classically complete*. That means that, for each way things might be, a world either rules it in or rules it out.[12]

This gives us a certain three-layered picture: (1) things are a certain way; (2) worlds represent classically complete ways things might be; (3) a proposition p is a set of worlds and true at a world w if and only if $w \in p$.[13]

Given an abstractionist account, arguing that multiple worlds are candidates for being actual amounts to arguing that no world is the uniquely correct abstract representation of how things are. Multiple worlds represent how things are equally well.

We can spell out this idea in various ways. On a metaphysical version of the view, things are genuinely indeterminate, which is why various worlds represent how things are equally well.[14] Another conception has to do with the metaphysics of representation. Many philosophers are drawn toward views on which representation is not a fundamental relation but is grounded in something else, such as speakers' activities or attitudes.[15] For example, on one version of this view, a drawing of something (e.g., of Obama) represents its object only because speakers interpret it as a representation (of Obama). One might argue that there are at least two different representation relations, R_1 and R_2, and at least two worlds, w_1 and w_2, so that w_1 best represents$_1$ how things are, while w_2 best represents$_2$ how things are. Both of these worlds are actualized. A third conception is more directly epistemological. On this view, there *might* be a unique world that is the best abstract representation of how things are. However, even *if* there is such a world, we cannot know which one it is.[16] My sympathies are with the

---

[12] This abstractionist view can be further fleshed out in various ways. For instance, a popular conception takes abstract *states of affairs* as fundamental and conceives of possible worlds as classically complete states of affairs, so that, for each state of affairs, a world either rules it in or rules it out. See Menzel (2017, §2.2) for an overview and references. The details will not matter in what follows.

[13] My distinction between "ways things might be" and worlds understood as abstract objects resembles Chalmers' (2009, §8) distinction between two senses of 'world': the world understood as "the huge concrete reality within which we live" and worlds understood as abstract objects that are stipulatively defined as coming with built-in domains. However, Chalmers and I make different uses of this distinction. Chalmers thinks that "the huge concrete reality within which we live" can be "furnished" in different ways and introduces the notion of a "furnished world".

[14] This view would need to be supplemented with certain epistemological principles, however. In more detail, the following view creates a problem for ontological expressivists: if things are genuinely indeterminate, then the best ontology is one that represents them as indeterminate. For example, if the existence of numbers is a genuinely indeterminate matter, then the best ontology is one that represents the existence of numbers as an indeterminate matter. But then it seems that a speaker who assesses the truth of propositions by considering only worlds at which numbers exist makes a factual mistake. (Likewise for a speaker who assesses the truth of propositions by considering only worlds at which numbers do not exist.) In order to avoid this conclusion, proponents of ontological expressivism need to supplement their view with certain epistemological principles, according to which speakers are epistemically speaking permitted to resolve indeterminacy in how things are one way or another. Thanks to Justin Clarke-Doane for helpful discussions of this point.

[15] See, for example, Jones (2019, §IV) for a discussion.

[16] Here is a possible line of argument: knowledge of which world best represents how things are requires knowledge of how things are. That is, one can know which world is the best abstract representation of how things are only if one is able to compare the various worlds with what they represent;

representationalist account, but nothing in what follows will depend on this choice.

Which propositions are non-objective? Well, the ones under discussion in ontology. This answer is in a way circular, since the difference between ontological and ordinary existence claims is that ontological existence claims concern non-objective propositions. However, this circularity is not a problem but part of the approach. As I said in §4.1, the goal here is to show that ontological disagreements can be analyzed along expressivist lines. I assume that we have a pre-theoretic grasp on which disagreements are ontological, and offer an expressivist account of these disagreements.

4.5 Which Mental State?

Norm-expressivists think that "murder is wrong" expresses the acceptance of a norm that prohibits murder. As discussed in §4.2, this attitude can be understood as a disposition to assess the truth of propositions in a particular way. The acceptance of a norm n that prohibits murder is a disposition to assess the truth of propositions only relative to hyperplan parameters that model n. We can now transfer this view to ontology. On my view, ontological existence claims express a disposition to assess the truth of propositions in a particular way.

It may help to begin by illustrating this idea with a nontechnical example. Here is the example. Teachers often use *grading scales* when they assess the work of students. For example, suppose that Alyssa and Brianna are the teaching assistants for a course on ancient philosophy and are jointly grading a stack of exams. They have assigned points on a scale from 0 to 100 to each exam and are about to assign a letter grade to each student on the basis of the number of points that they achieved in the exam. Cameron got 95 points. Alyssa looks at her grading scale, according to which 95 points are sufficient for an A, and says:

Alyssa: "Cameron achieved an A."

Alyssa can be seen as using her grading scale as a rule for assessing the truth of the proposition that Cameron achieved an A in the exam, which she affirms. We can now distinguish between two different contexts. First, in contexts where Alyssa and Brianna have agreed on a grading scale, Alyssa's utterance expresses her belief that, according to the established grading scale, Cameron achieved an A in the exam. But in contexts where Alyssa and Brianna have not yet

and this comparison requires knowledge of how things are. But knowledge is a propositional attitude. The objects of knowledge are not *things* but propositions. For this reason, it is in principle impossible for us to know how things are. This is why we cannot know which world is the best representation of how things are. For this reason, there is a range of distinct actualized worlds that constitute equally acceptable circumstances of evaluation for assessing the truth of propositions.

agreed on a grading scale, Alyssa's utterance rather expresses her acceptance of a grading scale that would result in the assignment of an A to Cameron's exam.

Back now to ontology. I think that ontological existence claims express similar dispositions. For example, the utterance "Numbers exist" in the context of an ontological disagreement expresses a noncognitive disposition to assess the truth of propositions in a particular way. Often, these dispositions are related to assumptions that speakers make, background beliefs on which they rely, or methodologies and heuristics that they employ. For example, speakers may be convinced that there are no abstract objects at all and (based on this background belief) conclude that numbers do not exist. Or speakers might assume that one should accept all and only the existence of entities that are required for the truth of our best scientific theories, and then assess whether numbers exist by considering whether they are dispensable (as Field (1980) does). Or speakers might take it for granted that 5 is a number and use this assumption to infer that numbers exist (as Thomasson (2015) does). In all these cases, speakers make use of a variety of rules that guide their assessment of whether numbers exist.

As the foregoing examples show, speakers' behavior is messy. Different speakers assess the truth of propositions in various ways. This observation raises a challenge. How can we develop a unified model that covers all the different cases? What, in general, does it mean to follow a rule of assessment? I will answer this question using the notion of a *circumstance of evaluation*, due to Kaplan (1989). Roughly, my proposal is that to follow a certain rule of assessment means to be disposed to consider only certain circumstances of evaluation when one assesses the truth of propositions. I'll first explain what circumstances of evaluation are, and then explain the role that it plays.

Kaplan (1989) models the truth-conditions of declarative sentences by means of two sequences of parameters: *context* and *index* parameters. Context parameters are needed to account for the context sensitivity of certain expressions, such as indexicals. For example, when Ida says on March 11, 2018, "I was in Berlin yesterday", she says that Ida was in Berlin on March 10, 2018. What is said by Ida's utterance depends on the context of utterance, which includes a speaker and a time. Context parameters model this sort of context sensitivity. Index parameters, in contrast, are needed to model the circumstances of evaluation of a proposition. The circumstances of evaluation of a proposition are the circumstances that determine its truth-value. For example, the circumstances of evaluation of the proposition that Ida was in Berlin on March 10, 2018 are Ida's whereabouts on that day. Modal operators shift the relevant circumstances of evaluation. For example, when we ask whether it is *possible* that Ida was in Berlin on March 10, 2018, we evaluate whether Ida's possible whereabouts on March 10, 2018 include Berlin. Modal operators thus "shift" the circumstances of evaluation, and index parameters are needed to model this shiftiness.[17] I will in what follows set aside context parameters, since context sensitivity plays no distinctive role in my view. Index parameters play an important role, however.

For Kaplan (1989), circumstances of evaluation play a purely *semantic* role: they determine the truth-value and the modal profile[18] of propositions. However, I think that circumstances of evaluation also play a certain *psychological* role: speakers so to speak "look at" or consider circumstances of evaluation when they assess the truth of propositions. This take on Kaplan's framework does not conflict with common interpretations; it constitutes a natural extension. Kaplanian characters, which are functions from contexts of use to semantic contents, are often described as "rules of use" that tell speakers what a given sentence can be used to say depending on the context of utterance (see e.g. Ninan 2010, §2). I here suggest, analogously, glossing semantic contents, which are functions from circumstances of evaluation to truth-values, as *rules of assessment*. A speaker who considers only circumstances of evaluation of a certain kind effectively follows a particular rule of assessment. This gets us to what speakers express when they make ontological claims: they express a disposition to follow particular rules of assessment. For example, "numbers exist", uttered in the context of an ontological disagreement, expresses a noncognitive disposition to assess the truth of propositions by considering only circumstances of evaluation that contain numbers.

The conception of propositions as sets of worlds yields a specific version of ontological expressivism.[19] If propositions are sets of worlds, they can be evaluated at different worlds. The conception of propositions as sets of worlds hence results in a version of ontological expressivism according to which "numbers exist" expresses a noncognitive disposition to assess the truth of propositions by considering only worlds at which numbers exist.

In what sense is this disposition "noncognitive"? I here assume a rough-and-ready definition of 'noncognitive' according to which a mental state is noncognitive if and only if it is neither true nor false. For example, beliefs are cognitive mental states since they are true or false. Distaste for cilantro is a noncognitive mental state, however. Someone who does not like cilantro does not make a factual mistake. Now, philosophers often assume that each proposition has a unique *actual* circumstance of evaluation that determines its truth-value. However, as discussed in §4.4, ontological expressivists reject this assumption.

---

[17] Kaplan (1989, p. 494) justifies the distinction between context and index parameters in brief as follows: "given a *use* of [an] expression, we may ask of *what has been said* whether *it* would have been true or false in various counterfactual circumstances".

[18] That is, a proposition that is true at all worlds is necessary and a proposition that is true at some worlds is possible.

[19] Kaplan (1989, p. 494) thought that *what is said* by a declarative sentence is a structured proposition that mirrors the structure of the sentence by which it is expressed.

They think that, for at least some propositions, multiple circumstances of evaluation are candidates for being actual. For example, the proposition that some things are composite can be evaluated either by considering worlds that contain things with parts, or by considering worlds that do not contain things with parts. When speakers assess the truth of the proposition that some things have parts, they have a choice with regard to which of these circumstances they consider, or "look at". This choice is a noncognitive choice, and a subsequent disposition to only look at circumstances of evaluation that contain composite objects therefore is a noncognitive disposition (in a derivative sense).[20]

4.6 Ontological vs. Ordinary Existence Claims

I have proposed an *expressivist* analysis of ontological existence claims, which (in my view) express dispositions to assess propositions in particular ways. Next, I will go on to present a *contextualist* account of the difference between ordinary and ontological existence claims. Sentences with a given semantic content can, in my view, be used to express either an ordinary or an ontological existence claim, depending on the context in which they are used. For example, the sentence 'some things are composite' has a specific semantic content (which is a proposition) and an utterance of this sentence can be used to express either an ordinary or an ontological existence claim, depending on the context.[21] To explain this view, I begin by discussing how utterances express mental states.

Meta-ethical expressivists commonly rely on a minimal characterization of the expression relation.[22] According to this minimal conception, utterances of normative sentences express noncognitive mental states in the same way that descriptive sentences express beliefs. Consider, for instance, the utterance "grass is green". This utterance does not *assert* that the speaker believes that grass is green, but nevertheless *expresses* the speaker's belief that grass is green. Meta-ethical expressivists think that utterances of normative sentences express

---

[20] In more detail, asking whether a disposition is true or false may appears like a category mistake. Dispositions are not the sort of thing that could be true or false. However, *dispositions* may be based on *choices*, and may inherit a noncognitive status from the noncognitive choices on which they are based. In particular, on my view, dispositions to assess the truth of propositions in particular ways may be based on choices that are neither true nor false, and may therefore be themselves noncognitive in a derivative sense. Thanks to David Chalmers for helpful discussions of this point.

[21] The sort of context sensitivity that is relevant here is not ordinary context sensitivity. Ordinary context sensitivity is a kind of dependence of what is said by the utterance of a sentence on the context in which it is used. For example, 'I am in Berlin' asserts different propositions depending on the speaker. This kind of context sensitivity can be ignored for present purposes. The sort of context sensitivity in which I am interested concerns the illocutionary act performed by the utterance of a sentence in a context.

[22] See Fogal et al. (2018, §1.4) for a general discussion of what could be meant by the expression of a mental state by a sentence.

noncognitive mental states in just the same way. For example, "murder is wrong" does not *assert* that the speaker disapproves of murder but nevertheless *expresses* the speaker's disapproval of murder. Meta-ethical expressivists often do not provide a more detailed account of the expression relation. However, more can be said.

A theory of the expression relation is best developed against the backdrop of a general theory of speech acts and communication. I here assume a broadly Stalnakerian background theory.[23],[24] The central concept in Stalnaker's (1970, 1999, 2002, 2014) theory of communication is the concept of the *common ground of a conversation*. The basic thought is that the participants in a conversation share certain common presuppositions, which constitute their common ground. The nature of these presuppositions can be explained in various ways. According to Stalnaker's (2002, p. 704) conception, the common ground of a conversation is a collection of *common beliefs*.[25] He defines: "a proposition φ is common belief of a group of believers if and only if all in the group believe that φ, all believe that all believe it, all believe that all believe that all believe it, etc.".[26],[27] Speech acts, from a Stalnakerian perspective, essentially are attempts at influencing the common ground of a conversation. A sentence 'p' is associated with a certain dynamic update potential. For instance, declarative sentences have the potential to make a proposition commonly believed. The essential effect of uttering "p" is to realize this update potential in the context of the conversation. For example, the essential effect of an utterance of "The sun is shining" is to make it commonly believed that the sun is shining. This utterance successfully communicates that the sun is shining only if, as an effect of this utterance, it becomes commonly believed that the sun is shining. Communicative success, in this view, requires that speakers coordinate their mental states and converge on a certain class of commonly held beliefs.

Ontological expressivism is a view about the function of certain sorts of communicative exchanges. Ontological disagreements, according to ontological

---

[23] Gibbard (1990) relies on a broadly Gricean theory. See van Roojen (1996), Schroeder (2015 (2008)), and Schroeder (2008, ch. 2) for criticisms of this view.

[24] See, however, Harris (2019) for a criticism of common ground theories of communication.

[25] In contrast, Yalcin (2018) proposes to simply postulate a basic mental state—"call it *presupposition*, or the *conversational state*"—to play the needed role. Furthermore, there is pressure from various directions to include more structure in a model of the common ground of a conversation. For instance, Roberts (2012) argues that the common ground of a conversation also includes *questions*, and Yalcin (2012) argues that the common ground of a conversation includes probabilistic structure.

[26] The iteration in this definition is needed to account for the requirement that elements of the common ground be truly public. If participants in a conversation are uncertain about whether the belief in p is iterated, then they won't have reason to believe that everyone will act as though p is commonly believed. See Lederman (2017, p. 3) for a good illustration and explanation of this point. See Lederman (2018) for a criticism of the iterative conception of the common ground of a conversation. Thanks to Matt Mandelkern for a helpful discussion.

[27] Propositions in the common ground of a conversation need not *actually* be commonly believed; it is sufficient that every member in the conversation treat them as such.

expressivists, do not concern matters of fact. Rather, ontological disagreements serve the purpose of coordinating speakers on a certain range of noncognitive dispositions. Stalnaker's account, according to which the essential effect of utterances is to update the common ground of a conversation, fits extremely well with this view. As just explained, updating the common ground of a conversation is a matter of coordinating the mental states of speakers. Ontological expressivism can be seen as a special instance of this more general thesis: the essential effect of ontological existence claims is to update the common ground of a conversation by adding a noncognitive mental state. However, some important adjustments to the standard Stalnakerian framework need to be made, since we need to explain the difference between ordinary and ontological existence claims.

Stalnaker's framework incorporates a distinction between two closely related notions: semantic contents and update potentials. A sentence with semantic content p has the potential to add a mental state with content p to the common ground. For example, the semantic content of 'grass is green' is the proposition that grass is green, and this sentence has the potential to add the belief that grass is green to the common ground of a conversation. The abstract representation of the common ground of a conversation as a set of propositions obliterates the distinction between semantic contents and update potentials. If the semantic content of a sentence is a proposition, then its update potential is likewise represented by a proposition. In reality, however, the sentence has the potential to update the common ground of a conversation by a *belief in p*.

I think that we need to draw a further distinction, and distinguish the *essential effect* of an utterance "p" from the *actual constraint* that this utterance imposes on a particular conversation. The essential effect of uttering "p" is closely related to the update potential of the sentence 'p'. If the update potential of the sentence 'p' is to add p to the common ground, then the essential effect of uttering "p" is to add the belief that p to the common ground. In other words, the essential effect of "p" is to realize 'p's update potential. However, the actual constraints that an utterance "p" imposes on the common ground of a conversation are the actual changes that need to take place so that the essential effect of "p" becomes realized. For example, the essential effect of an utterance of "The sun is shining" is to make it commonly believed that the sun is shining. However, in a context where it is *already* commonly believed that the sun is shining, no change needs to take place in order for this utterance to realize its essential effect. Uttering "the sun is shining" imposes no constraints on the common ground in this scenario, which shows that essential effects and actual constraints may come apart.

I will use this machinery to explain how utterances of sentences express mental states. By the "expression of a mental state", I mean the imposition of an actual constraint on the common ground of a conversation. This is a stipulative definition of what I mean by the expression of a mental state for the purposes of my theory. The account does not cover all cases that are ordinarily regarded as expressions of mental states. For instance, it does not readily explain how an utterance of "ouch" expresses pain. One can successfully express that one is in pain with an utterance of "ouch" without inflicting pain on anyone else, or making pain commonly felt. However, the account works well for the kinds of cases that ontological expressivists aim to explain. These are cases in which mental states are expressed with the goal of coordinating with other speakers on a common mental state, which isn't true in the pain case. Furthermore, my account of the expression relation is especially well suited for explaining the difference between ontological and ordinary existence claims, as I will go on to argue.

An important feature of this account of the expression relation is that it results in a form of contextualism. An utterance "p" of a sentence 'p' may impose a variety of different constraints on the common ground of a conversation, depending on the context in which it is used. For example, suppose that it is commonly believed in a context that Donald Trump is president of the United States but some people are confused on who is House Speaker. In this context, the communicative success of "Trump is president and Pelosi is house speaker" requires that some speakers adopt the belief that Nancy Pelosi is house speaker. In this context, the utterance expresses the belief that Nancy Pelosi is house speaker. However, consider a context in which it is commonly believed that Pelosi is house speaker, but some speakers are unclear on who is president. In this context, the communicative success of "Trump is president and Pelosi is house speaker" requires that some speakers adopt the belief that Trump is president. In this context, the same utterance therefore expresses the belief that Trump is president. So, if the expression of a mental state is the imposition of a constraint on the common ground of a conversation, then an utterance "p" of a sentence 'p' may express a variety of different mental states, depending on the context in which it is used. This is the case even if 'p' does not contain indexicals and is otherwise context-insensitive.

This observation puts me in a position to explain the difference between *ontological* and *ordinary* existence claims. I think that an utterance "p" of a context-insensitive sentence 'p' may express either ordinary or ontological existence claims, depending on the context in which it is used. To illustrate, consider the following utterance:

(1) "Some things are composite."

In general, an utterance like (1) could take place in contexts of two different kinds:

(i) either in a context in which all speakers assess propositions in a way that results in the assignment of the same truth-value to the proposition that some things are composite, or

(ii) in a context in which some of the speakers assess propositions in ways that result in the assignment of different truth-values to the proposition that some things are composite.

Suppose (3) takes place in a context of the first kind (i). In this context, there are no relevant differences among the speakers with regard to how they assess propositions. The dynamic change that needs to take place in order to achieve agreement among the speakers at most requires that some speakers acquire a belief. The constraint that (3) imposes on such a context is an ordinary factual belief. In a context of this kind, an utterance of (3) expresses an ordinary existence claim. Suppose, however, that (3) takes place in a context of the second kind (ii). In such a context, there are relevant differences among the speakers with regard to how they assess the truth of propositions. The dynamic change that needs to take place in order to achieve agreement among the speakers is a change in how some of the speakers assess the truth of propositions. The constraint that (3) imposes on such a context is a disposition to assess the truth of propositions in a particular way. In a context of this kind, an utterance of (3) expresses an ontological existence claim.

4.7 Ontological Disagreements

Ontological expressivists think that ontological debates concern whether one should accept a certain non-objective proposition. For example, the debate on whether objects with parts exist concerns whether to accept the proposition that some objects have parts, and this proposition is non-objective. In order to come to an agreement in these debates, philosophers have to coordinate how they assess the truth of propositions. For example, they need to coordinate their assumptions with regard to what is required for composition to occur. However, if that's right, what reasons do we have for engaging in ontological disagreement? Aren't these disagreements just as pointless on my view as on the anti- metaphysical views of Hirsch (2011) and Thomasson (2015)?

According to ontological expressivists, reality is in a sense standpoint-dependent. Specifically, let a *fact* be a true proposition, and let *reality* be the totality of facts.[28] We can then distinguish between two sorts of reality: objective reality, which is the totality of all objective propositions; and standpoint-dependent realities, which are determined by the totality of all objective propositions plus an ontology. Objective reality leaves the truth of some propositions undecided. Standpoint-dependent realities include, for each

---

[28] See Rayo (2017) for a defense of the view that reality is the totality of facts, not of things.

proposition p, either p or not-p. By changing which ontology they accept, speakers leave objective reality untouched; but they change their individual standpoint-dependent reality.

Through ontological disagreements, speakers do two things. For one, they try to influence other speakers to accept a specific ontology. Furthermore, speakers who are not yet sold on a specific ontology use ontological disagreements to clarify which reasons speak for specific ontologies. They thereby try to figure out which ontology they should accept.

We can now distinguish between two questions. First, what reasons do we have for trying to figure out whether we should accept a specific non-objective proposition? It is very hard to give a general answer to this question. As a matter of fact, many people already care about non-objective questions. For example, many philosophers wonder whether numbers exist, or whether there are past or future objects. These philosophers already have reasons for trying to figure out whether they should accept certain non-objective questions, and no further argument is needed. But it is hard to offer reasons to someone who is not already engaged in questions concerning non-objective matters for why they should care. Perhaps there just are no general reasons to care about non-objective questions (and this is why it is often hard to explain to non-philosophers why they should care about philosophy).

Second, what reasons could convince someone to accept or reject a specific non-objective proposition? In general, the key question is whether acceptance of the proposition would make for an overall better standpoint-dependent reality. But this question raises a further issue: when is a specific standpoint-dependent reality better than another? Here a variety of arguments may play a role. A pipe wrench is not "in itself" better than a toothbrush, though a pipe wrench is better suited for wrenching a pipe than a toothbrush. Similarly, no standpoint-dependent reality is "in itself" better than another, though some standpoint-dependent realities may be better for certain purposes than others. One such purpose could be the purpose of doing science. From this viewpoint, acceptable standpoint-dependent reality should contain all and only entities that are required for the truth of our best scientific theories. This particular heuristic in any case is often employed by philosophers, such as Field (1980), when they consider whether to accept a specific ontology.

4.8 Historical Background

The version of ontological expressivism I have developed in this chapter is inspired by Carnap's (1956) influential views on ontology. Carnap argues that metaphysicians debate misguided questions. He thinks that ontological questions, such as the question of whether numbers exist, can be understood in two ways. First, this question can be understood as internal to the framework of mathematics. Understood in this way, its answer is "yes". This answer can, moreover, be trivially read off the "rules of the framework" and is therefore analytic (p. 209). Ontologists presumably do not mean to debate this trivial question. Alternatively, ontologists could be asking whether numbers exist in an external sense of this question, where what is at stake is the existence of numbers in a framework-independent sense (p. 209). But, Carnap argues, this external question would be "non-cognitive" (p. 210). Either way, there is no philosophically interesting question with regard to the existence of numbers. However, even though something about what Carnap says seems to be deeply and importantly correct, "it all seems to vanish when one tries to get clear just what it is" (Field 1984, p. 662).

According to my interpretation (Flocke 2020), Carnap should be interpreted *literally*: a certain subclass of external statements is "noncognitive" because statements in this class express noncognitive mental states. In more detail, Carnap distinguishes between *purely external* statements, which are independent from all frameworks, and *pragmatic external* statements, which concern which framework one should adopt. I argue that the latter express noncognitive mental states. Specifically, I propose that Carnapian "frameworks" are systems of rules for the assessment of "statements", which are utterances of ordinary language sentences. Pragmatic external statements express noncognitive dispositions to follow only certain such rules of assessment. For instance, "numbers exist" understood as a pragmatic external statement expresses a disposition to assess statements using only rules according to which this statement is to be assessed as correct. This disposition is "noncognitive" since the relevant rules have no descriptive content.

The non-cognitivist interpretation contrasts with "language pluralist" accounts, as endorsed by Yablo (1998), Price (2009), Hirsch (2011), Thomasson (2015), Eklund (2016), and others, according to which frameworks simply are interpreted languages. According to this interpretation, the main difference between internal and external statements is that internal statements are meaningful while external statements are meaningless.

Language pluralist interpretations often are taken to inspire lightweight realist positions in meta-ontology. Hirsch's (2011) "quantifier variance" view and Thomasson's (2015) "easy ontology" view are two examples. On Hirsch's view, "frameworks" are languages, and ontologists of seemingly different viewpoints accept different frameworks, which means that they speak different languages. On Thomasson's view, ordinary language provides us with a "framework". Only existence questions asked using ordinary language are meaningful, and those questions can be answered "easily".

However, I think that language pluralist interpretations are mistaken (see Flocke 2020), and that Carnap's actual views should be taken as inspiration for an expressivist analysis of ontological debates. But my view is not *just* Carnap's.

For one, on Carnap's view, purely external statements—utterances made in contexts where speakers follow different rules of assessment but are not aware of this fact—are simply meaningless. Since metaphysicians typically debate purely external statements, on Carnap's view, metaphysicians typically make meaningless utterances. I agree that sometimes speakers don't realize that they follow different rules of assessment, and this ignorance may result in confusions and frustrating discussions. But I don't think that this ignorance makes their utterances meaningless. On my view, typical utterances by metaphysicians are not meaningless; their semantic contents are propositions and they express noncognitive mental states. Furthermore, on Carnap's view, framework rules are rules for the assessment of *utterances*, which are physical events that can be experienced. This view was presumably at least in part motivated by Carnap's empiricism. However, ontological expressivism as developed in this chapter is not motivated by empiricism, and I think that the relevant rules are rules for the assessment of *propositions* (or of *what is said*) by the utterance of a declarative sentence.

4.9 Conclusion

My goal in this chapter was to provide a possibility proof. I wanted to show that a coherent version of expressivism about ontological discourse can be had. To provide this possibility proof, I have developed a specific version of ontological expressivism. According to this version of ontological expressivism, "numbers exist" expresses a noncognitive disposition to assess the truth of propositions by considering only circumstances of evaluation at which numbers exist. On my view, this disposition is *noncognitive* because speakers have a choice between alternative circumstances of evaluation, only some of which contain numbers. Whichever way they decide, they do not make a factual mistake. However, not all utterances of quantified sentences express noncognitive mental states; some express beliefs. To explain the difference, I have distinguished between objective and non-objective propositions, and suggested that only utterances of quantified sentences whose semantic content is a non-objective proposition express noncognitive mental states.[29]

[29] I would like to thank David Chalmers for encouraging me to take up this project, and for supervising my dissertation on ontological expressivism. I would also like to thank for helpful comments and discussions two anonymous referees for Oxford University Press, Herman Cappelen, Justin Clarke-Doane, Cian Dorr, Gary Ebbs, Kit Fine, Anja Jauernig, Matt Mandelkern, Annette Martin, Daniel Nolan, David Plunkett, Agustín Rayo, Tobias Rosefeldt, Gideon Rosen, Chris Scambler, Jack Spencer, Barbara Vetter, and Stephen Yablo, as well as audiences at the University of Connecticut in 2014, at the 2016 Pacific APA, and at the University of Oslo and Trinity College Dublin in 2017. Work on this project furthermore benefited from two visits at the research project ConceptLab, located at the University of Oslo, spanning six months overall in 2017 and 2018.

References

Ayer, A. J. 1971 (1936). *Language, Truth and Logic*. London: Penguin Books.

Barnes, Elizabeth and Williams, J. Robert G. 2011. 'A Theory of Metaphysical Indeterminacy'. In Karen Bennett and Dean W. Zimmermann (eds.), *Oxford Studies in Metaphysics: Volume 6*, 104–147. Oxford: Oxford University Press.

Cappelen, Herman and Hawthorne, John. 2009. *Relativism and Monadic Truth*. Oxford: Oxford University Press.

Carnap, Rudolf. 1950. *Logical Foundations of Probability*. Chicago, IL: University of Chicago Press.

Carnap, Rudolf. 1956 (1950). 'Empiricism, Semantics, and Ontology'. In *Meaning and Necessity*, 205–221. Chicago, IL: University of Chicago Press.

Chalmers, David. 2009. 'Ontological Anti-Realism'. In David J. Chalmers, David Manley, and Ryan Wasserman (eds.), *Metametaphysics: New Essays on the Foundations of Ontology*, 77–129. Oxford: Oxford University Press.

Einheuser, Iris. 2006. 'Counterconventional Conditionals', *Philosophical Studies*, 127(3): 459–482.

Eklund, Matti. 2016. 'Carnap's Legacy for the Contemporary Metaontological Debate'. In Stephan Blatti and Sandra Lapointe (eds.), *Ontology after Carnap*, 165–189. Oxford: Oxford University Press.

Field, Hartry. 1980. *Science without Numbers*. Princeton, NJ: Princeton University Press.

Field, Hartry. 1984. 'Critical Notice of Crispin Wright: Frege's Conception of Numbers as Objects', *Canadian Journal of Philosophy*, 14(4): 637–662.

Fine, Kit. 2009. 'The Question of Ontology'. In David Chalmers, Ryan Wasserman, and David Manley (eds.), *Metametaphysics: New Essays on the Foundations of Ontology*, 156–177. Oxford: Oxford University Press.

Flocke, Vera. 2020. 'Carnap's Noncognitivism about Ontology', *Noûs* 54.3, pp. 527–548.

Fogal, Daniel, Harris, Daniel, and Moss, Matt. 2018. 'Speech Acts: The Contemporary Theoretical Landscape'. In Daniel Fogal, Daniel Harris, and Matt Moss (eds.), *New Works on Speech Acts*, 1–40. Oxford: Oxford University Press.

Geach, P. T. 1965. 'Assertion'. *The Philosophical Review*, 74(4): 449–465.

Gibbard, Allan. 1990. *Wise Choices, Apt Feelings*. Oxford: Oxford University Press.

Gibbard, Allan. 2003. *Thinking How to Live*. Cambridge, MA: Harvard University Press.

Harris, Daniel. 2019. 'We Talk to People, Not Contexts', *Philosophical Studies*, page forthcoming.

Hirsch, Eli. 2011. *Quantifier Variance and Realism: Essays in Metaontology*. Oxford: Oxford University Press.

Hirsch, Eli. 2011 (2008). 'Ontological Arguments: Interpretive Charity and Quantifier Variance'. In *Quantifier Variance and Realism: Essays in Metaontology*, 178–196. Oxford: Oxford University Press.

Jones, Nicholas K. 2019. 'Propositions and Cognitive Relations', *Proceedings of the Aristotelian Society*, 119(2): 157–178.

Kaplan, David. 1989. 'Demonstratives: An Essay on the Semantics, Logic, Metaphysics, and Epistemology of Demonstratives and Other Indexicals'. In Joseph Almog, John Perry, and Howard Wettstein (eds.), *Themes from Kaplan*, 481–563. Oxford: Oxford University Press.

Lederman, Harvey. 2017. 'Common Knowledge'. In Marija Jankovic and Kirk Ludwig (eds.), *The Routledge Handbook of Collective Intentionality*, 181–195. London: Routledge.

Lederman, Harvey. 2018. 'Uncommon Knowledge', *Mind*, 127(508): 1069–1105.

Lewis, David. 1986. *On the Plurality of Worlds*. Oxford: Blackwell.

MacFarlane, John. 2014. *Assessment Sensitivity: Relative Truth and Its Applications*. Oxford: Oxford University Press.

Markosian, Ned. 1998. 'Brutal Composition', *Philosophical Studies*, 92(3): 211–249.

Menzel, Christopher. 2017. 'Possible Worlds'. In Edward N. Zalta (ed.), *The Stanford Encyclopedia of Philosophy*. Metaphysics Research Lab, Stanford University, https://plato.stanford.edu/archives/win2017/entries/possible-worlds, Winter 2017 edition.

Ninan, Dilip. 2010. 'Semantics and the Objects of Assertion', *Linguistics and Philosophy*, 33(5): 355–380.

Price, Huw. 2009. 'Metaphysics after Carnap: The Ghost Who Walks?' In David Chalmers, David Manley, and Ryan Wasserman (eds.), *Metametaphysics: New Essays on the Foundations of Ontology*, 320–346. Oxford: Oxford University Press.

Rayo, Agustín. 2017. 'The World Is the Totality of Facts, Not of Things', *Philosophical Issues*, 27(1): 251–278.

Roberts, Craige. 2012. 'Information Structure in Discourse: Towards an Integrated Formal Theory of Pragmatics', *Semantics and Pragmatics*, 5: 1–69.

Schroeder, Mark. 2008. *Being For: Evaluating the Semantic Program of Expressivism*. Oxford: Oxford University Press.

Schroeder, Mark. 2009. 'Hybrid Expressivism: Virtues and Vices', *Ethics*, 119: 257–309.

Schroeder, Mark. 2015 (2008). 'Expression for Expressivists'. In *Expressing Our Attitudes: Explanation and Expression in Ethics, Volume 2*, 31–54. Oxford: Oxford University Press.

Sider, Theodore. 2001. *Four-Dimensionalism: An Ontology of Persistence and Time*. Oxford: Oxford University Press.

Sider, Theodore. 2011. *Writing the Book of the World*. Oxford: Oxford University Press.

Sider, Theodore. 2013. 'Against Parthood'. In Karen Bennett and Dean W. Zimmermann (eds.), *Oxford Studies in Metaphysics: Volume 8*, 237–293. Oxford: Oxford University Press.

Stalnaker, Robert. 1970. 'Pragmatics', *Synthese*, 1(2): 272–289.

Stalnaker, Robert. 1999 (1978). 'Assertion'. In *Context and Content: Essays on Intentionality in Speech and Thought*, 78–95. Oxford: Oxford University Press.

Stalnaker, Robert. 2002. 'Common Ground', *Linguistics and Philosophy*, 25: 701–721.

Stalnaker, Robert. 2014. *Context*. Oxford: Oxford University Press.

Thomasson, Amie L. 2015. *Ontology Made Easy*. Oxford: Oxford University Press.

van Inwagen, Peter. 1995. *Material Beings*. Ithaca, NY: Cornell University Press.

van Roojen, Mark. 1996. 'Expressivism and Irrationality', *The Philosophical Review*, 105(3): 311–335.

Yablo, Stephen. 1998. 'Does Ontology Rest on a Mistake?', *Australian Society Supplementary Volume*, 72(1): 229–283.

Yalcin, Seth. 2012. 'Bayesian Expressivism', *Proceedings of the Aristotelian Society*, 112(2).

Yalcin, Seth. 2018. 'Expressivism by Force'. In Daniel Fogal, Daniel Harris, and Matt Moss (eds.), *New Works on Speech Acts*, 400–430. Oxford: Oxford University Press.

5

Why Our Natural Languages Are Ideal Languages for Metaphysics

Thomas Hofweber

5.1 The Language of Metaphysics

Much of the debate about the language of ontology seems to me to be about the wrong thing. This debate focuses on the question whether ontological debates should be carried out in a language that carves nature at the joints and that in particular contains a joint-carving quantifier. This issue is exemplified in particular in the dispute between Eli Hirsch and Ted Sider,[1] and although this is an active and ongoing debate, it seems to me that there is another, much more central and important, issue connected to the language of ontology and of metaphysics. The central question is not about joints of nature and joint-carving quantifiers, but about the possibility of ambitious metaphysics as a project carried out by human beings. It concerns whether or not human natural languages and human thought are even minimally adequate to carry out metaphysics. Is it the case that the kind of languages that are in principle accessible to human beings are good enough to do metaphysics in an ambitious form? This question is the topic of the present chapter.

Almost everyone who is at least somewhat favorably inclined toward metaphysics agrees that metaphysics is in the fact-finding business. It tries to find out what reality is like, and thus what the facts are. Metaphysics is, of course, not concerned with all the facts, but only with a particular subclass of them. Which subclass is controversial, and rightly so. Is it very general facts, or the fundamental facts, or the structural facts, or normative facts about how reality ought to be described, something totally different, or a combination of the above? These are substantial questions connected to how one conceives of metaphysics, but whatever one says, one will hold that metaphysics has as its aim to find out about certain kinds of facts. We can call *the domain of metaphysics* those facts that are the target of metaphysical inquiry, whichever ones they might be. Or to put it differently, the domain of metaphysics is those questions of fact that are the ones

[1] See Hirsch (2011) and Sider (2011).

Thomas Hofweber, *Why Our Natural Languages Are Ideal Languages for Metaphysics* In: *The Language of Ontology.* Edited by: J. T. M. Miller, Oxford University Press (2021). © Oxford University Press. DOI: 10.1093/oso/9780192895332.003.0006

metaphysics is supposed to settle. Everyone who holds that metaphysics is in the business of fact-finding can agree, although they will disagree with what these facts are more precisely. The question for us here is: what language is suitable for representing these facts? Let us call *an ideal language for metaphysics* any language, natural or artificial, that is able to represent all the facts in the domain of metaphysics. Ideal languages in this sense are ideal for metaphysics in that they can represent all the facts in the domain of metaphysics, but they are not necessarily ideal in other ways. English might be ideal for metaphysics, but non-ideal otherwise, since it has an excess of grammatical rules, and too many letters, and some other imperfections. We should not concern ourselves with those dimensions of perfection and how a language might be perfectly ideal; that is, ideal in every respect, including alphabet, grammar, and so on. What matters for us here is being ideal when it comes to representing all the facts in the domain of metaphysics. An ideal language in this sense can be improved in several ways, but not in the way that matters for us here. It can represent all the facts in the domain of metaphysics, and no language can represent more facts in the domain of metaphysics than that.

A language can be pretty good for metaphysics without being ideal. We can say that a language is *adequate for metaphysics* if it can represent a good enough part of the facts in the domain of metaphysics. An adequate language might not be ideal, but at least it would be a good start. Our question in the following will be whether we should think that the languages that are accessible to human beings are ideal or at least adequate for metaphysics. Are the languages we can speak adequate or even ideal for metaphysics? And to carry it over to the level of thought, are the thoughts we can think adequate or ideal for metaphysics? If the answer is yes to both, then we are in great shape to carry out metaphysics. Metaphysics would be possible for human beings at least when it comes to representing the facts, although we might still be limited in when it comes to knowing the facts. Our concern here is not epistemic, but representational. On the other hand, if it turns out that the languages we can speak are neither ideal nor adequate, then metaphysics seems to be beyond what human beings can hope to do. Not only will we not be in a position to know what the metaphysically relevant facts are, we will not even be in a position to represent them. Any limitation on what we can represent in thought or language is a limitation on what we can know, since to know that p one has to be able to represent that p and to think that p. If our languages are not ideal but adequate, then metaphysics is in decent shape, but limited. That might not be too bad, depending on how far from ideal our adequate languages might be. So, are our human languages adequate, or even ideal, for metaphysics?

Considering this question brings up the thought that maybe we are not even close. The worry here is that metaphysics hopes to be ambitious: it aims to find out about reality as a whole, not merely to settle some local question of fact.

Metaphysics concerns what reality is like in general and overall. But why should we think that our human minds are adequate to represent all fact that obtains? Why should we think that our minds are good enough to represent all of reality? Our minds evolved in a very particular environment and we can grant that they are very good at representing the facts that we are commonly faced with. But reality might be very different in some of its parts than what we are accustomed to. And the kinds of representations that might be required to represent these other facts might be of a very different kind than what is accessible to us. We might be limited in a way that is irrelevant for ordinary life, and even for much of science, but highly relevant for metaphysics. Let us call *the Dark Vision* the worrisome possibility that our minds are limited in what they can represent in thought or language in such a way that ambitious metaphysics is not a reasonable project for creatures like us. The Dark Vision presents the possibility that reality in part is completely different from what we can represent, and completely alien to our way of thinking and speaking. And if so, then ambitious metaphysics would seem to be doomed for us, at least doomed in the sense of achieving its ultimate goal. Do we have to accept the Dark Vision as a legitimate possibility, or do we have any reasons to rule it out? And if we had to accept it, what would it show about the metaphysical theories we come up with? Would it put a shadow over all of them, and give rise to the worry that those theories are at best theories about reality as far as we can represent it, but possibly not about reality as a whole?

Let us call *an ineffable fact* a fact that we human beings cannot, in principle, represent in thought or language. The Dark Vision is closely tied to the question whether or not there are ineffable facts. In particular, it relates to the question whether any of the facts in the domain of metaphysics are ineffable. To illustrate the issue with an example: if metaphysics concerns at least in part the fundamental facts, as it does on one not unpopular conception of it, then there is the worry that even though we can easily represent facts like facts of objects having properties, we might not be able to represent the facts that give rise to such facts. We might be able to represent certain derivative facts, but possibly the fundamental facts are completely alien to our minds. Furthermore, if there are any ineffable facts at all, then this might suggest that our attempts at ambitious metaphysics, the kind that tries to come up with a metaphysics of all of reality, is bound to be limited. How can we hope to come up with a metaphysical story of all of reality when some parts of reality are beyond our minds in that we cannot even represent those facts? Shouldn't these facts also play a role in the metaphysics, and how could they if we can't even entertain them in thought?

Ineffable facts can be divided up into two kinds, which correspond to two ways in which our thinking might be inadequate. To illustrate, let us consider how a simple subject-predicate representation can fail to be good enough to represent a certain fact. First, it could be that the fact is the fact of an object having a property, but for some reason we are unable to represent the object or the property.

Second, it could be that a certain fact requires a representation of a different kind than a subject-predicate presentation. We could fail to be able to fill in the content of a kind of representation we have available, as when we are unable to represent an object or a property, or we might be unable to have a certain form or structure of representation available at all, as when we need a different kind of representing a fact than the kinds we have available. Facts of the former kind we can call *content ineffable*, and facts of the latter kind we can call *structurally ineffable*. Structurally ineffable facts are intuitively more alien to our minds than content-ineffable ones. The content-ineffable ones are at least of the same kind as the kinds of facts we can represent. They are facts of an object having a property, or some other kind that we can represent, even though we can't represent that particular object or property. Structurally ineffable facts are facts of a completely different kind than the facts we can represent. And structurally ineffable ones are what is truly worrisome and behind a certain way of thinking of the Dark Vision. Some parts of reality might be completely alien to our minds and languages, in the sense that the kinds of representation available to us are insufficient to even represent these kinds of facts. And if we can't even represent facts of this kind, how can we hope to have a complete general story of what reality is like? In particular, if some of these structurally ineffable facts are in the domain of metaphysics, then metaphysics can hope for partial success here or there, but its ambitions will have to be limited by that alone.

In the following, I will focus on structural ineffability. It is the most worrisome kind, and it is also in a sense the easier one to discuss. To properly discuss content ineffability, one needs to look more closely at the notion of what is in principle expressible by human beings. This notion is not easy to make clearer, although I believe it can be spelled out in more detail.[2] Doing so, however, will require almost as much space as I have here overall, and so it is best to leave it aside for now and focus on structural ineffability instead. Any fact that is structurally ineffable is in principle unrepresentable by us, in the sense that no matter what we do, no matter how long we live, our minds just aren't suitable to represent them. Our main question about the adequacy of human minds and languages for metaphysics thus turns into these: are there any structurally ineffable facts? And if so, are any in the domain of metaphysics?

In the rest of this chapter I would like to present an argument that answers this question. I will argue that there are no structurally ineffable facts at all, and thus that there are none in the domain of metaphysics. This might seem like a tough task, since to answer the question it would seem that one needs to know two things and put them together properly. First, one needs to know which facts can be represented in our thought or language, and second, one needs to know which

---

[2] I have done my best in Hofweber (2017).

facts obtain. Once one has both figured out, one can then answer the question by comparing the two. But that strategy is obviously hopeless. We won't be able to first figure out what reality is like and which facts obtain just so we can answer the question whether we can represent all of them. Instead I will argue from considerations about our language alone that we can see that structural ineffability can never obtain. By looking at our language alone, we can see that our language is able to represent all the facts, at least when it comes to their structure.[3] Furthermore, this argument can be extended to the conclusion that our language is able to represent all the facts full stop, not just with regards to their structure but also with regards to their content. However, this stronger claim requires some details that I have developed elsewhere but won't be able to discuss in this chapter. I will point to the relevant texts where appropriate, but even focusing on structure alone should be significant. That the structure of the facts matches the kinds of thoughts or kinds of languages we can have is not trivial, and that we can show this from considerations about our languages and thoughts alone, without looking at the facts, must seem hopeless. Nonetheless, just this is the case, or so I hope to argue in the following.

5.2 Talk about Facts

Before we return to our discussion of the language of metaphysics, we will need to consider how we talk about facts. I hope to make clear in section 5.3 that this is central for our main concern. The issues in this section are simply about our own natural language, and many of the questions raised here are simply empirical questions about this language—questions about what we do when we do certain things with certain phrases in our speech. As such empirical questions, they are complex and involved, and I can't hope to resolve any substantial issues about language in this chapter. Instead I hope to highlight that a certain debate about natural languages, one I will outline shortly, is closely tied to our main question of the adequacy of human natural languages for metaphysics. I will state below which side in this debate I have defended in some detail elsewhere. Furthermore, I will have to sideline some issues that give rise to further complexities. Here, first and foremost, I would like to sideline the issue whether or not all human languages are the same in the regard to be discussed shortly. The view defended here does not depend on all human languages being the same, but the situation gets easier if they are. I will therefore focus on talk about facts in the language in which I write: English. Thus in the following I will argue that largely empirical

---

[3] For a different argument that structural ineffability is impossible, see Filcheva (2020).

facts about English allow us to resolve the issue about the adequacy of human languages for metaphysics.[4]

Most directly we talk about facts with the use of that-clauses or phrases like 'the fact that p':

(1) a. That p is surprising.
     b. The fact that p is surprising.

That-clauses appear in many other contexts as well, and they do not always stand for facts, but the following question arises for them and our cases equally: when we use a that-clause, are we thereby attempting to refer to a thing or entity? Are we trying to pick out a thing with a that-clause, just as we try to do when we use a proper name? In other words, are that-clauses, and fact-terms more generally, referential expressions? An expression can be referential in two ways: first, it could aim to refer to something, whether or not it succeeds; second, it could succeed in referring to something. Only the former concerns language alone, and only in the sense of attempted reference do we ask here whether that-clauses and fact-terms refer. This question is actively debated in the philosophy of language and in semantics.[5] Some reasons speak for them being referential, and some speak against it. What speaks against it is that they are clauses, and on the face of it clauses are very different than names. They complement or modify something, but don't pick out a thing like a name. What's more, fact-terms don't seem to have the same features as names; in particular, they can't be substituted for each other even if they refer to the same thing. There seems to be an important difference in truth conditions between fearing that one's mother will find out and fearing the fact that one's mother will find out, even if it is a fact that one's mother will find out. The former is fear concerning one's mother; the latter is fact-phobia, fear of a fact itself.[6] So, maybe fact-terms are not referential. But there are also good reasons to think that they are. First and foremost is that they give rise to valid quantifier inferences that seem to settle the issue right away. (1) immediately implies that

(2) Something is surprising.

and if that is so, then it would seem that that thing which is surprising is just the thing that 'that p' was referring to. And if so, then that-clauses must be referential after all.

But is this quantifier inference really a decisive reason for fact-terms being referential? Quantification in natural language might not always be used in just this

---

[4] For more on this issue, see Hofweber (2006).
[5] See Bach (1997), King (2002), Moltmann (2003), Hofweber (2016b), and many others.
[6] See the references in footnote 5 for more on this 'substitution problem'.

way in which it concerns a domain of objects or entities. One alternative view could go as follows. Quantifiers are semantically underspecified. They are used with different readings on different occasions. One reading is just the one discussed above. When we use a quantified sentence like

(3) Something is F.

we claim that the domain of things or entities contains at least one thing which is F. Let us call this the *domain-conditions reading* of the quantifier. But it is plausible that quantification in natural language is also used on a different reading. In this reading various inferences are trivial, as the inference from

(4) I need an assistant.

to

(5) I need something.

On this reading quantifiers are used for their *inferential role*. They are used in such a way that the inference from 'F(t)' to 'Something is F' is always and trivially valid. Now, whether quantifiers really have these two readings is simply a question about our own language. Maybe they do, maybe they don't, but this is an issue just about our own language. Suppose, then, that they do have these readings, as I believe they do.[7] We can note first that these two readings must differ in truth conditions. If the inference from (4) to (5) is valid, but if there is no assistant in the domain that I need, then the two readings come apart in truth conditions, and thus they make different contributions to the truth conditions. But what then are the truth conditions of the inferential-role reading of the quantifier?

Those truth conditions need to be such that they give rise to the inferential role. And that role is that for any instance in our language F(t), it implies that something is F. There are different truth conditions that would give rise to this inferential role, but there is one that is the simplest one: the quantified sentence 'something is F' needs to be truth-conditionally equivalent to the disjunction over all the instances that imply it. If there are only three instances, and if 'something is F' is truth-conditionally equivalent to 'either F(a) or F(b) or F(c)', then it will have just the inferential role for which we want it. In our case there are infinitely many instances, but that doesn't change the main point. To have the inferential role of being implied by any instance in our language, the simplest truth conditions that give it this inferential role are to be equivalent to the disjunction of all

---

[7] I argued for this in much more detail in chapter 3 of Hofweber (2016b).

the instances that are supposed to imply it: all the instances in our language. Thus if the quantified statement is truth-conditionally equivalent to the infinite disjunction over all the instances in our language, then it will have the inferential role for which we want it. And what's more, those are the simplest and optimal truth conditions that give it this inferential role. And for universal quantifiers it is correspondingly the conjunction over all the instances. That gives it the inferential role of implying each instance.

I will in the following call the domain-conditions reading of the quantifier also the *external reading*, since it requires something language-external: a domain of things. I will call the inferential-role reading the *internal reading*, since it is language-internal: it relates sentences within the language to another one with the language. Using this terminology, we can thus sum up that on this view of quantification, quantifiers are semantically underspecified and they have an internal and external reading. And these are congenially paired with the views that that-clauses are or are not referential. If that-clauses are not referential, then we would really mess things up if we used quantifiers over facts in the external reading. And if that-clauses are referential, then the external reading of the quantifier would be a perfect match for that. If we aim to pick out things in a domain of entities with that-clauses, then naturally we should quantify over that domain when we quantify over facts. And if that-clauses are not referential, then it would be confused to quantify over facts by quantifying over a domain of entities. There are thus two kinds of views about what we do when we talk about facts:

(6) **Externalism**: Fact-terms are referential, and quantifiers over facts are generally used on their external, domain-conditions, reading.

(7) **Internalism**: Fact-terms are not referential, and quantifiers over facts are generally used on their internal, inferential, reading.

Which one of those is correct is central for our main question, or so I hope to argue in section 5.3.

To be sure, the above was merely an outline of a view of quantification in natural language. The proper story is a lot more complicated, since the above outline neglects contextual contributions to content and truth conditions, and it is only outlined for the simplest cases of quantifiers. But this story can be spelled out more properly, and I have done my best to do so in chapters 3 and 9 of Hofweber (2016b). Furthermore, these complications that I skip actually matter for our issue here, but they are too involved to properly discuss now. We can avoid these issues by focusing on structural ineffability instead of full ineffability, and I will return to this issue later on. For now, let's put this aside and consider only the simplified proposal. Here, too, we should say that this is a question about our own language; it is an issue that concerns what we do when we quantify and use quantifiers. As such, it is a largely empirical issue that is reasonably up for debate. But let's consider what would happen if internalism turns out to be correct as the proper view of what we do when we talk about facts.

5.3 Internalism and the Language of Metaphysics

Whether internalism or externalism or some other view is correct for talk about facts is an empirical question about our own language and what we do with it. We won't be able to settle it here, of course, but suppose that internalism is indeed correct, and suppose that internal quantifiers indeed have the simplest truth conditions as outlined above. This is not a far-fetched assumption; I believe that it is correct, and I have argued for it in detail in Hofweber (2016b). Whether or not these arguments are in the end correct is again beyond what we can settle here, but let us suppose for the moment that internalism is correct. What would follow from it for our main concern about the language of metaphysics?

If internalism is true, then our present natural language is an ideal language for metaphysics. No fact is or could be structurally ineffable for it. This simply follows from the truth conditions of quantified statements that range over facts. To see this, consider the sentence

(8) Every fact is structurally effable.

Assuming internalism is true, this sentence is truth-conditionally equivalent to

(9) $\bigwedge$ if it is a fact that p then that p is structurally effable.

But each of those conjuncts is true. Each conjunct is an instance where 'p' is replaced with a sentence in our own language. And for each such instance, the fact that p is structurally effable by us. Thus the big conjunction is true and therefore (8) is true.

We can thus see that if internalism is true, then there are no structurally effable facts. Since structural ineffability is ruled out, we can say that our thought and reality are in *structural harmony*. The totality of facts and what thoughts or sentences are available to us are in harmony in that any structure that is to be found in the facts is also to be found in our representations of the facts. We focused on structure here, in good part so that we can simplify along a number of ways. The semantics of quantification given was too simple in certain ways, and the notion of the ineffable was not properly spelled out. However, both of those limitations can be overcome, and I have done my part in doing so in, for example, Hofweber (2017) and Hofweber (2016b). Once we do not make these simplifications, we can see that we get an even stronger sense of harmony, which we can call *complete harmony*. Complete harmony holds when any fact that obtains is representable by a sentence in our language or a thought available to us, assuming some idealization, in particular with regards to length of sentence and complexity of thought. Either structural or complete harmony gives rise to a certain position about the language of metaphysics. Our human languages are structurally ideal if structural harmony obtains, and they are simply ideal if complete harmony obtains. If complete harmony obtains, then all facts can be represented in our languages. Thus all facts in the domain of metaphysics can be represented by our languages. No other language can do better in principle when it comes to representing the facts. We have already got them all. Other languages can be an improvement on our present natural languages in that they represent the facts more simply or more elegantly or in some other way, but they can't improve our present language in representing more facts. We can already represent all of them.

This argument must seem puzzling, to say the least. We were able to argue that our natural language is ideal, or at least structurally ideal, by relying only on considerations about our own language. No assumptions were made about which sentences are true or false; the argument simply proceeded from a view about what we do when we talk about facts, and thus a view about what we aim to do when we talk this way, without assuming that our aims are met. We never made any assumptions about what reality in general is like. But how could it be that one could argue for the adequacy of our own language to represent all of reality by looking only at our language, and not otherwise at reality at all? No such argument should be possible, since the issue is about the match between two things—language and reality—and one can't determine that by looking at just one of these two things: language. What's more, the argument seems to be the kind of an argument that we have reason to believe is never a good argument. It seems to aim to draw metaphysical conclusions about reality from merely how we aim to represent reality. And this seems to be impossible, since metaphysics concerns reality, not what we aim to do with reality. It is one thing to aim to represent reality in a particular way, and another thing for those representations to be accurate. Only the latter allows for conclusions about what reality is like. There seems to be a gap, which we can call *the language-metaphysics gap*, that needs to be bridged for the above argument to get off the ground, and it seems that this gap can't be bridged.[8] And thus the above argument must go wrong somewhere.

Although in general one can't draw conclusions from how we represent the world to how the world is, there are exceptions, and this is one of them. To see this, let us consider what conclusions we can draw merely from the fact that that-clauses and fact-terms are non-referential. On the internalist view they are not just non-referential in that they aim to refer but fail, but rather in the sense that

---

[8] Heather Dyke calls drawing conclusions about the world from how we talk about the world 'the representational fallacy' in Dyke (2008), something she rejects. As will become clear, I do not agree that this is indeed always a mistake.

they do something different altogether than referring. The former is not a claim about language alone, but about language and the world. The latter, however, is about language alone. It is merely about what we do or don't do when we use certain parts of language. But if our fact-terms are non-referential in this sense, then it follows that facts do not exist. It follows that the domain of things or the collection of all that exists does not contain any facts. If fact-terms are non-referential, then nothing in the domain of things is the fact that snow is white. The reason simply is that if internalism is true and fact-terms are non-referential, then I just used the term 'the fact that snow is white' in this non-referential way in the last sentence. That term was not in the business of referring to anything, and so whatever things there may be, none of them were referred to with the fact-term I just used. So none of the things in the domain are the fact that snow is white. And similarly for all other facts. So, there are no facts in the domain, and there is no ontology of facts. And we could see this merely by thinking about our language and what we do when we talk about facts. Since the non-existence of facts is a metaphysical claim, we did bridge the language-metaphysics gap. We were able to draw a metaphysical conclusion. And once the gap has been bridged, there can be further consequences from what we were able to conclude more directly. And similarly here. Although the non-existence of facts is at first only a rather negative conclusion, it has a number of positive consequences, only some of which are directly at issue in this chapter.

Even if it is possible to draw conclusions about reality from considerations about our own language, it might be argued that this is only a shallow victory, and the true metaphysical issues remain. One thought that motivates this reaction is that if internalism is indeed true for our talk about facts, then we made a mistake in thinking of reality as the totality of facts. The totality of facts is too closely tied to us and our talk about reality. We thus need to talk about something else instead. Maybe not facts, but truths, or maybe something totally different altogether. Although this sounds good at first, it quickly goes nowhere. First, switching from facts to truths won't change the overall situation. Not only are facts closely connected to truths, in the sense that for every fact there is a corresponding truth, and the other way round, but also the arguments in favor of internalism about talk about facts carry over to arguments in favor of internalism about talk about truths. If we shift away from facts, it would need to be something rather different. Some substitute for them, but something not of the kind that we generally talk about with a that-clause. We need to move away from facts to facts*, or whatever that substitute for facts might be called. But such a shift in focus and target of inquiry also shifts us away from reality. Reality is the totality of facts, not the totality of facts*, or so is our concept of reality. We will then need to direct our attention not to reality, but to reality*. But how could we ever rationally move away from facts, truth, and reality, and instead make facts*, truth*, and reality* our target of inquiry? Inquiry aims at the truth and the facts. To truly follow this line of thought to its natural end, we would have to abandon inquiry for inquiry*, which aims at the truth*. But could it ever be rational for us, given our present starting point, to abandon inquiry in favor of inquiry*, and to give up the aim of truth in favor of the aim of truth*? I believe no such transition could be rational, and I have argued for this in more detail in Hofweber (2020) as well as Hofweber (2019). Instead of giving it all up, we should instead accept that reality is that totality of facts, but the facts are not independent of our talk about the facts. Internalism, if it is indeed correct, does not suggest that inquiry should have a completely different target, or should be replaced altogether, but instead it shows something about what reality is like. The target is and remains the truth, and reality is the totality of facts, but the facts are tied to us and our minds and language. This might sound like idealism, and I think it is. Internalism leads to idealism, but how precisely and in what sense of idealism is not really the topic for the present chapter. I have done my best to work out these connections in Hofweber (2019) and Hofweber (forthcoming), and the details require quite a bit more than what we can do here. Internalism has substantial metaphysical consequences, and most pressing for now, it has consequences for determining what language is perfectly matched to reality. It shows that our human natural languages are ideal languages for metaphysics, which is the consequence that is the focus of this chapter.

5.4 Conclusion

Whether our human natural languages are ideal or even adequate languages for metaphysics is a substantial question, tied to the question whether or not there are any ineffable facts. I have argued above that if internalism is true for our own talk about facts, then ineffable facts are ruled out. This argument was only given in outline, with many of the details missing. To spell it out more fully, we need to look at quantification in natural language more carefully and what the truth conditions of the inferential-role reading of quantifiers are, as well as whether that-clauses and fact-terms indeed are non-referring expressions. I have tried to do all this in Hofweber (2016b), which contains a detailed defense of internalism for talk about facts, as well as a few other things. On this proper formulation of internalism it indeed follows that there are no ineffable facts. And that in turn implies that our language can represent all the facts, and thus all the facts in the domain of metaphysics, whatever that domain might be. Thus our language is not only adequate for metaphysics, but ideal. It can't be improved in a way that matters for us now: representing facts in principle. And thus there is no representational limitation on ambitious metaphysics. We are in a perfect position to represent all the facts, and whatever obstacles we face in metaphysics, representing the facts is not one of them. As I suggested above, I hold that this internalist picture not only supports that there are no ineffable facts and that our minds and reality are in perfect harmony in this regard, but also a closely connected form of idealism. How that is supposed to go is another story. But our main lesson for the language of ontology and the language of metaphysics is this: if internalism is true, then there is a close connection between what we can in principle represent and which facts can in principle obtain. If this connection obtains, then there is no limit to the ambitions of metaphysics as carried out by us from a possible representational limitation of our thoughts and languages. But if externalism is true, then there is no such guarantee of our representational tools being adequate to carry out metaphysics. If the facts are independent of our representations, then there is no guarantee that the language required to represent all of them or just the ones most relevant for metaphysics is a language we humans can speak. In fact, we should expect to be limited in this regard, and thus take more caution in metaphysics. If externalism is true, then a form of intellectual humility is appropriate in metaphysics, as argued for in Hofweber (2016a). But if internalism is true, then metaphysics does not face any representational obstacles to its ambitions, in part because of a connection between the totality of facts and our languages. Ambitious metaphysics stands or falls with idealism, or so this argument suggests.

References

Bach, K. 1997. 'Do Belief Reports Report Beliefs?', *Pacific Philosophical Quarterly*, 78: 215–241.

Dyke, H. 2008. *Metaphysics and the Representational Fallacy*. London: Routledge.

Filcheva, K. 2020. 'Can There Be Ineffable Propositional Structures?', *Journal of Philosophical Research*, 44.

Hirsch, E. 2011. *Quantifier Variance and Realism: Essays in Metaontology*. Oxford: Oxford University Press.

Hofweber, T. 2006. 'Inexpressible Properties and Propositions'. In K. Bennett and, D. Zimmerman (eds.), *Oxford Studies in Metaphysics: volume 2*, 155–206. Oxford: Oxford University Press.

Hofweber, T. 2016a. 'Intellectual Humility and the Limits of Conceptual Representation', *Res Philosophica*, 93(3): 553–565.

Hofweber, T. 2016b. *Ontology and the Ambitions of Metaphysics*. Oxford: Oxford University Press.

Hofweber, T. 2017. 'Are There Ineffable Aspects of Reality?' In K. Bennett and D. Zimmerman (eds.), *Oxford Studies in Metaphysics: volume 10*, 124–170. Oxford: Oxford University Press.

Hofweber, T. 2019. 'Idealism and the Harmony of Thought and Reality', *Mind*, 128(511): 699–734.

Hofweber, T. 2020. 'Inescapable Concepts'. Unpublished manuscript.

Hofweber, T. forthcoming. *Idealism and the Harmony of Thought and Reality*. Oxford: Oxford University Press.

King, J. 2002. 'Designating Propositions', *Philosophical Review*, 111(3): 341–371.

Moltmann, F. 2003. 'Propositional Attitudes Without Propositions', *Synthese*, 35(1): 77–118.

Sider, T. 2011. *Writing the Book of the World*. Oxford: Oxford University Press.

6

What Counts as a 'Good' Metaphysical Language?

J. T. M. Miller

One recent metaontological debate focuses on the significance of alternative languages. We talk about tables as composite objects, but it is possible for there to be a linguistic community that substitutes our table-talk for talk of particles-arranged-tablewise. The deflationist thinks that this shows that some ontological debates are non-substantive. The possible language is no better than our actual language for the purposes of metaphysics, so if it is true for us that there are tables, this is due to nothing more than the shallow fact that we happen to speak English. The realist, by contrast, thinks that among the possible languages some are metaphysically better than others.[1] For the realist, we can settle the metaphysical debate about the existence of tables by identifying which is the best of the candidate languages, and determining whether tables exist according to that language.

Claims that there are multiple 'equally good' languages to describe the world and that we cannot compare those languages to see which is the best can be found throughout the metaontological deflationist literature.[2] But both the deflationist and the realist rely on qualitative comparisons of languages: the deflationist thinks some are equally good, while the realist thinks that one is best, or that one can be better than another. This leaves us with a question: what determines the metaphysical 'goodness' of a language?

This kind of normative question is not new to philosophy. Attempts to define the 'good' have been a central part of meta-ethics since Moore's argument that the most important question in ethics is 'how is "good" to be defined?' (Moore [1903] 1993, p. 58). The focus of this chapter is to consider, in a sense, that same question but in the context of the debate between metaontological realists and deflationists. My contention in this chapter is that the debate turns significantly on what each side means by 'good' or 'better' when they say that one metaphysical language can

---

[1] I use the terms 'objectively best language', 'metaphysically privileged language' (or just 'privileged'), and 'fundamental language' interchangeably here.
[2] Sider (2009, p. 3 fn.10) identifies, as well as what he calls a 'silent majority watching from the sidelines', the following: Carnap (1950/1956); Chalmers (2009); Hirsch (2002a, 2002b, 2005); Peacocke (1988); Putnam (1975, 1987); Sidelle (2002); Sosa (1999); Thomasson (2007, 2008, 2009, 2015).

J. T. M. Miller, *What Counts as a 'Good' Metaphysical Language?* In: *The Language of Ontology*. Edited by: J. T. M. Miller, Oxford University Press (2021). © Oxford University Press. DOI: 10.1093/oso/9780192895332.003.0007

be 'better' or that all languages are 'equally good'. More specifically, I will argue that there is a way in which at least some deflationists and realists are talking past each other, employing different normative notions to compare languages so that, I argue, the attempt to deflate metaphysical arguments in this way fails to hit its intended mark.

To make this argument, I will make use of the concept of 'semantic purpose' that is present in the metaontological realist work of Sider (2011), and used in an argument in favour of deflationism by Irmak (2013). 'Semantic purpose' will be used as a way to understand what languages are *for*—that is, what they, as languages, are intended to help us capture or describe, and hence provide a criterion against which to judge how 'good' those languages are. Semantic purpose is therefore a highly useful concept to understand whether or how languages might be compared to see which is 'best', or to see if languages are really 'equally good'.

After outlining Irmak's argument against Sider, I will contend that the argument rests on too narrow a conception of the semantic purpose of languages proposed by metaphysical theories as being privileged or fundamental. I argue that this undercuts the conclusion that there are 'equally good' languages as this conclusion can only be reached if the semantic purposes of the putative privileged languages are the same.

I argue that if we do wish to consider comparing putative privileged languages, then we should (i) understand the idea of a semantic purpose in a coarse-grained (rather than fine-grained) way; and (ii) distinguish between two tasks where the first is to decide whether there is an objectively best language, and the second is to debate the content of that fundamental language. I argue that once we have done this, candidate metaphysically privileged languages can, in principle, be compared to see which is metaphysically best. Actually comparing languages will still be very hard. Indeed, if I am right, comparing languages, including for the conclusion that they are equally good, will require engaging in various debates about what metaphysical principles we accept as we start to create a putative privileged language. However, to debate those principles is to engage in substantive metaphysical disputes, and hence supports a metaontological realist position.

A brief note before the main substance of this chapter. A central claim of this chapter is that we must be careful to distinguish between arguments that there is a metaphysically privileged language and arguments about what that language looks like (or how we can find out what it looks like). Beyond agreeing with Sider's metaontological realism, I will be silent about other commitments that he defends, including his use of notions such as 'joint-carving' and his focus on structure. My claims stand independent of whether we wish to accept those commitments.

6.1

Irmak (2013) produces a typical reconstruction of an argument for the existence of a privileged or fundamental language, taking his cues from Sider (2011):

1. There are objective similarities and differences 'out there' in the world.
2. The point of human inquiry is to conform itself to the world in a way that correctly represents these similarities and differences rather than to make or construct them.
3. There might be different languages that state true propositions. But when there are, one must be the better description of reality. A description is better than the others just in case the propositions in that description are cast in joint-carving terms so that its ideology better matches the range of differences in the world.
4. There is an objectively privileged language which best carves nature at the joints and can be used for 'writing the book of the world'. (Irmak 2013, p. 4)

These four theses lead to the argument:

(a) The language that best carves nature at the joints is the best language (from 3 above).
(b) The language of physics is the language which best carves nature at the joints.
(c) Therefore, the language of physics is the best (most objectively privileged) language. (Irmak 2013, p. 5)[3]

Irmak concludes his reconstruction by stating that:

According to Sider, given that there is a best, objectively privileged language that can describe the world as it is, we can say that ontological questions are substantive because they can be formulated in this fundamental language. An ontological debate when it is done in this fundamental language, then, is a serious, quasi-scientific debate about which answer gives a better description of reality. What is at stake in those debates, in this account, is discovering the most fundamental structure of reality. Even though rival ontologies might state true propositions about the world, one is the best.   (2013, p. 5)

---

[3] Note that the language of physics does not only contain 'physical' predicates (leaving aside the question of which predicates should be admitted as being 'physical'). For Sider, the best language also contains basic logical notions (such as quantification, negation), plus a predicate for set membership (Sider 2011, p. 292).

In order to defend the substantivity of metaphysical debates, Sider wishes to defend the possibility and intelligibility of an objectively privileged language. This is a fundamental language, which provides the best description of reality. It is this realism about there being a fundamental language that Irmak focuses his argument on, thereby attempting to undercut the claim of substantivity in metaphysical debates.

Usefully for the dialectic that I am engaging with here, Irmak also provides an overview of the structure of an argument against Sider (numbers and letters referring to the above quotes):

> In what follows I will argue that knee-jerk realism and particularly the claim that the language of physics is objectively privileged are false. I grant (1) and (2) above which assures that there is a mind-independent reality with objective similarities and differences that we try to wrap our minds around. Together they are enough to provide a modest form of realism that many are eager to preserve. I argue that (3) is false and once we reject it we also lose (4). Therefore, I reject (a), which depends on the truth of (3), on the implicit argument for (c); that the language of the physical is objectively privileged. My arguments against (3) and (4) rely on the idea of a semantic purpose. I argue that once we acknowledge the roles of purposes where we introduce new terms to our language (locally) and when we adopt new languages or provide descriptions (holistically), we no longer are able to claim that there is a single fundamental and objectively privileged language. Therefore, I conclude that knee-jerk realism is wrong and there is no single best language that one can use to 'write the book of the world'.
>
> (2013, p. 5)

Before unpacking this argument in detail, it is worth noting a possible tension in the stated aims. At the beginning of this quote, the aim of the paper is to 'argue that knee-jerk realism and particularly the claim that the *language of physics* is objectively privileged are false' (my emphasis). Later, it is stated that 'therefore, I conclude that knee-jerk realism is wrong and *there is no single best language* that one can use to "write the book of the world"' (my emphasis). These two conclusions are clearly not the same. One can hold that there is a single best language that one can use to write the book of the world without thinking that it is the language of physics that is objectively best. I will discuss the importance of how these two claims come apart in relation to broader metaontological issues in later sections.

It is worth stressing here that Irmak's claim is not that there are *no* objective similarities or differences in reality, or that as humans we do not attempt to express these similarities and differences. For Irmak, and other deflationists, we do not create or construct differences and similarities in the world. Or, more precisely, we do not create them *all*. Some social facts may have objective status, and yet are constructed by individual (or groups of) humans.

Rather, the claim is that there can be no single objectively best language to express these pre-existing objective similarities and differences. This is a crucial commitment, common across the metaontological literature, to what I will call 'minimal realism'. Minimal realism is the view that the world contains some similarities and differences that are entirely independent of us and our language choice, yet we nonetheless are trying to express those differences within our language and general inquiries into the world. This is a conjunction of (1) and (2) above. Crucially, Irmak wishes to hold onto these claims, whilst rejecting (3). Irmak is not alone in his acceptance of minimal realism, but rejection of a privileged or objectively best language. Similar views can be found in the highly influential work of Hirsch (2011) and Thomasson (2015). Whilst Hirsch and Thomasson put forward different versions of neo-Carnapianism, both wish to hold that there are multiple equally good ways but no *best* way to describe the world.[4]

We should note that these aspects of minimal realism might come apart. That is, it may be possible to think that there are objective similarities and differences in the world but that our language is not intended to, or simply cannot, represent them. I leave that form of anti-metaphysical argument aside here, and focus solely on those that would accept minimal realism as the conjunction of these two theses.

As also expressed in the above quote, the argument against theses (3) and (4) comes from the idea of a 'semantic purpose'. Semantic purpose refers to the idea that when we introduce a new term to a language, then we do so for a particular reason. The semantic purpose associated with a new term allows us to fix the meaning of the new term from amongst the infinite number of candidate meanings. We can explain this idea with reference to the word 'inch'. The semantic purpose of introducing this word into our language is to measure the size of smallish things. This purpose could be achieved in a number of different ways, each of which would satisfy this goal equally well. The two sentences,

S: Let 'inch' be that unit such that fifteen of them add up to the length of my computer screen.

S': Let 'inch' be that unit such that thirty of them add up to the length of my computer screen.

---

[4] Irmak's, and other deflationists', commitment to 'minimal realism' is tied to their claim to be putting forward a realist position, and not a conceptualist, anti-realist, or idealist position. For example, Hirsch stresses that his view does not endorse 'an absurd form of linguistic idealism' (2002b; 2011, p. 70). Here, I accept this claim to be realist; see Miller (2016) for a response.

pick out instances where we have simply stipulatively defined 'inch' differently. It just so happens that the convention followed in S' defines 'inch' as half the size of the convention followed in defining 'inch' in S. However, what the sentences express is empirically identical. My computer screen is only one length across, and both sentences equally well express this fact. In this case, neither S nor S' carve at the joints better than the other.

We are then told to take the idea of semantic purpose, and generalize it. First, semantic purpose is extended from the convention-based examples such as 'inch' to technical terms within different forms of discourse. Take the term 'elementary particle':

> The meaning of this physical term is not fixed conventionally yet the semantic purpose has the same role as in the case of determining the meaning of 'inch': it narrowed down the range of candidate meanings. Had the purpose for introducing the term 'elementary particle' been different and instead of naming the most fundamental physical particle, it was, say, naming the elementary basic unit of life, then DNA, cells, or organs might have been among the candidate meanings for the term 'elementary particle.' The reason why we don't realize that we have semantic purposes when we do science, ethics or economics might be that those purposes are so obvious that they often need no explicit discussion.
>
> (Irmak 2013, p. 7)

In this case, the meaning of the term 'elementary particle' can only be identified given a particular semantic purpose: that of naming the most fundamental physical furniture of the universe. Comparing any candidate meanings requires specifying this purpose. It is only with respect to this purpose that candidate meanings can be seen as better or worse than each other (as is the case for 'elementary particle') or equally good (as is the case for 'inch'). This is an extension from the initial convention-based notion of semantic purpose, to cover also the introduction of new concepts into more technical languages.

Semantic purpose is subsequently generalized even further, to cover *entire languages*:

> I want to take the idea of semantic purpose seriously and generalize it in the following way: Different choices of candidate meanings for terms (locally) and of *different languages and descriptions (holistically)* may be evaluated as better or worse only relative to their purpose.   (Irmak 2013, p. 7, my emphasis)

It is the generalization of semantic purpose to entire languages that is crucial to these kinds of arguments against the idea of an objectively best language. The argument is that once we recognize that languages, like terms and concepts before, can only be compared relative to the semantic purpose for which they are introduced, then we 'must reject the claim that where we have different languages to describe reality one must be (absolutely) better' (Irmak 2013, p. 10).

I confess that I find the notion of a 'semantic purpose' for an entire language unclear and cannot offer any major insights into the idea. It is not obvious at all that the generalization from how single terms are introduced to how *languages* are is possible. For instance, one issue is that whilst we can relatively easily isolate a single term within a language and assess its semantic purpose, it is not entirely clear that we can isolate any language from any other language. This is not to support a holism about all languages. It is instead that it is not clear what the semantic purpose of English is opposed to that of French, or that of the language of physics, or the language of economics (etc.). For starters, these languages overlap in semantics, grammar, and what they seek to describe. Irmak's argument relies on there being some way to distinguish between the semantic purposes of languages, but gives us no tools about how to do so. From the discussion, it seems clear that Irmak does not claim that different natural languages might have different purposes. But they do not provide us with a method to know why it is that natural languages do not differ in semantic purpose, but the languages of physics and economics do. It is at least possible that natural languages were introduced with different purposes. However, I only note this lack of details, and will leave this to one side in this chapter; and assume, with Irmak, that semantic purposes for whole languages can be given.

6.2

As we have seen above, the claim is that there is no shared purpose through which we can judge languages so as to see which is the objectively best language. The support for the claim comes in considering an example that Sider (2011) uses in defence of knee-jerk realism—the view that at least some parts of human inquiry aims to conform itself to the world. As Irmak states: '[t]he example is important because it is supposed to show how and why physics is objectively privileged' (2013, p. 10). Sider's example compares the relative 'betterness' of physics and shmysics, where shmysics is the subject matter of a set of propositions arrived at via an arbitrary function that creates a different interpretation of a set of propositions that express the set of physical truths (of which physics is the subject matter). These two languages share the same purpose: that of explaining the fundamental physical structure of reality, and so Irmak agrees with Sider that in this case physics is the objectively better language.

This kind of assessing of languages is not possible when the languages do not have the same purpose. We are asked to imagine two languages (or sets of propositions) S and P, where P is the set of physics propositions, and S is a set of propositions that express some aesthetic judgements. Say further that for a statement T there is a corresponding aesthetic proposition in S. But, '[c]an we say that P is better than S? No—it doesn't make sense to say so. Better for what? On what basis will we compare them? We cannot evaluate them by assuming that they both have the same purpose; this is just not the case' (Irmak 2013, p. 11).

Irmak continues: '[t]hus, there are two possibilities. First, we might say that even though P and S are intended to serve different semantic purposes, we can still compare them. Second, and more plausibly, we can concede that P and S are "just different"; they are different ways to describe reality' (2013, p. 11). Neither option is a good one for anyone who wishes to claim that there is an objectively best language. Therefore, if two sets of propositions S and P have different purposes, then we cannot objectively compare them.

The question at hand then is: is there a relevant criterion that putative privileged languages share that would allow us to compare them? If there is not, and there are only the different purposes that the different languages have, then Irmak is correct. If there is, then the realist can hold that we can, in principle at least, compare languages to see which is the best. My claim will be that Irmak is wrong to say that in relevant cases S and P are intended to serve different purposes, and hence the realist can provide a shared purpose to compare them against.

In order to do this, I need to make a distinction between narrow and broad semantic purposes. Narrowly, the semantic purpose of the term 'inch' is to measure smallish things. However, semantic purposes come with varying degrees of breadth. 'Inch' also has the broader semantic purpose to measure all things. Perhaps 'inch' is less good at measuring the distance from here to the moon than the term 'mile' in part because one of the reasons we introduced the term 'mile' was to measure longer distances and objects.

Let us try to put this more precisely. A semantic purpose is a reason for which a term or language is introduced. Such reasons can vary, and some can be more general, or broad, than others. 'Measuring smallish things' and 'measuring longer distances' are both semantic purposes that are narrower than 'measuring things', and if we want to compare our use of 'inch' and 'mile', which purpose we compare them against will be relevant to which we think is better. Against the first, 'inch' is better; against the second, 'mile' is better; and it is unclear which is better against the third. In this case, it is plausible to believe that 'inch' and 'mile' are equally good terms relative to the purpose of 'measuring things', unless, perhaps, we have reason to believe that there are more small things than large things, or vice versa.

Let us now apply this to languages. As Irmak defends, we can take the language of physics to have a semantic purpose of representing the objective *physical* similarities and differences in the world, and a semantic purpose of the language of economics is to represent the objective *economic* similarities and differences in the world. Are these narrow or broad semantic purposes? This depends on how we look at them. Relative to representing the objective *physical* similarities and differences in this room, representing the objective *physical* similarities and differences in the world is a broad semantic purpose. Relative to representing the objective similarities and differences in the world, representing the objective *physical* similarities and differences in the world is a narrow semantic purpose as it *only* aims at the *physical* similarities and differences and we might think that there are non-physical similarities and differences in the world. Similar claims can be made about the language of economics, and its semantic purpose to represent the objective *economic* similarities and differences in the world, or just those within, say, one country.

Where does this leave us? Irmak's claim is that we cannot compare the language of physics and the language of economics as they have different purposes: representing the objective *physical* similarities and differences in the world, and representing the objective *economic* similarities and differences in the world, respectively. On this, I agree with Irmak. We cannot compare these languages relative to these semantic purposes, and if we do try to, we should accept that they are just different.

What if we just pick one? Relative to the semantic purpose of representing the objective *physical* similarities and differences in the world, it seems clear, to me at least, that the language of physics is better. Physics represents better physical similarities and differences than economics. In contrast, relative to representing the objective *economic* similarities and differences in the world, economics is better, as economics represents better economic similarities and differences.[5] That this is the case should not be surprising. Each of these languages aims to represent those similarities and differences, and those developing the languages have got very good at creating language that fulfils that purpose.

It also gets us nowhere if we want to defend a realism about a metaphysically best language. This is because we must be careful not to import first-order metaphysical claims into our metametaphysical theorizing. We cannot assume what kinds of similarities and differences the world actually contains. We can assume that it contains some, as this was the commitment to minimal realism that was discussed earlier. Minimal realism held that the world contains some similarities and differences that are entirely independent of us and our language choice, yet we nonetheless are trying to express those differences within our language and general inquiries into the world. What we cannot assume is that the differences and similarities in the world are physical in nature, or that they are economic, aesthetic, ethical, modal, or any other kinds of distinction we might think of.[6] To do so would be to beg the question. If we *assume* that realism only

---

[5] This is an empirical claim perhaps, but I think a reasonable assumption. Some (reductive) physicalists might deny this assumption, but as I will discuss in detail in a moment, this is to assume first-order metaphysical claims that we should not in this metametaphysical debate.

[6] The same goes for the notion of 'fundamental'. If we think that the best language contains only those terms that refer to fundamental entities, then we cannot build that commitment into our notion of semantic purpose.

concerns physical similarities and differences, then representing the objective *physical* similarities and differences and representing all objective similarities and differences collapse into each other. If a language satisfies one, then it must satisfy the other. But we cannot assume that in our metametaphysics.

In light of this, I argue that we can instead take the semantic purpose of a putative privileged language is to represent *all* objective similarities and differences in the world. The metaphysically best language is introduced in order to represent all the ways that the world really is, however that may be; what such a language is *for* is to represent *all* objective similarities and differences in the world, not just some subset of them. Absolutely we cannot compare languages relative to different semantic purposes, but we can compare them relative to the *same* semantic purpose, and the semantic purpose intended by the metaphysician when introducing terms or a language that they think is best is to represent all similarities and differences in the world.

If we think that the language of physics is the best metaphysical language, then we think that it is a good language *both* at representing *physical* similarities and differences in the world and at representing *all* objective similarities and differences in the world. The same holds, *mutatis mutandis*, for the language of economics, or the language of biology, or any other terms or language that we might adopt. If someone thinks that unrestricted mereological composition is correct, then a language that expresses those claims will be a language that they think satisfies the semantic purpose of representing objective similarities and differences in the world, and they will think that it does it better than a language that expresses the claims of mereological nihilism. To tell which is the best, there has to be a shared semantic purpose. We, I argue, have that shared semantic purpose in virtue of the broad semantic purpose I have identified.

Is comparison relative to this broad semantic purpose possible? I think it is. To compare the language of physics to the language of economics is to ask which represents better the genuinely occurring similarities and differences in the world. If the language of physics represents better the objective similarities and differences, then it is a better language relative to the metaphysically relevant broad semantic purpose; if the language of economics does, then it is better. To know this, though, we have to know, or at least put forward, arguments about how the world really is, and what similarities and differences it contains.

That is, making *any* claim about their relative goodness, including that they are equally good, requires first-order metaphysics of the sort that deflationists wants to resist. That is, deflationists must either accept that physics is a better candidate for being the privileged language, a worse candidate, or equally good. Each of these claims, though, rely on first-order metaphysical claims about what kinds of objective similarities and differences exist in the world. We must accept that there are substantive first-order metaphysical disputes in order to both accept and deny that there are equally good languages relative to the semantic purpose of representing all objective similarities and differences in the world. This form of deflationism can only support the claim that there are multiple equally good languages by making first-order metaphysical claims about the nature of the world.

Why, though, should we adopt this broader semantic purpose? Instead, we might just think that it is enough that we introduced the language of physics on the grounds that it is an additional linguistic tool to understand, represent, and predict physical features of the world. After all, a language is a kind of social artefact that is created, maintained, and revised to fulfil various goals. The answer, I think, is in this last claim already. We have various goals with languages. Some are big, some small, and some of them will overlap with each other. I am not making the claim that we should all adopt this broader semantic purpose, or consider it when we speak. I am only claiming that it is this semantic purpose that the metaphysical realist intends to adopt. Others might find this purpose a boring one to adopt, but just because adopting a metaphysically relevant purpose will not be useful in other cases, or be seen as a fulfilling endeavour by all, does not result in the conclusion that such a semantic purpose does not exist.

I am also not claiming that we, with our finite abilities, *can* create a language that fulfils this purpose. There may be reasons for thinking that we cannot. There might be epistemic reasons for thinking that we could never know if a language we have fulfils the broad semantic purpose I have identified. My claim has only been that what a metaphysician is doing when they introduce a putatively best language is to introduce a language that has the semantic purpose of representing all similarities and differences in the world. What determines the metaphysical goodness of a language is relative to this semantic purpose, not some narrower one. Likely there will still be some cases—some impasses—where we cannot decide which putative metaphysically best language is actually better. Such impasses will not always arise, though, and the metametaphysical claim that the realist needs here is only that two languages have a shared semantic purpose against which they can be judged, contra deflationism.

6.3

The immediate response will be that I have somewhat missed the point. Two sets of propositions can be taken to share this broad purpose, but comparing them would still be impossible. After all, is a language that has expressed some aesthetic objective similarities *better* or *worse* than a language that has expressed some physical objective similarities? This is ultimately the main deflationist claim that I am concerned with here.

However, this still relies on an assumption about the underlying metaphysical nature of reality. Take Sider again as an example. Sider discusses the view that for every aesthetic judgement, there is a physical property P that is the linguistic meaning of 'is beautiful' (Sider 2011, pp. 58–59). This is a statement of his physicalism. Under this view, the physical language is metaphysically better because the aesthetic judgement can be reduced to the physical—the physical property is what is picked out by the predicate 'is beautiful'.

Physicalism, though, is a metaphysical commitment to the idea that, for example, aesthetic judgements can be reduced to statements about physical properties. But physicalism in this sense is a claim about *what the objective language looks like*, not about *whether there is one*. In order to conclude that two sets of propositions—those of physics and those of aesthetics, for example— cannot be compared, we have to assume that one or both of these languages is not the language that represents all objective similarities and differences in the world. We have to assume that there are no fundamentally aesthetic objective similarities and differences.

If we have a prior commitment to physicalism, the narrow semantic purpose representing the objective physical similarities and differences in the world and the broad semantic purpose of representing *all* objective similarities and differences in the world collapse into each other. The purposes collapse into each other as we have antecedently assumed that *all* of the world's objective similarities and differences in the world are physical. But we of course need not accept this if our aim, as mine is, is to discuss the metaontological issues as opposed to the first-order metaphysical claims.

The mistake lies in confusing the claim that physics is the objectively best language, and hence why it seems as though other languages must have a different semantic purpose, with an argument that defends that there is an objectively best language. The purpose of physics is to explain the fundamental physical structure of reality. But that physics has the purpose of explaining the fundamental physical structure of reality tells us nothing about the fundamental nature of reality unless we independently assume that the fundamental nature of reality is physical. This is clearly a first-order claim, and other languages will be worse relative to the narrow purpose of explaining the *physical* structure of reality. But this is not the semantic purpose of a fundamental language, as the semantic purpose of a fundamental language cannot, prior to investigation, be assumed to only be interested in *physical* reality.

Answering whether a language that has expressed some aesthetic objective similarities is better or worse than a language that has expressed some physical objective similarity depends then on some underlying metaphysical claims about the nature of reality. Perhaps the language of aesthetics in fact best carves up the world. Whether this is the case is a matter of first-order debate within metaphysics about what joints in nature there are, what similarities and differences really exist, and what language best describes those that do exist. In our scientifically inclined world, many typically assume that it is physics that does this. We could, though, instead make arguments for aestheticalism, the view that the objective similarities and differences in the world are all fundamentally aesthetic in nature. If we thought this, then we presumably defend the idea that physical entities should be reduced to aesthetic ones, and thus that the aesthetic language is better than the physical language. Comparison of candidate privileged languages becomes an issue about what first-order metaphysical claims, such as physicalism or aestheticalism, we wish to endorse.

A pluralistic metaphysics where there are many different types of joints in reality is not a denial of the claim that there is a fundamental language, or a language that is objectively best. It is a denial that physics (or any single language or theoretical scheme)[7] alone can provide that objectively best language to represent all objective similarities and differences. That is, it is a denial of the first-order commitment to physicalism. Many would be sympathetic to this claim, but it does not touch upon the truth of (3) and (4). It may help illuminate that some physicalist might be making an assumption about what the content of the best language will be like, but not about there being such a fundamental language.

Perhaps, instead, we object that neither language is better. The concern might be that comparing language is trivial if the languages compared all successfully track similarities and differences, or do so equally well. Perhaps both the physical and aesthetic languages carve reality at objectively real joints. If this is the case, then it does not suggest that (3) is false. Rather, it suggests that the objectively best language needs to be broad enough to include elements of *both* physical and aesthetic languages, contra Sider's first-order metaphysical claim that we should reduce aesthetic talk to physical properties, but in line with the metaontological realism Sider defends.

If all that we are interested in is arguments for and against the possibility of an objectively best language, then we should not antecedently adopt any metaphysical principle such as physicalism or aestheticalism that would dictate what that language's contents might be like. The argument of Sider's that Irmak focuses on is not entirely about whether (3) and (4) are correct, but is also about (b): that the language of physics is the language which best carves nature at the joints. Once we separate these two aspects, and ignore for present purposes whether (b) is correct, we can see that (3) and (4) are not threatened by the notion of semantic purpose once we understand it, as the metaphysician does, to be coarse-grained.

There is, though, a broader point about different languages and the objectively best language, one that metaphysicians are perhaps too quick to ignore. It is that we should not, without good reason, rule out any language as potentially contributing to the objectively best language. Those good reasons are going to be arguments in favour of or against some metaphysical principle, such as physicalism. If

---

[7] Insofar as physics is in some sense isolated from other sciences.

we have good independent reasons to accept physicalism, then we can start to restrict which languages we think might contribute to the objectively best language. But for many it is far from clear that we have those reasons currently or that we could ever have those reasons.[8] Progress is only going to be made on providing the content of the objectively best language once we recognize that a large part relies on the metaphysical principles that we take to be important to restricting its contents. If I have no good independently motivated reason for ruling out a language as being interested in representing objective similarities and differences in the world, then it must be considered as potentially being (or contributing to) the objectively best language. That is what my toy example of aestheticalism was intended to show. Of course, providing arguments for or against metaphysical principles of the sort I have been discussing is difficult, and I can provide none here in favour of aestheticalism.[9] But it does indicate the need for metaphysical debate, and why it is substantive, highly non-trivial debate (at least not for any reasons discussed here).

6.4

My claim is that we can define the relevant semantic purpose of a language that purports to be objectively best or privileged as being that of an attempt to represent all of the objective similarities and differences in the world. What, though, about a language that does not have this as a purpose at all? For example, take a language that by stipulation is introduced with a semantic purpose that does not include an attempt to describe objective similarities and differences in the world.[10] It is unclear, though, why the realist about a metaphysically best language should be concerned with such languages. If they are not intended to be candidates for being the best language, then we simply have no need to consider them when we are seeing which language is the best candidate we have for being the metaphysically best language. Such languages, if there are any, might of course

---

[8] Physicalism is, of course, a far from universally accepted claim. See, inter alia, Chalmers (1996), Chomsky (2000), Hempel (1969), Jackson (1986), and Kripke (1982) for just some of the arguments against the view.

[9] Indeed, whilst the aesthetic language might be the best to use relative to the semantic purpose of talking about the beauty of artwork, it seems hard to believe that it would be sufficiently complete when comparing that language *qua* being a putative privileged language. This, though, is a first-order issue independent of my metaontological arguments in this chapter.

[10] This cannot be just to say that that language is allegorical or metaphorical, as it might be reasonable to suppose that even allegorical and metaphorical language is intended to describe some objective similarities and differences at least some of the time. If this was not the case, then those languages would not be useful in the way that they are at teaching children lessons about life, or highlighting some otherwise overlooked aspect of the world (assuming that they are useful in this way on at least some occasions). Some might hold that moral or modal talk is of this sort, though. If I am a modal sceptic, then I could believe that no modal talk tracks any real distinction in the world, and that it is mere fiction.

be highly useful and important for other reasons. They simply are not aiming to describe objective similarities and differences in the world. Nothing can be inferred from this as to their usefulness without some further claim about what pragmatically could be a useful language. The language that does not have this purpose should only be rejected if we are currently interested in representing those similarities and differences.

However, we must also remember here that economic, sociological, aesthetic languages, and ordinary language, are not like this language. At least part of their semantic purpose is to describe the objective similarities and differences in the world. Deflationists must hold this if they wish to maintain a belief in minimal realism, the view that the world contains some similarities and differences that are entirely independent of us and our language choice, yet we nonetheless are trying to express those differences within our language and general inquiries into the world. This follows simply from the conjunction of (1) and (2) above. Most (if not all) language that we care about in our lives will therefore not be like the language that has no part of its semantic purpose as representing objective similarities and differences in the world. To compare the putative privileged languages, we must do so relative to the coarse-grained semantic purpose.

The conclusions of this chapter, though, are more significant than this precisification of which semantic purpose is the relevant one. My ultimate point has been to argue that in order to know whether two putative privileged languages are equally good, relative to the coarse-grained semantic purpose I have identified, we have to engage in substantive first-order metaphysical disputes. In order to know whether the languages of physicalism and aestheticalism are equally good, we need to consider whether we think that there are objective physical and/or aesthetic similarities and differences in the world. Assessing the languages to see which are the 'good' metaphysical languages requires us to assess the metaphysical principles that underlie those languages. It is this that ultimately undercuts the deflationist argument.

The deflationist faces a dilemma. Either languages do (at least in part) share the coarse-grained semantic purpose and so we can evaluate which language is better (even if the objectively best language might end up being a mixture of a number of somewhat different language), but to evaluate them requires first-order metaphysical commitments; or the languages do not have as any part of their semantic purpose the purpose of representing objective similarities and differences in the world, in which case we have no reason to suppose that they were ever intended to be metaphysically privileged languages. I have provided no solution to what the metaphysically best language looks like, but hope to have shed some light on how we can decide which languages are good.

References

Carnap, R. 1950/1956. 'Empiricism, Semantics and Ontology', *Revue International de Philosophie*, 4: 20–40. Reprinted in *Meaning and Necessity: A Study in Semantics and Modal Logic*, 2nd edn. Chicago, IL: University of Chicago Press.

Chalmers, D. 1996. *The Conscious Mind*. New York: Oxford University Press.

Chalmers, D. 2009. 'Ontological Indeterminacy'. In D. J. Chalmers, D. Manley, and R. Wasserman (eds.), *Metametaphysics*, 77–129. Oxford: Oxford University Press.

Chomsky, N. 2000. *New Horizons in the Study of Language and Mind*. Cambridge: Cambridge University Press.

Hempel, C. 1969. 'Reduction: Ontological and Linguistic Facets'. In S. Morgenbesser et al. (eds.), *Essays in Honor of Ernest Nagel*. New York: St Martin's Press.

Hirsch, E. 2002a. 'Against Revisionary Ontology', *Philosophical Topics*, 30(1): 103–127.

Hirsch, E. 2002b. 'Quantifier Variance and Realism', *Noûs*, 36(1): 51–73.

Hirsch, E. 2005. 'Physical-Object Ontology, Verbal Disputes, and Common Sense', *Philosophy and Phenomenological Research*, 70: 67–97.

Hirsch, E. 2011. *Quantifier Variance and Realism: Essays in Metaontology*. New York: Oxford University Press.

Irmak, N. 2013. 'The Privilege of the Physical and the Status of Ontological Debates', *Philosophical Studies*, 166(1): 1–18.

Jackson, F. 1986. 'What Mary Didn't Know', *Journal of Philosophy*, 83: 291–295.

Kripke, S. 1982. *Wittgenstein on Rules and Private Language: An Elementary Exposition*. Oxford: Basil Blackwell.

Miller, J. T. M. 2016. 'Can an Ontological Pluralist Really Be a Realist?', *Metaphilosophy*, 47(3): 425–430.

Moore, G. E. 1993. *Principia Ethica*. Cambridge: Cambridge University Press: 1903. *Revised edition with 'Preface to the second edition' and other papers. In T. Baldwin (ed.), Cambridge: Cambridge University Press.

Peacocke, C. 1988. 'The Limits of Intelligibility: A Post-Verificationist Proposal', *Philosophical Review*, 97: 463–496.

Putnam, H. 1975. 'The Refutation of Conventionalism'. In H. Putnam, *Mind, Language and Reality: Philosophical Papers, volume 2*, 153–191. Cambridge: Cambridge University Press.

Putnam, H. 1987. *The Many Faces of Realism*. La Salle, IL: Open Court.

Sidelle, A. 2002. 'Is There a True Metaphysics of Material Objects?', *Philosophical Issues*, 12: 118–145.

Sider, T. 2009. 'Ontological Realism'. In D. Chalmers, D. Manley, and R. Wasserman (eds.), *Metametaphysics*, 384–423. Oxford: Oxford University Press.

Sider, T. 2011. *Writing the Book of the World*. New York: Oxford University Press.

Sosa, E. 1999. 'Existential Relativity'. In P. French and H. K. Wettstein (eds.), *Midwest Studies in Philosophy XXIII: New Directions in Philosophy*, 132–143. Oxford: Blackwell.

Thomasson, A. L. 2007. *Ordinary Objects*. New York: Oxford University Press.

Thomasson, A. L. 2008. 'Existence Questions', *Philosophical Studies*, 141: 63–78.

Thomasson, A. L. 2009. 'Answerable and Unanswerable Questions'. In D. J. Chalmers, D. Manley, and R. Wasserman (eds.), *Metametaphysics*, 444–471. Oxford: Oxford University Press.

Thomasson, A. L. 2015. *Ontology Made Easy*. New York: Oxford University Press.

7

The Questions of Ontology

Richard Woodward

Questions of ontology are at once both familiar and mysterious. Their familiarity has recently been nicely expressed by Theodore Sider:

> Ordinary ontology is no more remarkable than wondering about the weather. We ask whether there is ice-cream in the freezer, whether there is a twenty for a cab, whether there is a game on television. In more expansive moments we ponder the existence of black holes, gods, UFOs, or anything at all beyond the world of space and time. We understand these questions, and we know, more or less, how to go about answering them. (2011, p. 179)

The mysteriousness of ontological questions arises when we consider not questions of ordinary ontology but those that are asked by philosophers in their professional capacities. When philosophers ask whether or not there are such things as numbers or composite objects, eyebrows are raised not only about how we should go about answering the questions but also about how we should even understand them in the first place. Moreover, insofar as questions of philosophical ontology are strange beasts, it is unfortunate that philosophers tend to retreat to weasel words and metaphors to demarcate their topic. Whatever content might subsequently be attached to such intriguing locutions, a research project founded on questions of whether there are 'really' such things as numbers or whether composite objects are 'out there' and part of 'the furniture of the world' is one whose foundations will naturally be taken to be rather shaky.

The work of W. V. O. Quine constitutes one way of trying to remove the mystery that shrouds questions of philosophical ontology. Quine (1948) proposes that we understand questions of philosophical ontology as being on a par with more familiar ontological questions. For Quine, the question of whether there are numbers or composite objects is the same kind of question as that of whether there are black holes or arctic penguins. In each case, the question is of the same form—are there Fs?—and all ontological questions are thus taken to be quantificational questions. And Quine thinks that the method we should employ to answer them is the same in each case: inference to the best explanation. If we cannot formulate our best theory of the world without quantifying over things of a certain sort, then we should believe that there are things of that sort; otherwise,

Richard Woodward, *The Questions of Ontology* In: *The Language of Ontology*. Edited by: J. T. M. Miller, Oxford University Press (2021). © Oxford University Press. DOI: 10.1093/oso/9780192895332.003.0008

we should not believe that there are such things. Even the question of whether there is such a thing as the external world is, for Quine (1969), answered by assessing whether or not we need to posit an external world in order to best explain the appearances.

Despite its enduring influence, Quine's conception of how we should both understand and go about answering ontological questions has come under fire. My focus here is on one important and influential critique of Quine's views, due to Kit Fine (2009), who argues that Quine's picture of ontology is thoroughly misguided. Fine tells us that Quine's approach is based on a 'double error' since he both 'asks the wrong question' and then 'answers the question he asks in the wrong way' (p. 161). Indeed, the fact that Quine's approach gives pride of place to existential quantification means that his approach is vitiated 'by the failure to recognize the most elementary logical form of [ontological] claims' (p. 167). On Fine's own approach, ontological questions do not have the form 'are there Fs?' but instead 'are Fs real?', and one answers such questions not by existentially quantifying and saying 'there are Fs' but by universally quantifying and saying 'every F is real' (p. 168).

In this chapter, I take up the defence on behalf of Quine and argue that Fine's central objections to the Quinean approach are unsuccessful.

7.1 Metaontology, from Quine to Fine

The ontological question, Quine (1948) tells us, is curiously simple. It can be asked in only three English words—What is there?—and answered in just one: Everything. But the project of ontological inquiry survives as there is room for disagreement about cases. Thus two philosophers might disagree about whether there are mathematical objects like numbers and sets, or about whether there are any composite objects like tables and chairs, or about whether there are objects that lie beyond the realms of actuality. Such philosophers will, of course, agree that there is what there is. But they disagree nonetheless, since they disagree about what there is, and thereby about to what 'everything' amounts.

For Quine, then, the subject matter of ontological inquiry is what there is and the goal of ontological inquiry is to give a true and comprehensive account of what there is. Ontological questions obviously arise in different disciplines and different contexts, but the ontological questions that arise within philosophy are, for Quine, the same kind of questions as those that arise in science and everyday life. Quine did not simply identify the questions ontologists aim to answer: he also provided a methodology for their inquiry. Roughly, the question of whether there is a certain sort of thing is to be answered by considering whether our best theories of the world are committed to that sort of thing: if our best theories of the world are so committed to there being things of that sort—if the truth of our best theories requires that there are things of that sort—then we ought to believe that there are such things, otherwise we should at least not believe that there are such things and probably we should believe that there are no such things. The naturalistic component here is that the standards for betterness that are appropriate when comparing theories in the context of ontological inquiry are the same as those that are appropriate when comparing theories in the context of scientific inquiry. In particular, when applied to the case of ontology, Quine's naturalistic rejection of the idea of a 'first philosophy' means that there is no place for an extra-scientific tribunal: if by scientific standards a given theory T is judged to be the best theory, then there is no possibility of a further philosophical assessment of the merits of that theory that could justify either the rejection of T's ontological commitments or the acceptance of further commitments over and above those incurred by T. All of our attempts at knowledge, and therefore all of our attempts at knowledge about what there is, are 'subject to those standards of evidence and justification which are most explicitly displayed, and most successfully implemented, in the natural sciences' (Hylton 2014, p. 151).

Fine's critique is wide ranging, but his central complaints are two-fold:

- **Substantiality.**

Insofar as the Quinean takes ontological questions to be existential questions about what there is, the Quinean cannot make sense of the supposedly substantial nature of ontological inquiry. For existential questions are easily answered by trivial considerations, whereas ontological questions are not supposed to be easily answered.

- **Autonomy.**

Insofar as the Quinean takes ontological questions to be existential questions about what there is, the Quinean cannot make sense of the autonomy of ontological inquiry. For even if we accept that there are certain sorts of things, there remains the possibility of holding that things of that sort do not really exist, so that answering the existential question in the affirmative leaves open the possibility of giving a negative answer to the corresponding ontological question.

Here, Fine objects not only to Quine's conception of the subject matter of ontology, i.e. the identification of ontological questions with questions about what there is, but also to the methodology that Quine proposes we use for answering ontological questions so conceived. That is, Fine takes the Quinean approach to be based on a 'double error' since Quine 'asks the wrong question...and answers the question he asks in the wrong way' (2009, p. 161). But rather than dealing with these complaints at this stage, I will begin by focusing on a third objection that Fine lodges against the Quinean approach. For whilst Fine takes this third complaint to be less fundamental than those that concern the substantiality and autonomy of ontological questions, it provides a useful springboard from which we can address the others.

7.2 Comparing Commitments

According to the Quinean conception of ontological commitment, someone is ontologically committed to certain sorts of things just in case they accept the truth of a theory that entails that there are those sorts of things. But, according to Fine, powerful considerations show that this approach, the dominant account of ontology and ontological commitment found in the contemporary literature, is vitiated by 'a failure to recognize the most elementary logical form of ontological claims' (2009, p. 167).

Fine asks us to compare a realist about integers, who is committed to integers and is able to express his commitment in familiar fashion by means of the sentence 'integers exist', with a realist about the positive integers (i.e. natural numbers), who is committed to the positive integers and is similarly able to express his commitment in familiar fashion by means of the sentence 'positive integers exist'. Intuitively, Fine thinks, it is the realist about integers who has the stronger position here: after all, she is committed to all the integers and not merely to the positive ones. Put otherwise, it is the realist about positive integers who has the weaker position, for she is committed only to the positive integers, leaving it open whether she might also be committed to the negative ones. As Fine (2009, p. 165) puts it, the realist about integers has a more thorough-going commitment, since she is committed to all the integers, whilst the realist about positive integers only has a partial commitment, since she is committed only to the positive integers.

On the Quinean picture, however, this intuitive picture is reversed. For on this picture, to be committed to integers is to accept that there are integers, i.e. that there is something such that it is an integer—that is, to accept $\exists x(\text{Integer}(x))$—whereas to be committed to positive integers is to accept that there are positive integers, i.e. that there is an integer such that it is positive—that is, to accept $\exists x(\text{Integer}(x) \land \text{Positive}(x))$. But since the claim that there are integers is logically weaker than the claim that there are positive integers, the quantificational account of ontological commitment 'gets the basic logic of ontological commitment wrong' because the commitment to integers should be stronger than the commitment to just the positive ones (2009, p. 166; compare Fine 2001, pp. 5–6).

In light of this observation, Fine suggests that we reject Quine's identification of ontological questions with existential quantification about what there is and instead identify ontological questions with universal quantification about reality. That is, when the realist about integers expresses her commitment by means of the sentence 'integers exist', she is not, contra Quine, claiming that there is something such that it is an integer, but that each and every integer is such that it really exists.[1] And now the previous difficulty disappears: the commitment to integers will be stronger than the commitment to positive integers since the claim that all of the Fs really exist (i.e. $\forall x(F(x) \supset Real(x))$) is in general stronger than the claim that all of the Fs that are Gs really exist (i.e. $\forall x((F(x) \wedge G(x)) \supset Real(x))$). Moreover, the Finean picture of ontology can now readily accommodate the felt substantiality and autonomy of ontological inquiry. For even if it is a trivial matter to establish that there are certain sorts of things, the corresponding question of whether all things of that sort are real remains unresolved. Hence, the question of whether all of the Fs, or none of the Fs, or exactly those Fs that meet some further condition are real can be held to be nontrivial and independent of the question of whether there are Fs, thereby respecting the felt substantiality and autonomy of questions of philosophical ontology.

Now, even if the commitment to Fs (integers, e.g.) is in general weaker than the commitment to Fs that are also Gs (integers that are also positive, e.g.), it is worth noting that the kind of sentence-by-sentence comparisons that Fine focuses on have the capacity to be highly misleading in the context of the Quinean approach. When we ask whether or not one theorist has a stronger or weaker position than another theorist, the primary comparison the Quinean will make is between the existential consequences of their respective theories. And whether or not one theorist has a stronger position than another theorist will in turn depend on exactly which theory each theorist accepts. Now, consider Fine's description of the case:

> Intuitively, the realist about integers holds the stronger position. After all, he makes an ontological commitment to the integers, not just to the natural numbers, while the realist about natural numbers only commits himself to the natural numbers, leaving open whether he might also be committed to the negative integers. The realist about integers—at least on the most natural construal of his position—has a thorough-going commitment to the whole domain of integers, while the natural number realist only has a partial commitment to the domain.   (2009, p. 165)

It is clear from the context that we are supposed to associate certain theories with each theorist. The former theorist, Fine's 'realist about integers', is ontologically committed 'not just to the natural numbers', whereas the latter theorist, the 'realist

---

[1] Fine initially expresses this as 'every integer exists' but later comes to construe the relevant sense of 'exists' in terms of what exists 'in reality' (see Fine 2009, p. 168ff.). Hence, the relevant statement of the realist position is $\forall x(Integer(x) \supset (In\ Reality,\ \exists y(x=y)))$. I'll shorten this to $\forall x(Integer(x) \supset Real(x))$ for brevity.

about natural numbers', is 'only committed to the natural numbers'. Hence, the former theorist is naturally taken to accept a theory that not only entails the existence of positive integers but also entails the existence of negative integers, whereas the latter theorist is naturally taken to accept a theory which entails that there are positive integers but does not entail that there are negative ones. Accordingly, even though the sentence 'There are integers' is logically weaker than the sentence 'There are positive integers', the theory that is to be associated with Fine's realist about integers is in fact stronger than the theory that is to be associated with Fine's realist about natural numbers.

To be clear: the idea is not the idiotic one that to believe in Fs is thereby to believe both in Fs that are Gs and in Fs that are not Gs. Rather, the idea is that in the Finean example, the relative strength of the two positions is determined not on the basis of a sentence-to-sentence comparison but on the basis of a theory-to-theory comparison. And so everything depends upon which theory is being associated with each theorist. The Quinean is committed to holding that the realist about integers has a weaker position than the realist about positive integers only if the realist about integers takes no stance on the existence of positive and negative integers. And since Fine describes the realist about integers as being committed not just to the positive integers, this condition fails since we naturally assume that the realist about integers is committed to negative integers too. And since the realist about integers also believes in the existence of both positive integers and negative integers, then her theory will in fact be stronger than someone who only accepts the existence of positive integers. In that case, her theory has commitments over and above those of her rival's theory, for her theory is committed to the existence of negative integers and her rival's theory is not. To stress, this is not to say that there is no general answer to the question of the conditions under which someone is committed to Fs: to be committed to Fs is to accept a theory that entails that there are Fs. Rather, the point is that there are various theories that entail that there are Fs, and so whether or not one theorist has a stronger position than another depends on the existential consequences of the specific theories they respectively accept. And even though the sentence 'there are Fs' is by itself only committed to Fs, the theory in which that sentence is embedded may be committed not only to Fs but also to Fs that meet various other conditions.[2]

If the above thoughts are correct, Fine's argument against the Quinean conception of ontological commitment is unsound insofar as Quine can explain why, in the example at hand, the realist about integers (at least as Fine describes her) has a stronger view than the realist about positive integers (as Fine describes her). With

---

[2] Or it may not. A theory that says that there are Fs (integers, e.g.) but does not make any claims about the further kinds that the Fs fall under (positive, negative, prime, e.g.) will be committed only to Fs. That only serves to underwrite the crucial point: the results of taking on a commitment to Fs will vary depending on the wider theoretical context in which that commitment is accepted. Ontological commitment, as we might put it, is a holistic matter.

that initial skirmish out of the way, we can now proceed to examine the more central components of Fine's critique, viz. the felt substantiality and autonomy of ontological inquiry that Fine contends cannot be captured on Quine's view.

7.3 Moorean Manoeuvres

Recall that Fine holds that the Quinean approach is vitiated by its failure to secure the substantiality and autonomy of ontological inquiry. Properly understanding these complaints requires us to tread carefully, however. For one thing, Fine does not claim that all existence questions are easily answered by trivial considerations: he explicitly acknowledges that some existential questions—whether there are electrons, for example—are substantial (2009, p. 158), so the charge of triviality is perhaps best localized to the existential questions that arise in philosophical contexts. For another thing, it is worth noting that Fine is committed by his own lights to holding that certain ontological questions are insubstantial and answered by trivial considerations. On his account, after all, ontological questions are of the form 'is every F real?' and that question will be trivially answered in the affirmative whenever there are no Fs (since if there are no Fs, then every F will trivially meet any arbitrary condition including that of being real). Given that certain existence questions are easily answered in the negative—are there round squares, are there things such that 2+2=5?—it will follow that the corresponding universal questions about reality will in turn be insubstantial too.

In light of these observations, Fine's complaint is not that all existence questions are easy, or that no ontological questions are insubstantial, but rather that Quine's approach renders trivial certain specific ontological questions: ontological questions about numbers, properties, propositions, tables, chairs, and the like. And this complaint, I think, doesn't so much concern Quine's conception of the subject matter of ontological inquiry so much as it concerns his naturalistic methodology. As we saw, Quine's naturalism entails that the evidence that is required in order to justify our belief in the existence of numbers or tables is the same kind of evidence that is required in order to justify our belief in the existence of electrons. In each case, it needs to be established that the existence of things of the target sort is a pre-condition of the truth of our best explanations, where the relevant standards of theoretical betterness are those found in the natural sciences. Hence, if Fs were dispensable for the purposes of scientific explanation, there would be no reason left that could justify belief in their existence. And whilst Fine concedes that this kind of methodology may be appropriate in the case of the theoretical entities of science, he contends that it is inappropriate when applied across the board:

> Our reason to believe in couples or in chairs and tables [...] has nothing to do
> with their role in explanation. John and Mary are 'together' and that is reason

enough to suppose that they are a couple; the object over there has a certain form and function and that is reason enough to suppose that it is a chair....My own view is that something similar should be said in the case of the objects of mathematics. Just as the fact that two people are married is reason enough to think that a couple is married, so the fact that there are no goblins is reason enough to think that the number of goblins is 0 (and hence that there is a number).   (2009, p. 161)

It should hopefully be clear how this dovetails with Fine's complaints about the substantiality of ontological questions: if the existence of numbers and tables can be easily established on the basis of compelling inferences from eminently justified premises, it would seem that the substantial question of philosophical ontology cannot be identified with the quantificational question of whether there are such things. To focus attention on a particular case, consider the inference from the premise that there are no married bachelors to the sub-conclusion that the number of married bachelors is zero, and then to the final conclusion that there are numbers. According to Fine, the compelling nature of this inference gives us a reason to believe in numbers that is independent of any explanatory role that numbers may or may not play in our scientific theorizing. Let us call this the Moorean Complaint.

The immediate worry about the Moorean Complaint is that Fine's 'easy' argument for the existence of numbers looks question-begging: the move from there being no married bachelors to the number of married bachelors being zero will only be granted by someone who already accepts the existence of numbers. That is, it is only in the context of an antecedent commitment to the principle that the number of Fs is n iff there are exactly n Fs—which logically entails that there are numbers, given that it is logically true that there are no Fs such that some contradiction is true—that the initial step of the Moorean argument will be granted.[3] In the same way, consider Jonathan Schaffer's expression of the Moorean Complaint:

Existence debates are trivial, in that the entities in question obviously do exist. Start with the debate over numbers. Here, without further ado, is a proof of the existence of numbers:

(1) There are prime numbers

(2) Therefore there are numbers

(1) is a mathematical truism. It commands Moorean certainty, as being more credible than any philosopher's argument to the contrary. Any metaphysician

---

[3] As Daly and Liggins (2014, p. 1472) note, Fine seems to conveniently neglect to mention that even the most vocal defenders of that principle acknowledge that its status and justification is controversial at best: see Hale and Wright (2001).

who would deny it has ipso facto produced a reductio for her premises. And (2) follows immediately, by a standard adjective-drop inference. Thus numbers exist. End of story. (2009, p. 357)

Again, the Moorean Complaint that Schaffer articulates here is not that all existence debates are trivial, since he would accept that there are no easy arguments for the existence of electrons or black holes. And again, it is difficult to see why this 'proof' isn't anything other than question-begging: the validity of the argument notwithstanding, the initial premise of Schaffer's 'proof' will only ever be granted by someone who is antecedently committed to the existence of numbers. Moreover, if Schaffer is right that the existence of prime numbers is a Moorean certainty, it becomes unclear to what extent the 'proof' is needed since the Moorean could have just insisted that our belief in the existence of numbers is itself better justified than any philosopher's argument to the contrary. And that contention will be dialectically ineffective against an opponent who directly questions whether we are justified in believing in the existence of numbers, especially so in contexts where our existential beliefs are questioned because of their apparent inconsistency with other beliefs that we cherish. (Think here of arguments for eliminating ordinary objects based on paradoxes of material constitution and the like. Such arguments work by attempting to show that our belief in the existence of ordinary objects is undermined by its inconsistency with other commonsensical beliefs we want to hold on to.) It is in this context difficult to see exactly how the Moorean argument is meant to give us a reason to believe in numbers or how its proponents hope to establish that mathematics and common sense are somehow hermeneutically sealed from philosophical criticism.[4]

The nature of the Moorean Complaint, then, is murky and at the very least there is a range of very subtle epistemological issues that need to be addressed before the complaint can be properly assessed: for headway in that direction, see Daly and Liggins (2014). But it bears emphasis that the naturalistic methodology advocated by Quine is consistent with the considerations Fine and Schaffer outline, at least on one articulation of those considerations. For whilst it is true that the Quinean denies that the existence of numbers is so certain that no considerations could ever justify revising our belief in the existence of numbers, it is also true that the Quinean thinks that our belief in the existence of numbers is especially secure insofar as our mathematical beliefs lie close to the centre of our web of belief, being deeply implicated in, and intimately bound up with, the rest of

---

[4] Compare here Field (1989, pp. 11–13) and Williams (2012, p. 167). Schaffer for his own part thinks that doubts about mathematical knowledge systematically require epistemological premises that are always less plausible than the mathematical beliefs they seek to undermine. For a discussion of why that response rests on a misunderstanding of the challenge Field raises for Platonist epistemologies, see Daly and Liggins (2014, p. 465).

what we believe. Hence, when our theory of the world proves flawed, our practice is to retain our mathematical beliefs and instead make adjustments elsewhere in the system. That is not to say that our mathematical beliefs are more justified than many of our empirical beliefs: the relative immunity to revision possessed by our mathematical beliefs is the same as that enjoyed by any belief to the extent that it lies near the centre of the web. But the point is that many of our existential beliefs—in numbers, in cats, in people—are so deeply embedded in the web of belief that abandoning them would be to give up on almost everything that we currently take to be true. To give up those beliefs would, to continue the joke, be to lose our Moore-ings. Moreover, the kind of picture of inquiry suggested here is also attractive insofar as it is in a position to acknowledge the relative security of the things we ordinarily think and say without thereby forcing us to make bold claims to the effect that philosophical reflection can never undermine common sense, or that mathematics and science can never be questioned on philosophical grounds. All of this, to stress, is perfectly consistent with naturalism: rather than showing that our justification for believing that there are numbers is radically different from our justification for believing in electrons, naturalism and Mooreanism are natural bedfellows.

Once it is recognized that the Quinean is perfectly willing to accept the centrality of certain existential views in our web of belief, there is a certain mundane sense in which she can equally accept the 'obviousness' and 'triviality' of certain existential questions, at least under one understanding of those terms. But their obvious and trivial answers notwithstanding, the crucial point is that ontological questions remain substantial questions about the world and there remains the possibility that even those beliefs that lie at the centre of our web of commitments are false. Whatever other merits a theory that rejected numbers or cats or people might have, the radical conflict that such a theory would have with our present commitments would thereby be a heavy theoretical cost. Though that cost could in principle be outweighed by other theoretical virtues, the point remains that the Quinean's emphasis on scientific standards does not mean that our ordinary mathematical and empirical beliefs are called into immediate doubt or that our ordinary mathematical and empirical beliefs are not massively justified by scientific standards. Insofar as scientific explanation is taken by the naturalist to be an extension and refinement of our everyday explanatory practices, she will think that these beliefs figure in scientifically respectable explanations on a daily basis. As Christopher Hookway puts it: 'For Quine, our scientific beliefs—and our common-sense beliefs—stand firm; we experience no inclination to doubt them and it is easy to dismiss anyone who doubts them as a crank. If there are no controversies about how we ought to conduct our inquiries, the only tasks we face are explanatory ones' (2004, pp. 39–40).

7.4 Autonomy and Reality

In section 7.3, I focused mainly on defending the Quinean approach from Fine's complaint that it fails to underwrite the felt substantiality of ontological questions. I turn finally to the remaining component of Fine's critique: his allegation that the Quinean cannot account for the felt autonomy of ontological inquiry. In some ways, this complaint is the hardest to address since it is premised on the seemingly thoroughly anti-Quinean idea that, even once existential questions are answered positively, further ontological questions, questions that are distinctively philosophical in character, remain unanswered. Moreover, the central concept that Fine deploys in order to demarcate an autonomous domain of ontological inquiry—the concept of Reality—seems exactly the kind of concept that Quine would have viewed with the utmost contempt. Put bluntly, there seems to be so little common ground here that any hopes of conducting a fruitful exchange seem forlorn. I am slightly more optimistic that there is more to be said than might meet the eye, however, since Fine's concerns are not as alien to the concerns of those working in the Quinean tradition as one might suspect.

To begin, it bears emphasis that the notion of Reality that Fine has in mind is not the notion familiar from the distinction between appearance and reality. That latter distinction is a distinction between how things seem to be and how things are: the stick appears bent but is in fact straight, the distant elephant appears small but is in fact big. Fine's distinction, by contrast, is a distinction between two kinds of facts: those that are really the case and those that are merely the case. The idea in the mereological case, for example, would not be that the world appears composite but is in fact simple: rather, it would be that the world is composite even though only simple objects exist in reality. Hence, even once we have settled that there do not only merely seem to be tables but there are in fact such things, we would still be left with the question of whether some, all, or none of the tables exist in Reality.[5]

Though many will find Fine's distinction opaque, the central idea is part and parcel of any approach to metaphysical questions that allows that one can maintain an anti-realist position about a certain domain even if one accepts that the contested claims made in that domain are true. Crispin Wright (1992), for instance, is another philosopher who allows for this possibility: on his approach,

---

[5] As Lipman (forthcoming) observes, the precise formulation of the negative import of anti-realism raises delicate issues for Fine. For if it is true in reality that everything is simple, we cannot maintain that the reality operator is factive without contradicting our antecedent commitment to the existence of composite objects. But if, on the other hand, it is not true in reality that everything is simple, it would seem to follow that reality is incomplete, since the anti-realist will deny that it is true in reality that something is composite and hence accept that it is not true in reality that it is not the case that everything is simple.

the analogue of Fine's distinction emerges as a distinction between the relevant truth predicate that the target claims satisfy. Transposed into the ontological key, Wright's idea is that the realist and anti-realist about colours disagree not over *whether* it is true that there are coloured things but over *how* it is true that there are coloured things.

Many metaphysics working in the Quinean tradition have been sympathetic to a similar idea. Thus Jonathan Bennett (2001, pp. 147–148) writes:

> The work of any interesting metaphysician involves two or more levels. I do not mean levels of reality: the metaphysicians I am talking about do not describe reality as stratified; rather, they stratify their accounts of it. At the basic level of speech, thought and conceptualization, they express truths that directly reflect the metaphysical situation; at the less basic level, they say things that are still true, but, as stated, are bad pointers to the metaphysical situation, and one needs an account of what their truth amounts to, comes down to, arises from, in terms of facts expressed at the basic level. The non-basic level gets a hearing only because it involves ordinary, familiar ways of saying things.

Obviously there are different ways of fleshing this basic idea out. One might hold, with Peter van Inwagen (1990), that the things we ordinarily say ('there are chairs', e.g.) are, whilst true, less than perspicuous ways of representing the metaphysical situation because their surface forms do not align with the structure of the propositions they express (the proposition that there are some things arranged chairwise, e.g.). Or one might hold, with Cian Dorr (2005) and Theodore Sider (2011), that the things we ordinarily say are, whilst true, less than perspicuous ways of representing the metaphysical situation because ordinary quantificational expressions do not carve nature at its joints.[6] And the positive proposal is then that ontological claims can still be perspicuously expressed either because existential claims work differently in philosophical contexts (van Inwagen) or because we can introduce new, more faithful quantificational expressions into natural language (Dorr, Sider). In any case, where Fine sees the distinction between the relevant notion of appearance and reality as a metaphysical distinction between those facts that are merely the case and those that are really the case, such metaphysicians conceive of the relevant contrast in representational terms; that is, as a distinction between more and less faithful and perspicuous ways of truly representing the way the world is.

Fine is aware of such strategies to create a distance between ordinary existence questions and ontological questions, but finds them inadequate, complaining that

---

[6] Sider (2013) distances himself from this position. For discussion of how a similar distinction might be articulated in a setting closer to Quine's own views about representation, see Williams (2012) and von Solodkoff and Woodward (2013).

there is no independent reason to accept the bold semantic hypotheses other than the fact that they make certain ontological positions more viable: as he puts it, such philosophers are guilty of putting 'logico-linguistic beliefs...at the service of ontological prejudices' (2009, p. 162). And whatever else we think of Fine's own proposal, one of its good-making features is precisely that it allows us to create a distance between ordinary existence questions and ontological questions without thereby making bold and controversial claims about the workings of ordinary language.

Note, however, the theoretical role played by the semantic claims entertained by people such as van Inwagen: they give us a way of expressing our ontological views in a perspicuous way. Given that we accept that we speak truly when we say, in the ordinary business of life, that there are tables for sale at IKEA, we need to find some other way of more perspicuously expressing certain views about the underlying metaphysical situation. Here we face a dilemma: either (a) we find some way of expressing those views in ordinary language or (b) we dump ordinary language and express those views in a new language that is more fit for metaphysical purpose. There is a sense in which Fine too faces this dilemma: by his lights, the things we say in the ordinary business of life are true, and so he needs to find some way of expressing his ontological and metaphysical views. And he resolves this dilemma by grasping its first horn and expressing his ontological views by means of the operator 'it is really the case that'. Fine is playing the same game as people like van Inwagen: the difference is that the strategy he pursues in order to provide a way of expressing ontological claims is free from the troubling kind of semantic speculations offered by his rivals. And whilst Fine's aim to avoid bold linguistic speculation is to be applauded, it is an aim he shares with many Quineans: for example, Williams (2012) and Sider (2013) can both be read as aiming to give broadly Quinean accounts that avoid linguistic revisionism.

Moreover, Fine's own proposal suffers from analogous difficulties. For instance, the central resource in Fine's account is the concept of something being constitutive of Reality. And Fine claims that we have a good intuitive grip on this concept (and cognate concepts such as the concept of one thing being nothing over and above another) and that our good intuitive grip on these concepts is reflected in our ability to make coherent sense of metaphysical positions such as Democritus' view that there is nothing more to the world than atoms in the void. Whether or not we agree with Democritus, Fine claims that our grasp of Reality is manifested in our ability to find his position intelligible. I cannot resist a parody:

Thales thought that everything is water. I take this to be an intelligible position, whether correct or not. I also assume that his thinking that everything is water can be taken to be shorthand for there being nothing more to the world than this being hot water and that other thing being cold water..., or something of this sort. I assume further that this position is not incompatible with his believing in things other than water. To be sure, the existence of things other than water creates a prima facie difficulty for the view that everything is water, but as long as the existence of things other than water can be seen to consist in nothing more than water, the difficulty will have been avoided....Of course, it is always open to the sceptic to doubt the coherence of Thales' position. It simply follows from the existence of things other than water that there is more to the world than water. But I hope I am not alone in thinking that such a philosopher is too sophisticated for her own good.   (Cf. Fine 2009, p. 175)

I hope that I am not alone in thinking that Fine's claims to understanding have been put at the service of his metaphysical prejudices. That is not to say, of course, that these Finean concepts are unintelligible (though see Daly 2012 for scepticism on that front). But it is to say that anyone who attempts to reconcile bold metaphysical claims with the things we ordinarily think and say will need to hope for an interlocutor who will meet them halfway and not begrudge them a pinch of salt. With Rosen (2014, p. 568) I believe that Quine's own view would have been that the onus is on Fine to show that the relevant notions play entrenched roles in the sciences or can be deployed in order to improve science on its own terms. If this challenge cannot be met, Quine's objection will not be that Fine's notions are meaningless, but rather that they serve no purpose in the improvement and systematization of total theory. Relatedly, Quine would not object in principle to the deployment of notions like reduction in philosophy: some things do reduce to, and consist in, other things. But he would hold that reduction is something that stands in need of philosophical explication, rather than something in terms of which philosophical explications can be given.

The original objection from autonomy, recall, was this: given that the Quinean identifies ontological questions with existential questions about what there is, she cannot make sense of there being another possibility—that of maintaining an anti-realist view about Fs whilst maintaining that there are such things. As we have seen, however, the Quinean's identification of ontological questions with existential questions needs to be handled carefully. For various metaphysicians working in the broadly Quinean tradition have attempted to make room for precisely that possibility, by holding that even if existential questions asked in the ordinary business of life are answered positively, there remains the possibility of holding that our answers to ordinary existence questions are not perspicuous ways of representing the underlying metaphysical situation. In that sense, Fine is not so much pursuing a strategy that is diametrically opposed to those strategies offered by various Quineans, but rather offering an alternative solution to the expressive problem that everyone faces.

To be clear, I do not mean to suggest that the Finean distinction between what is the case and what is really the case is marking the same distinction as those drawn in the Quinean tradition. One immediate difference is that Fine's distinction is most naturally understood in a metaphysically inflationary way, as a distinction between two kinds of facts, whereas the distinctions we find in the Quinean tradition are most naturally understood in a metaphysically deflationary way, as distinctions between two ways in which representations can be related to the underlying structure of the world.[7] Be that as it may, the point remains that the distinctions all play a similar role, viz. that of providing a subject matter for ontological inquiry that means that the ontological project is not finished once we have answered existence questions as they are couched in ordinary language. On this way of seeing things, the debate is not whether ontological questions are autonomous from ordinary existence questions, but how they manage to be.

7.5 Concluding Remarks

Fine, as we have seen, argues that the Quinean conception of ontological inquiry, according to which ontological questions concern the existence of a given kind of thing, should be abandoned and replaced with a conception according to which the primary focus of ontological disputes should be universal questions about the reality of things of the relevant kind. In this chapter, I have argued that the negative complaints that Fine lodges against the Quinean approach are unpersuasive. In particular, I have argued that the two central components of Fine's critique— the objections based on the felt substantiality and autonomy of ontological inquiry—are in fact misdirected since the proponent of a Quinean approach is well positioned to explain both the apparent triviality of many existential questions and how ontological questions might remain open, even once existence questions have been answered in the ordinary business of life.

References

Bennett, Jonathan. 2001. *Learning from Six Philosophers, volume 1*. Oxford: Oxford University Press.

Daly, Chris. 2012. 'Scepticism about Grounding'. In Fabrice Correia and Benjamin Schnieder (eds.), *Metaphysical Grounding*, 81–101. Cambridge: Cambridge University Press.

---

[7] Thus Williams (2010, p. 127) writes: 'Fine's defence of a distinction between what exists and what really or fundamentally exists might be given a thoroughgoingly metaphysical reading. But it need not be' because such operators can be understood as 'allowing us to give expression to genuinely metaphysical theses amidst a thicket of true but metaphysically misleading existence claims'. His disagreement with traditional Quineans is then over their understanding of the way representations are connected to reality (cf. Williams 2012).

Daly, Chris and Liggins, David. 2014. 'In Defence of Existence Questions', *The Monist*, 97: 469–478.

Dorr, Cian. 2005. 'What We Disagree about When We Disagree about Ontology'. In Mark Kalderon (ed.), *Fictionalism in Metaphysics*, 234–286. Oxford: Oxford University Press.

Field, Hartry. 1989. *Realism, Mathematics and Modality*. Oxford: Blackwell.

Fine, Kit. 2001. 'The Question of Realism', *Philosopher's Imprint*, 1: 1–30.

Fine, Kit. 2009. 'The Question of Ontology'. In David Chalmers, David Manley, and Ryan Wasserman (eds.), *Metametaphysics*, 157–177. Oxford: Oxford University Press.

Hale, Bob and Wright, Crispin. 2001. *The Reason's Proper Study*. Oxford: Oxford University Press.

Hookway, Christopher. 2004. 'Quine and Skepticism', *Quaderns de Filosofia i Ciència*, 34: 31–40.

Hylton, Peter. 2014. 'Quine's Naturalism Revisited'. In Gilbert Harman and Ernest Lepore (eds.), *A Companion to W.V.O. Quine*, 148–162. Oxford: Blackwell.

Lipman, Martin. forthcoming. 'Against Fundamentality-Based Metaphysics', *Noûs*.

Quine, W. V. O. 1948. 'On What There Is', *Review of Metaphysics*, 2: 21–38.

Quine, W. V. O. 1969. 'Epistemology Naturalized'. In *Ontological Relativity and Other Essays*, 69–90. New York: Columbia University Press.

Rosen, Gideon. 2014. 'Quine and the Revival of Metaphysics'. In Gilbert Harman and Ernie Lepore (eds.), *A Companion to W.V.O. Quine*, 552–570. Oxford: Blackwell.

Schaffer, Jonathan. 2009. 'On What Grounds What'. In David Chalmers, David Manley, and Ryan Wasserman (eds.), *Metametaphysics*, 347–383. Oxford: Oxford University Press.

Sider, Theodore. 2011. *Writing the Book of the World*. Oxford: Oxford University Press.

Sider, Theodore. 2013. 'Against Parthood'. In Karen Bennett and Dean W. Zimmerman (eds.), *Oxford Studies in Metaphysics, volume 8*, 237–293. Oxford: Oxford University Press.

van Inwagen, Peter. 1990. *Material Beings*. Ithaca, NY: Cornell University Press.

von Solodkoff, Tatjana and Woodward, Richard. 2013. 'Noneism, Ontology, and Fundamentality', *Philosophy and Phenomenological Research*, 87: 558–583.

Williams, J. Robert G. 2010. 'Fundamental and Derivative Truths', *Mind*, 119: 103–141.

Williams, J. Robert G. 2012. 'Requirements on Reality'. In Fabrice Correia and Benjamin Schnieder (eds.), *Metaphysical Grounding*, 165–185. Cambridge: Cambridge University Press.

Wright, Crispin. 1992. *Truth and Objectivity*. Cambridge, MA: Harvard University Press.

8

What "X Does Not Exist" Says About We Who Do Exist

Stephen Yablo

8.1 Overdetermination

Imagine an empty world *e*. *Dogs exist* is going to be false in a world like that. But *why* is *Dogs exist* false in *e*? We are pulled in two directions, I think. One reason *Dogs exist* is false there is the lack of dogs in *e*. Another, though, seemingly just as good, is the lack of *anything* in *e*. Unless the two reasons are somehow in competition, the falsity of *Dogs exist* is (very slightly) overdetermined.

How strange should we find this? Not very. Explanatory overdetermination is a fact of life.[1] Say the doorbell button was depressed by you yesterday, and the neighbor's cat today. Did the bell ring "for the same reason" both days? Yes, since some*thing* pushed the button both days. And yet no, since it was only yesterday that some*one* pushed it. But then it seems that there were two reasons at work yesterday: someone's pushing the button, and something's pushing it.

Consider now whether *Dogs exist* is false for "the same reason" in *e* as in a world *f* that contains cats, but no dogs. Thinking of *e*'s absolute emptiness as the falsemaker, we want to say no. Thinking of the lack of dogs, we want to say yes. It is hard to see how these judgments can be reconciled without allowing *Dogs exist* to be false in *e* both because *e* is empty, and because it is free of dogs.

If the falsity of an existence-claim can be overdetermined in this way, then the question arises whether one falsemaker could be in play without the other. Certainly we can imagine a nonempty world which is lacking in dogs—*f* was one—but I am wondering about our same old empty world *e*. Could there be an existence-claim *Ks exist* that is false there solely because *e* has nothing in it whatsoever—not because of any fact about *Ks* in particular?

Objection 1: If the world is empty, then a second fact obtaining in it is that it is free of *Ks*. And the second fact is another falsemaker for *Ks exist*. But, plausible as this seems, the argument has a gap. That *e* is empty ensures there is a fact obtaining in it about the number of *Ks*, only if facts like that exist in the first place.

---

[1] Sider (2003).

Stephen Yablo, *What "X Does Not Exist" Says About We Who Do Exist* In: *The Language of Ontology*. Edited by: J. T. M. Miller, Oxford University Press (2021). © Oxford University Press. DOI: 10.1093/oso/9780192895332.003.0009

Sometimes a kind term is semantically defective in a way that prevents it from figuring in the specification of facts. *K* might be a nonsense or dummy predicate, for instance, like *whatsit*. *Whatsits exist* is false in *e*, not because *e* is free of whatsits, but because nothing exists in *e* whatsoever.

Objection 2: *Whatsits exist* contains a nonsense-word. Doesn't that make it unevaluable? The principle that nonsense-words absolutely prevent evaluation is hard to take seriously. It is often thought—see section 8.2—that *A&B* can be false wholly on account of whatever it is that makes *A* false. Whether *B* is false, whether it is even evaluable, is beside the point; *B* might as well be pure nonsense. *0=1 & BLAH* is false, even if *BLAH* lacks truth-value, because of facts about 0 and 1. *Whatsits exist* is admittedly not a conjunction. But it appears at least to be logically equivalent to a conjunction, viz. *Some things exist, and among the existing things are some whatsits*. Since the first conjunct here is false in *e*, the conjunction is false too. Assuming that logical equivalents agree in truth-value, *Whatsits exist* will have to be false in *e* as well.

8.2 Propositions

Discussions of nonexistence often proceed on the assumption that a sentence is evaluable only if it expresses a proposition. Here is Kripke on the apparent falsity of *Bandersnatches exist*:

> [A] certain sentence about bandersnatches seems to have a truth-value, but this does not mean that sentences containing "bandersnatch" express ordinary propositions. And this I regard as a very substantial problem.   (2011b, p. 65)

There is no such "ordinary proposition" as the proposition that bandersnatches exist, because the term *bandersnatch* lacks a referent. If the sentence strikes us as evaluable, that, Kripke proposes, is because we associate with it (by a kind of semantic courtesy) a higher-order proposition to the effect that there are no true propositions about bandersnatches to the effect that they exist. Similarly, *Holmes exists* is false only insofar as we associate with it the second-order proposition that there is a true proposition about Holmes to the effect that he exists.

You might wonder why, if the name's emptiness makes trouble for the alleged proposition that Holmes exists, it doesn't make trouble as well for the proposition that *There is a true proposition about Holmes to the effect that he exists*. Kripke points in reply to a difference in how the names are used. *Holmes* occurs in the first sentence in a regular old referential position. But not the second; the phrase 'about Holmes' has in the second sentence "a special sort of quasi-intensional use" (2013, p.156).

Before getting into the details of this special usage, it is puzzling why S should go unevaluable, in Kripke's view, when there is no such thing as the proposition that S. The observation above, that $0=1$ & B would normally be counted false just on the strength of its first conjunct, was made by Kripke himself in "Outline of a Theory of Truth." Given that initial conjunct, whether B is paradoxical, or non-sensical like *BLAH* or *Bandersnatches are frumious*, or fails for these or other reasons to express a proposition, doesn't save the conjunction from falsity.[2] $0=1$ & B looks like a counterexample, then, to the notion that S is evaluable only if "the proposition that S" exists, assuming at least that there can be no proposition that A&B unless there is a proposition that B.

A second, related, point is that it should be enough for S's falsity that it say *something* false—even something which, for whatever reason, cannot be regarded as *the* proposition that S.

A third point grows out of what Kripke calls "the risky nature of truth." Evaluability is too variable across worlds to be underwritten by an on-off property like proposition-expressingness. Just as "heterological" puts clear demands on "short" but not on itself, a sentence may put clear demands on some worlds while making no logical contact with others. $0=1$ & *BLAH* gets traction in every world. But suppose that $0=1$ is replaced with a contingent falsehood like *Dogs rule Mars*. *Dogs rule Mars* & *BLAH* gets traction in our world, but not in worlds where Mars is ruled by dogs. *Whatsits exist* gets traction only perhaps in the empty world.

If a sentence does not inherit its truth-value from the proposition it expresses—from what it overall says—then how *does* it get to be true (false)? This is a fair question, but not unanswerable; for while propositions in the what-is-said sense figure in one model of truth-value acquisition, other models have been suggested. One associates sentences with truthmakers and falsemakers, and links S's truth-aptitude in w to the issue of whether any -makers obtain there. This model appears indeed to lie behind the Strong Kleene valuation scheme alluded to above, on which $A \lor B$ is true when a disjunct is true, and A&B is false when a conjunct is false. These are the truth-tables you'd expect if

   i. truth (falsity) goes with possession of a truthmaker (falsemaker),
   ii. disjunctions inherit their truthmakers from their disjuncts, and
  iii. conjunctions inherit their falsemakers from their conjuncts.

Kripke's puzzle about the truth of nonexistence claims can be accused with some justice of overlooking Kripke's theory of truth. Sentences are true, on that theory, not because of what they say all in all, but because their truth is grounded *somehow or other* in the non-semantic facts. More generally S gets traction (is

[2] Kripke (1975).

evaluable) in w if it has a truthmaker or falsemaker there. The point is not just that other putative truth- or falsemakers need not obtain in w. They may not even "make sense" in w, as it makes no sense to speak of something being a bandersnatch in the empty world.[3]

8.3 Traction

The sentence *Bandersnatches exist* strikes us as false. How can it be false, Kripke wonders, when it fails to express a proposition? Of course, Kripke is talking about falsity in our world. But the question arises already for e, the empty world. How can *Bandersnatches exist* be false in e, when it fails to express a proposition?[4]

The view we've been toying with is that there is more than one possible reason why an existence-claim should be false. The specific reason, to do with Ks in particular, indeed fails for bandersnatches. But the general reason—that nothing exists—holds in e in full glory. And it is all one needs to falsify *Bandersnatches exist*. Once again, *Bandersnatches exist* does not need to express a proposition to be false.

This is all fine, you may say, but what we *really* want to know is, not how *Bandersnatches exist* can be false in the empty world, but how it can be false in a nonempty world like our own. Does the falsemaker idea extend to worlds that are populated?

Imagine a world v stipulated to contain only concrete, as opposed to abstract, objects. Why is it false in v that the Russell set ($\{x \mid x \notin x\}$) exists? Again, the result seems overdetermined: the sentence is false both for logical reasons—nothing *could* satisfy its existence-conditions—and metaphysical ones—sets are abstract and v contains only concreta.

Now let's consider instead the Russell *schmet*: the schmet of all x that do not belong to themselves. *Schmets* here are a made-up category, like *whatsits*, except that schmets are stipulated to be like sets abstract. Does the Russell schmet exist in v?

The set failed to exist because $\{x \mid Fx\}$, if it exists, contains all and only Fs, and this leads to contradiction if F expresses non-self-membership. But the schmets

---

[3] The point can be taken further. Although all truths have a truthmaker on the Strong Kleene version of Kripke's theory, they may not on other versions. $B \vee \neg B$ is true on the supervaluational scheme because its structure ensures that it is true on the (possibly false) hypothesis that B is evaluable. The most we can ask in such cases is an *account* of why S counts as true (false), for instance, that S is entailed by a truth P (entails a falsehood Q). This will not be much pursued in the present chapter. But we should keep an open mind about whether a theory of negative singular existentials must provide truthmakers for these statements, as opposed to reasons of another sort—*accounts* of why they are true. (See in this connection Baron-Schmitt forthcoming; Skiles 2015; and Muñoz 2019, 2020.)

[4] "It is not sufficient just to be able to say that it is false, [if there is to be a proposition] one has to be able to say under what circumstances it would have been true, if any" (Kripke 2011a, p. 68).

are subject to no such principle—not because they violate the principle, but because they are radically underdefined. Of the two reasons we gave for the Russell set not existing, then, the first does not apply. The Russell schmet does not fail for *logical* reasons to show up in v. That still leaves, however, the second, non-logical, reason, that the Russell schmet would be abstract, and v contains only concreta.[5]

But although this is progress, it does not help much with bandersnatches. Bandersnatches are supposed to be concrete, not abstract. And the actual world is more ontologically varied than v. But there is a deeper problem. Sets are not just *supposed* to be abstract, they on many views *have* to be abstract.[6] And it is not clear that bandersnatches *have* to be concrete.

8.4 Contingency

What is the necessity involved when one says that sets "have to" be abstract? The phrase could be taken metaphysically, to mean that sets are essentially, or by nature, abstract. It could be read semantically, to mean that sets are analytically abstract. Or it could be read epistemically, to mean that sets are abstract as an a priori matter. Any of these "have to"s could be used to argue that sets' abstractness prevents them from existing in v.

Now, bandersnatches are in some sense *supposed* to be concrete. Whether they *have* to be concrete, though, in any of the three ways just mentioned, is a further question. There are reasons to doubt their destiny is quite so inescapable as that of sets.[7]

Metaphysical: That things of kind K are necessarily concrete would ordinarily be sourced either in the generic essence of the kind, or the individual essences of its instances. But neither party exists in this case. Bandersnatches have no essence that needs respecting, since there aren't any around to set the standard. Here I am echoing Kripke on unicorns. Just as one can't say of a possible beast that to be a unicorn, it needs to be of the same kind as *these* unicorns, one can't demand of a candidate bandersnatch that it be of the same kind as these bandersnatches.[8]

Semantical: Bandersnatches are not analytically concrete either. They have often been regarded, by those who believe in them, as abstract, even the frumious ones portrayed as concrete in the poem. This is the view, for instance, of Nathan

---

[5] A third reason to count the sentence false will be brought in later. The Russell schmet exists only if something is a schmet; something is a schmet only if it satisfies the predicate $\hat{x}$ (x is a schmet); nothing does satisfy that predicate. See Stalnaker (1977).

[6] *Pace* Lewis on the empty set (Lewis 1986).

[7] Similar questions could in principle be raised about sets.   [8] Kripke (1980).

Salmon.[9] Salmon's theory of bandersnatches may be mistaken, but it is not *analytically* wrong.

Epistemic: Could it be *epistemically* necessary (a priori) that bandersnatches are concrete, or that Vulcan is closer to the Sun than Mercury? Kripke's notion of reference-fixing seems to provide a model here.

(1) Suppose the reference of *n* is fixed by *the F*.
(2) Then we know a priori that *n if it exists is an F (and nothing else is F)*.
(3) *n exists* thus a priori implies that *Something is F*.
(4) To learn *n doesn't exist* is to learn that some such implication is false.

But it is the rare name that has its reference fixed by a description in the strong sense here supposed.[10] This is why Kripke quickly moves on to his preferred model of initial baptism followed by chains of reference-preserving intentions.

Some have argued that the initial baptism has no chance of success unless a sortal comes in to disambiguate ostension, and that we know a priori that the sortal attaches if the referent exists. Kripke considers this in connection with referents that do exist and strongly rejects that they must turn out to be of the kind initially stipulated or supposed:

> Even if a sortal is used to disambiguate an ostensive reference, surely it need not be held a priori to be true of the object designated. Couldn't Dobbin turn out to belong to a species other than horses (though superficially he looked like a horse), Hesperus to be a planet rather than a star, or Lot's guests, even if he names them, to be angels rather than men?   (Kripke 1980, p. 116, n. 58)

If an existing animal like Dobbin could turn out not to be a horse, it is hard to see why other animals, thought to be nonexistent, could not surprise us both on the score of existence and biological type. Why should unicorns, if there are any, not turn out to be a previously unknown sort of horse? This is one of the likelier scenarios, surely, on which unicorns turn out to exist. But then it is not a priori that unicorns, if there are any, are non-horses.

That names do not tend to be *acquired* ostensively only strengthens the point. Suppose that someone has "picked up the name by a chain of communication leading back to an ostension." Why in that case would

---

[9] Salmon (1998).
[10] "I also think, contrary to most recent theorists, that the reference of names is rarely or almost never fixed by means of description. And by this I do not just mean what Searle says: 'It's not a single description, but rather a cluster, a family of properties that fixes the reference.' I mean that properties in this sense are not used at all" (Kripke 2011c, p. 21).

the sortal allegedly used in the ostension be, in any sense, part of the "sense" of the name for them?...An extreme case: A mathematician's wife overhears her husband muttering the name "Nancy." She wonders whether Nancy, the thing to which her husband referred, is a woman or a Lie group.   (Kripke 1980, loc. cit.)

To bring this closer to our present concerns, we should throw in as a third possibility that Nancy, despite figuring somehow in the husband's dream, does not in fact exist. Nancy might turn out to be (i) a living thing, or (ii) a group, or (iii) nothing at all. Suppose now that it's the third option that obtains: there is no such thing as Nancy. Although she turns out not to exist, she *might* have turned out, if existent, to be either a group or a living thing. She might even have turned out to be a group *played* in the dream by a human being–– the so-called Monster group played by a monstrous woman. Similarly bandersnatches might turn out, if they exist, to be mathematical objects played in the story by monstrous animals.[11]

Now we begin to see how a nonexistent item, presumed to be of one ontological category, could if existent have turned out to be another kind of thing entirely. The mathematician's wife might conjecture, based on particulars of the muttering, that Nancy, though presenting in the dream as a woman, is really the Monster group. This would be to conjecture, of an unreal concrete thing, that it was a real non-concrete thing. The wife is wrong, as we've told the story. But she could have been right. This gives us a model of how bandersnatches could have turned out to exist otherwise than as concreta (see also footnote 12).

8.5 Turning Out

The idea that unreal characters might have turned out to be real—might yet, not that this is expected, turn out to be real—runs deep in our understanding of existence-statements. Kripke says that "I of course acknowledge that it might turn out that there really are unicorns." How would this occur? Holmes was supposedly based on Joseph Bell, a "scientific surgeon" for whom Doyle had clerked at the Edinburgh Royal Infirmary. Holmes is *not* Bell, as matters stand; otherwise we should say Holmes exists, or existed. But one can imagine tweaking the scenario so as to make an identification plausible.

What sort of tweaks would be needed? When Kripke allows that there might turn out to be unicorns, or that it might *have* turned out there *were* unicorns, he is careful not to confuse that scenario with the one we imagine when considering

---

[11] If it seems strange that a group would be personified, consider this from Wikipedia: "The Monster group (also known as the Fischer-Griess Monster, or the Friendly Giant) is the largest sporadic simple group, having order [about] 8×10^{53}...The Monster group contains 20 other sporadic groups as subquotients. Robert Griess has called those 20 groups *the happy family*, and the remaining 6 exceptions *pariahs*."

what is true according to the unicorn myth. Whether unicorns are thus and so, according to the myth, is going to depend in considerable part on how the myth depicts them. But whether they will have turned out to exist, if it turns out that *P*, is somewhat independent of how they are traditionally depicted:

> one shouldn't regard this question [of their turning out to exist] as simply a question about whether there is an animal matching the description in the myth.
> (Kripke 2013, ch. 2)

In wondering whether unicorns turn out to exist, if *P*, we are guided more by the origins of the myth than its descriptive content. It is the same presumably with bandersnatches. Kripke imagines at one point that Carroll was writing about a genuine sort of animal, albeit perhaps misdescribed in the poem:

> I once read a hypothetical story about Lewis Carroll in which it turned out that that was the case. Contrary to what we thought, he was writing a straightforward report about bandersnatches. (Actually I didn't read a story; it was a comic strip.) At any rate this could turn out to have been the case. Suppose we had asked him and he said he was quite surprised that people thought he was talking about imaginary animals here; why, he himself used to be warned to avoid them when he walked through the park as a child, and that is what they were always called in his little region, though apparently the term has passed out of usage. So one could discover that, contrary to what we thought, bandersnatches are real.   (Kripke 2013, ch. 2)

To fill this out a bit, let us say that it was Tibetan mastiffs, a particularly scary sort of dog, that Carroll ran into in the park. They were called bandersnatches in his corner of Oxford, or maybe he believed this to be their name. Carroll meant on this hypothesis to be using the word literally in the poem, in reference to an actual class of animals. Perhaps he was writing a report about these animals; in that case the poem may describe them more or less accurately. More likely he was taking liberties with their properties so as to weave an appealing yarn. This is the case that primarily interests us. Bandersnatches exist in the taking-liberties scenario but are not quite as portrayed in the poem.[12]

Or consider the bedtime stories I myself used to tell about the family dog (Sparky). The stories made him out to be clever and brave, which was not strictly the case. Still the Sparky in my stories really existed. Kurt Vonnegut

---

[12] Our position where bandersnatches are concerned is not so different from the mathematician's wife's with respect to Nancy. Carroll was a mathematician after all; it seems not out of the question epistemically speaking that some group was endowed with animal-like properties in one of his dreams, a dream he later set to verse as "Jabberwocky." Bandersnatches would in that case have turned out to be mathematical objects.

Figure 8.1 A Tibetan mastiff. © iSTock/guojieyi

writes, helpfully enough, about a dog of the same name, where this time it is not so clear whether Sparky exists[13] How does the story go?

Vonnegut's narrator, call him Al, lived in Menlo Park, New Jersey, next door to Thomas Edison. Edison was working, Al tells us, on something called an "intelligence analyzer," a device to determine a test subject's level of braininess. Al makes a surprising suggestion: "Mr. Edison, sir, let's try it on the dog." I will let Vonnegut take it from here:

> Edison held him down while I touched the wires to his ears. And would you believe it, that needle sailed clear across the dial...
>
> And then is when Edison showed me what a great scientist he was. He was willing to face the truth, no matter how unpleasant it might be. "So!" said Edison to Sparky. "Man's best friend, huh? Dumb animal, huh?"
>
> That Sparky was a caution. He pretended not to hear. He scratched himself and bit fleas, anything to get out of looking Edison in the eye.
>
> "Look," said Sparky, "why not keep quiet about this? You forget all about it, destroy the intelligence analyzer, and I'll tell you what to use for a lamp filament." The last words Sparky ever spoke were, "Try a piece of carbonized cotton thread." Later, he was torn to bits by dogs that had gathered outside the door, listening.

---

[13] "Tom Edison's Shaggy Dog," by Kurt Vonnegut.

Now, perhaps Vonnegut wrote this story for his children about a dog known to all of them (along the lines of the stories told at 395 Washington Street, in 2006 or so, about the resident cockapoo); old Sparky then turns out to really exist. You can imagine, I am sure, an alternative hypothesis about the story's origins where our verdict is different.

This is the kind of decision-point we are confronting when we ask about the existence or not of a character encountered in fiction. Vonnegut's Sparky turns out to really exist in the scenario just described. But he could equally have turned out not to exist. Does the Sparky in "Tom Edison's Shaggy Dog" exist in fact? I don't know, and it doesn't matter.[14] The point for us is that a purported object may turn out either to exist or not to; the contrast is clear, if not what Descartes would call distinct. The question now is, how much of a grip does the turning-out contrast give us on the content of singular (non) existence claims?

8.6 To Exist Is to Be One of Us

Kripke asks at one point what it is that we are excluding, when we say that Holmes does not exist. One thing we are certainly excluding is that Holmes turns out to be "one of us" along the lines suggested. What are we *in*cluding? Kripke ventures the guess that we use *Holmes doesn't exist* (*Bandersnatches don't exist*, etc.) to "express the fact that such a discovery hasn't occurred" (Kripke 2013, ch. 2).

Can that be right? It does of course *follow* from Holmes, or bandersnatches, not existing that such a discovery has not occurred. The reverse implication fails, though, for it might occur tomorrow. The discovery might *never* be made; the world goes up in smoke before we stumble on Carroll's notes about encountering bandersnatches in the park. Only a verificationist could think that their existence never being established means that bandersnatches never existed.

Now, if we could discover that bandersnatches are real, we could also discover (and presumably *have* discovered) that bandersnatches are not real. We could learn, for instance, that Carroll told his friends that he made the idea up out of whole cloth, that he was not lying or misremembering, and so on.

But if bandersnatches' nonexistence does perhaps follow from discoveries of these sorts, the reverse implication is now in trouble, for the same old verificationist reasons. Bandersnatches might fail to exist, though this is never established. *Bandersnatches don't exist* does not express either that a certain positive

---

[14] For those who want to dig deeper, Vonnegut's own dog was named Pumpkin. There is a Sparky too in *Breakfast of Champions,* modelled on a dog of his brother's.

discovery has not occurred (that's too weak), or that the corresponding negative discovery has occurred or will do (that's too strong). Our topic in the ontology room is not our discoveries, but what was there to be discovered.

How do we move the spotlight away from the first issue—actual existential discoveries—and towards the second—the facts up for discovery?

Suppose that x_1, x_2, x_3, ... are all the things that exist. Then for Holmes to exist is for Holmes to be one of x_1, x_2, x_3, ...; and for Holmes not to exist is for Holmes to be none of x_1, x_2, x_3, ... Whether Holmes is x_2, or x_{99}, seem in principle like factual questions open to empirical investigation. These questions could in principle give us a handle on the content of *Holmes exists*. But only if it is possible to ask (and answer) them without prejudging the issue of whether he exists or not.

How would this work exactly? There might be Holmes-free properties Q such that if a thing is in actual fact Q, then it is Holmes. Q would involve, I guess, being thus and so connected to Doyle, and his use of *Holmes*, when he was conceiving and writing the stories. To discover that x_{99} is Q would be a way of discovering that x_{99} = Holmes, and hence (since the x_is are the existing things) that Holmes exists.

Then too, there might be properties R such that if a thing is R, it is not Holmes. To discover that each x_i has some such property (different presumably in each case) would be a way of discovering that each $x_i \neq$ Holmes, and hence, given that the x_is are the existing things, that Holmes does not exist.

Note that the question of whether any x_i has a Q-type property (a "qualifying" property) makes sense independently of any investigations we might undertake, nor does it prejudge the results of such investigations. We don't have to know beforehand that Holmes exists to discover that x_i is Q, and thereby come to know of his existence. The question of whether each x_i has an R-type property (a "disqualifying" property) also makes sense independently of whether Holmes exists. We can well imagine that even granting Holmes's existence, still, x_i isn't Holmes if it is R. That x_i is R shows that *it*, at any rate, can't be Holmes, never mind Holmes's actual ontological status.

A tempting first hypothesis about the cognitive cash value of *Holmes does not exist* is the following: every x has properties R_x such that if a thing has those properties, it is not Holmes (even if Holmes exists). On second thought, though, the properties seem out of place. x's properties certainly have a role to play in why we *think* it is not Holmes, even if Holmes exists. But reasons for believing a thing do not figure (normally) in the thing believed. This suggests a different and cleaner version: *n does not exist* says of every x that *n* is not x even if *n* exists. The cognitive difference between *Holmes does not exist* and *Vulcan does not exist* is akin to that between *No x is such that: x = Holmes if Holmes exists* and *No x is such that: x = Vulcan if Vulcan exists.* How exactly we are to understand the embedded conditionals (with their empty names) is considered next.

8.7 Quasi-Intensionality (1)

Kripke starts from the fact that there is no such "ordinary proposition" as the proposition that Holmes exists, because the term *Holmes* lacks a referent. We proposed in section 8.2 that there does not need to be a proposition for the sentence to be evaluable. *S* can have a falsemaker in *w* even if there is no such thing as what it overall says. (Or it can be groundlessly false—false without benefit of falsemaker—provided an account is available of why the truth-value it groundlessly possesses is FALSE rather than TRUE.) The proposal in section 8.6 was that this falsemaker, or account, could take the form: every *x* is distinct from Holmes.

You might wonder whether any real progress has been made. What does it mean for *x* to be distinct from Holmes, when there is no such person? This seems hardly clearer than the meaning of *Holmes does not exist*, when there is no such person. Kripke considers an analog of this problem for his own account, and suggests a response we can build on. *Holmes exists* counts as false, Kripke says, because we associate with it a higher-order proposition to the effect that there are no true propositions about Holmes to the effect that he exists. If one asks why the name's emptiness does not deprive *There are true propositions about Holmes* of meaning, the way it did *Holmes exists*, Kripke replies that *Holmes* is used referentially in *Holmes exists*, while it has in *propositions about Holmes* "a special sort of quasi-intensional use." The time has come to look at this special use, for the light it may shed on our own use of *Holmes* in *x is not Holmes even if Holmes exists*.

Quasi-intensionality comes up first for Kripke in connection with "reportorial" claims like *Holmes is a great detective, according to the story*. The question as ever is, how can this be true, in the absence of a proposition about Holmes for the story to endorse?

> "The story has it that Sherlock Holmes is a great detective." What is it that the story has it that? There is supposed to be no such proposition as that Sherlock Holmes is a great detective which the story has it that. I said of this,...that one should speak of a kind of proposition which is being asserted to exist and to be true. The story has it that there is a true proposition about Sherlock Holmes, namely that he is a great detective.   (Kripke 2013, Lecture 6)

A proposition's nonexistence doesn't prevent the story from endorsing "it," if it exists according to the story. Nor do empty names in *S* make *According to the story, S* unevaluable, Kripke thinks, if the story assigns them referents. This is because of something called the *Pretense Principle*:

> Isn't it a problem for Mill's theory, where there cannot be names with no referent, as appears to be the case in fiction? Well, no,..., because when one writes a

work of fiction, it is part of the pretense of that fiction that the criteria for naming, whatever they are, are satisfied. I use the name "Harry" in a work of fiction;
I generally presuppose as part of that work of fiction, just as I am pretending
various other things, that the criteria of naming, whatever they are…are satisfied. That is part of the pretense of this work of fiction. Far from it being the case
that a theory of the reference of names ought to make special provision for the
possibility of such works of fiction, it can forget about this case, and then simply
remark that, in a work of fiction, it is part of the pretense of that work of fiction
that these criteria are satisfied. Perhaps what makes it a work of fiction is that
these criteria are not in fact satisfied (and usually other things in the story), but
the pretense is just that: a pretense.   (Kripke 2013, Lecture 1, 23–24)

Kripke never doubts for a moment our ability to *pretend* or *imagine* that Holmes
exists. We do it every time we read the story; we treat the sentences as true and continue along the imaginative path they lay down. For Holmes to be a great detective
according to the story amounts to this: those on the right imaginative path will suppose, *of a person they are already imagining to exist*, that he is a great detective.
Holmes is used quasi-intensionally when it serves to mark out an imaginative path—
the one we are meant to be travelling when considering whether Holmes is thus and
so, with a view to evaluating *He is thus and so, according to the story*.

8.8 Quasi-Intensionality (2)

So much for the work an empty name *n* does in conveying the content of a fiction.
Kripke now moves on to *n*'s role in the phrase *proposition about n* that is supposed to explicate *n does not exist*. *Holmes does not exist* says or conveys that there
are no true "propositions about Holmes" (*Holmes* is used quasi-intensionally in
this phrase) to the effect that he does exist. Quasi-intensional uses are imaginative
path markers, we decided. All that remains is to specify the sort of imaginative path we are meant to be traveling, when we ask if there are true propositions
"about Holmes" to the effect that he exists.

Kripke never quite tells us, and it is hard to see how the thing could work
even in principle. A pretense within which propositions can be assessed for
Holmes-aboutness would seem to be a pretense within which Holmes exists!
But, if we are pretending that he exists, then we are very much *not* pretending that
there are no truths attributing existence to Holmes. This is where Kripke's account
runs into trouble. He needs us on the one hand to pretend that Holmes is somehow
"present," to give sense to the notion of Holmes-aboutness. But he expects us at the
same time to judge, within the pretense, that there are no true existence-propositions
about Holmes. Why would there be no true existence-propositions about him, if
Holmes within the pretense exists?

Existential pretenders are left by Kripke in a tight corner. The judgments they are called on to make—the ones that confer truth outside the pretense on *Holmes does not exist*—cannot be to the effect that Holmes fails to exist, or that truths attributing existence to him fail to exist. They need to be judgments taking Holmes's existence for granted, as the intra-pretense judgment that Holmes is a great detective takes his existence for granted.[15] The challenge is to find Holmes-assuming statements *S* whose acceptance within the pretense affords a way of rejecting Holmes's existence outside it. *Holmes does not exist* cannot play this role, for reasons just discussed. What can?

The beginnings of an answer were given in section 8.6. To judge within the scope of a Holmes-assuming pretense that he is at any rate not you, or me (and here we run through every last existing thing...through all of *us*), is a way of judging outside the pretense that the world contains no such individual as Holmes. *Holmes is in my back pocket* is as good as false if my pocket is empty, because he is not, given its emptiness, in my pocket even if he exists. But then *Holmes is one of us* is as good as false too, because none of us is Holmes even if he exists.

8.9 Finding the Path

Holmes is used quasi-intensionally when it serves to indicate a suppositional or imaginative path. The path it indicates in *According to the stories, Holmes did so and so* is the one marked out by...—and here we point to some texts in which *Holmes* occurs; we are to pretend, more or less, that the texts constitute true reports of interesting events. I said that it was obscure, at least to me, what path Kripke wants the name to put us on, when the question is whether Holmes exists.

The difficulty was partly met by replacing Kripke's candidate for the pretend-hypothesis to be pretend-accepted (*No true propositions attributing existence to Holmes exist*) with a different hypothesis compatible with Holmes's existence—*Holmes is not one of us*, where *we* are the things that exist, as opposed to the things that exist if Holmes does. But this substitution does not tell us *how* to judge externally that Holmes does not exist while supposing internally that he does. Against the background of what pretense, exactly, are we to assess whether Holmes is one of us?

Kripke is very clear that we are not supposed to pretend in line with the stories, as we do when evaluating *Holmes noticed a curious fact about the dog in the night, according to "Silver Blaze."* For one thing, we mostly do not exist in the stories, making us unavailable for pretend comparison with Holmes. The real problem,

---

[15] The pretenses at work in the two cases are otherwise quite different.

though, is that those of us who do exist in them—Prince Albert, say—may not be credited with the properties that in fact distinguish them from Holmes. Holmes might even have been *identified* with Prince Albert, in some strangely neglected passage. If so then Holmes *is*, in the relevant pretense, one of us, since Prince Albert really existed. But that hardly means that Holmes is in truth one of us; Holmes = Prince Albert only fictionally.

The alternative to imagining in line with the stories is to imagine simply that Holmes exists, scholarly opinion to the contrary; or to imagine learning that scholars had reversed themselves on the matter. Traveling this alternative path, will we imagine that the stories give a true account of him? Surely not. Doyle will have mucked about with his properties if Holmes exists, as Carroll mucked about with the properties of Tibetan mastiffs in *Jabberwocky* (if that is what bandersnatches are) and Alice Liddell's properties in *Through the Looking Glass* (if that is who Alice is).

The best approach for metasemantic purposes is to imagine that a trusted informant has said: *Holmes exists*. This has the advantage of locating us (qua imaginers) in the kind of referential tradition that gains one access to a proposition attributing existence to Holmes. The analogy with Kripke on reportorial claims should be clear. Just as the nonexistence of a proposition attributing great-detective-hood to Holmes does not prevent readers from endorsing "it," provided it exists according to the story, the nonexistence of a proposition expressed by *Holmes exists* does not prevent would-be recipients of *Holmes exists* in testimony from endorsing "that proposition," if it exists on the imaginative path they are then traveling.

8.10 If-Prefixes and Story-Prefixes

Story-prefixes are not the same as if-prefixes (antecedents), but the two have much in common. *S, according to fiction F* has often been explained as a conditional—along the lines of *If F is the case, then so is S*, or *If F were told as known truth, then S would be the case*.[16] Going from right to left, we're encouraged by Ramsey and others to process a conditional by pretending that we have been informed of the antecedent and assessing the consequent from that put-on perspective:

> If two people are arguing "If *p*, then *q*?" and are both in doubt as to *p*, they are adding *p* hypothetically to their stock of knowledge and arguing on that basis about *q*.[17]

---

[16] Lewis (1978).
[17] Ramsey, "General Propositions and Causality," in Ramsey and Mellor (1990).

The disputants in Quine's version of this idea "feign belief in the antecedent and see how convincing [they] then find the consequent" (Quine 1960, p. 222). Given that we can sensibly ask, under the scope of a fictional pretense that assigns *Holmes* a referent, whether Holmes is a great detective, we should also be able to ask, under the scope of a factual supposition that assigns *Holmes* a referent, whether Holmes is identical to x.[18]

That supposition will have two parts: first, that Holmes exists, and second, that x has thus and such properties S_x, qualifying or disqualifying as the case may be. To decide whether x is identical to (distinct from) Holmes, if Holmes exists and x is S_x, we imagine ourselves (i) acquiring both pieces of information, and (ii) asking, under the scope of that imagining, whether x is (is not) identical to Holmes. Kripke seems to be engaged in some such exercise in passages like the following:

> Without being sure of whether Sherlock Holmes was a person,...we can say "none of the people in this room is Sherlock Holmes, for all are born too late, and so on"; or "whatever bandersnatches may be, certainly there are none in Dubuque." (Kripke 2011b, pp. 71–72)

None of us in the room can be Holmes, even if he exists, for we all have properties (being born too late, e.g.), such that if a thing is *R*, it is not Sherlock Holmes. I would add only that this applies not merely to the individuals in this room, but to every existing thing whatsoever. Every x that there is has properties R_x given which it fails to be Holmes, even if Holmes exists; or, simpler still, not a single one of us is, even if Holmes exists, identical to Holmes.

8.11 Content or Truthmaker?

Earlier we put $\forall x$ (*x ≠ Holmes, even if Holmes exists*)—$\forall x$ (*Eh → x ≠ h*)—forward as a candidate for the role of *Holmes does not exist*'s cognitive content.

But, $\forall x$ (*Eh → x ≠ h*) has *Eh* (*Holmes exists*) in it. Pending an account of *its* cognitive content, we seem not much further ahead. Also, the idea of *If Holmes DOES exist* figuring in a statement of the content of *Holmes does NOT exist* sounds improbable. Do we really need to condition on an entity's existence to form the thought that there is no such entity? If we do not find ourselves assuming, provisionally, that Holmes exists, in judging that he does not exist, then the content of *Holmes does not exist* doesn't perhaps condition on such an assumption either.

Maybe we got it wrong, then, when we suggested that $\forall x$ (*En → x ≠ n*)—ANI for short—gave the cognitive cash value of *n does not exist*. This does not

---

[18] This kind of question brings us as close as we dare approach to the "sense" of *Holmes*. (Cf. Hartry Field's suggestion in Field (1977) that conditional probability may be all we need, or can hope for, in a theory of sense.)

necessarily make *ANI* irrelevant to what *n does not exist* says. For another line of attack on what *S* says is via the kind of fact that makes *S* true, or false (as we saw in section 8.2). What about recasting *ANI* (or the fact it expresses) as *n does not exist*'s truthmaker? The chapter could then end as follows: Just as *Holmes does not exist* is true in the empty world *e*, because there is nothing *there* for Holmes to be, it is true in our world @ because there is nothing *here* for Holmes to be. @ is not devoid of things altogether, but it is devoid of things that stand a chance of being Holmes.

Shall we say that *n does not exist* owes its truth to the fact that *ANI*—the fact that $\forall x \, (En \rightarrow x \neq n)$? This is what I am ultimately going to suggest. A couple of worries might be raised, however, about the *ANI*-fact's ability to play this role.

One concerns subject matter. *ANI* looks to be about everything whatsoever. Does *Holmes does not exist* owe its truth to a fact of such scope and generality? Granted that Alpha Centauri and Mike Pence are not Holmes (even if he exists), these facts do not seem to play much of a role in *Holmes does not exist* having *TRUE* as its truth-value. Further along the same lines, *ANI* expresses different facts, one might think, in worlds with differing populations. But then *Holmes does not exist* will have to be true for distinct reasons in our world @, and a world just like it except for an extra electron millions of light years away. Are we to suppose that *Holmes does not exist* changes why it is true whenever a new electron pops into being? These are good questions, but I want to put them aside in this chapter, both because they're too broad—one could raise them equally about the standard equation of *The Eiffel Tower exists* with $\exists x \, x = the \, Eiffel \, Tower$—and because we arguably *are* talking in the ontology room about everything whatsoever.[19]

A more serious obstacle to treating "the fact that *ANI*" as a truthmaker for *Holmes does not exist* is that *ANI* has an indicative conditional in it. Indicative conditionals are widely suspected of not stating facts in the first place.[20] The only facts in the neighborhood are "subjective" facts of the wrong sort to serve as -makers. *Holmes exists* does not owe its falsity to anyone's personal credences; it is false for objective reasons that are the same for each of us.[21]

8.12 Unconditional Truthmakers

Are there ways of getting the arrow out? A point of clarification before exploring this. The question of why *Holmes does not exist* is true can be taken in two ways.

---

[19] At least in a weak, de dicto, sense of "about everything."

[20] Some give them acceptability conditions, equal to the probability of the consequent conditional on the antecedent, rather than truth-conditions (Adams 1975, Lewis 1976, Skyrms 1994, Bennett 2003, Yalcin 2011).

[21] The subject-matter worry emphasizes variation across worlds, the objectivity worry variation across thinkers.

Table 8.1 Negation

NOT-A is	if A is
FALSE	*TRUE*
TRUE	*FALSE*
TRUE	*NEITHER*

One might be seeking an explanation in semantic terms of how given its compositional structure the sentence comes out true. Or one might be looking for an explanation of what *makes* the sentence true.

Take these in order. *Holmes does not exist* will certainly be true if we take the *not* to express strong negation, the connective taking truths to falsehoods and untruths (falsehoods and gaps) to truths:[22]

Holmes does NOT exist is true on this account provided that *Holmes exists* fails to be true. The name's emptiness, rather than preventing this outcome, ensures it, insofar as it prevents *Holmes exists* from being true or false. Whether a truth-maker is needed for NOT-A when A lacks truth-value is a good question. But the maneuver does not in any case get us quite what we wanted. Our feeling intuitively about *Holmes does not exist* is that its truth reflects, not that *Holmes exists* is unevaluable, but that it is false. If we can find a compositional structure for *Holmes exists* on which it comes out false, strong negation will not be needed.

The simplest way to arrange for the falsity of *Holmes exists* (Eh) is to let *all* atomic sentences with empty names be false, as is done in negative free logic.[23] But this rests too much on linguistic contingencies. What if we'd had, instead of a predicate E for existence, a predicate A for absence (nonexistence)? Ah comes out in that case just as false as Eh did, which seems like the wrong result. Stalnaker develops a more nuanced approach in "Complex Predicates."[24]

Start with the fact that Rab is read in some contexts—those where a is "topical"—as predicating $[\hat{x} : Rxb]$ of a, while in others it predicates $[\hat{y} : Ray]$ of b. *Descartes was born in France* predicates born-in-France of Descartes if we are talking about Descartes, birthplace-of-Descartes of France if we are talking about France. A subject-predicate sentence Fa generally predicates $[\hat{x} : Fx]$ of a, but it may occasionally predicate $[\hat{X} : Xa]$ to something in the neighborhood of F.

How does it go with existence claims? They seem at first to be about their grammatical subjects. It turns out, though, that n is by the usual tests *not* topical in *n exists*. One test calls on us to identify the implied question, the one that *Pence exists*, say, would normally be taken to address. Most people judge it sounds strange as a reply to "What is Pence like?", more so anyway than if the question

[22] As observed by Salmon and others (Salmon 1998).
[23] See the Stanford Encyclopedia of Philosophy entry on free logic.
[24] Stalnaker (1977).

Table 8.2 Predication

$[\hat{z}: Fz]$ is	if Fz is
TRUE of o	*TRUE* of o
FALSE of o	*FALSE* of o
FALSE of o	*NEITHER* of o

was "What is there?".[25] Plausibly, then, the name figures in the description that is being offered of something other than Pence: the existing things overall.[26] Can we find among them anything of which $[\hat{z}: z=p]$ is true? To say that Pence exists is to answer that we can; there really is such a thing. A plausible analysis of *Pence exists* thus puts *Pence* into the predicate: $\exists x\, [\hat{z}: z=p](x)$.

Incorporating n into the predicate has semantic consequences too, as Strawson observed in various places. When is $[\hat{z}: Fz]$ true (false) of an object o? The standard line is that $[\hat{z}: Fz]$ is true of o if Fz is true of o, and false of o if Fz fails to be true of o, either by being false of it or neither true nor false (See Table 8.2).

Writing h for *Holmes*, that the name is empty means that $z=h$ is neither true nor false of any o.[27] But then $[\hat{z}: z=h]$ is false of every o, making $\exists x\, [\hat{z}: z=h](x)$ false simpliciter.[28] That completes our "explanation in semantic terms of how, given its compositional structure, *Holmes exists* comes out false."

But our main goal in this chapter is a specification of what *makes* the sentence false. The semantic explanation *seems* to put one on our doorstep. For in addition to the sentence $\exists x\, [\hat{z}: z=h](x)$, we have the fact that $\forall x\, \neg[\hat{z}: z=h](x)$. It ensures the falsity of *Holmes exists*, when the latter is analyzed as $\exists x[\hat{z}: z=h](x)$. It appears to explain the sentence's falsity as well. Maybe, then, the fact that nothing is Holmes-identical can serve as *Holmes exists*' falsemaker.

8.13 Discerning Truthmakers

If it was so easy to find a fact making *Holmes exists* false, why not mention this earlier? The falsity of *n exists* could have been blamed right from the start on the fact that

$$(ANI^*)\, \forall x \neg \big[\hat{z}: z=n\big](x).$$

---

[25] Especially on a "mention some" reading of that second question. See Atlas (1988).

[26] Compare *The king of France is bald*, uttered in response to *Tell me about the bald people*. Kripke discusses related cases in Kripke et al. (1973).

[27] Contra negative free logic.

[28] This for Strawson is why *A bald person is the King of France* sounds falser than *The King of France is bald*.

The fact, or quasi-fact, that

$$(ANI)\forall x (En \rightarrow x = n)$$

would not have come into the picture at all. Something should be said about why we didn't take this quicker route, especially when ANI^*, being $\rightarrow$-free, does not run into the objectivity worries raised above for ANI. Here is why we should be reluctant to make this move. There is a danger, if we drop ANI for ANI^*, of all (false) singular existence claims winding up false for the same reason. One and the same nonexistence fact will underwrite the falsity of *Holmes exists*, *Vulcan exists*, and so on down the line. This is hard to take seriously. Singular existentials have, we think, *discerning* falsemakers—"one per nonexistent object," so to speak. They *need* to have discerning falsemakers, if the difference in content between *Holmes exists* and *Vulcan exists* is to be accounted for (as suggested in section 8.2) in terms of their verifiers and falsifiers.

Holmes exists is false, to go by ANI^*, because every object o is $\neg[\hat{z}: z=h]$, while *Vulcan exists* is false because every o is $\neg[\hat{z}: z=v]$. Of course, $\neg[\hat{z}: z=h]$ is a different (complex) *predicate* from $\neg[\hat{z}: z=v]$. But do they apply for different reasons? This will be so only if the predicates differ in semantic value—not to be fancy about it, in the property they express. But any difference on that score will have to derive from a semantic difference between the empty names involved. And the names are semantically indiscernible on present (Millian) assumptions. Thus both predicates express the same uninstantiated property, what we may as well call the null property. *Holmes exists* and *Vulcan exists* are both false (to go by ANI^*) because nothing has the null property. True, $[\hat{z}: z=h]$ expresses the null property because one name is empty, while $[\hat{z}: z=v]$ expresses it because another is empty. But we are interested not in why the semantics spits out a certain truth-value (the names are admittedly relevant to that), but the worldly basis for that truth-value.

Again, one would like to think that *Holmes exists* and *Vulcan exists* express different hypotheses, failing for different reasons. There ought to be a separate hypothesis of this sort for, forgive the expression, each and every nonexistent object. But then a whole lot of discerning falsemakers will be needed. If we cannot get them from ANI^*, we are driven back to ANI, the offending conditional notwithstanding.

A possible upside should be noted concerning the truth-conditional contribution of empty names. Those who agree with Kripke that a name's truth-conditional contribution is in *most* contexts exhausted by its referent, or lack of one, sometimes make an exception for epistemic contexts. Certainly, Kripke wanted to leave this door open:[29]

---

[29] Crucially, this need involve no departure from Millianism. For instance, some contexts are "Abelardian": the name bears on the proper interpretation of the predicate (Noonan 1991). In Quine's Giorgione example (*Giorgione was so-called because of his size*), the name employed sets the value of

The entire apparatus elaborated in *Naming and Necessity* of the distinction between epistemic and metaphysical necessity, and of giving a meaning and fixing a reference, was meant to show, among other things, that a Millian substitutivity doctrine for modal contexts can be maintained even if such a doctrine for epistemic contexts is rejected. *Naming and Necessity* never asserted a substitutivity principle for epistemic contexts.   (Kripke 2011a, p. 158)

Whatever one thinks about epistemic contexts generally, the case for nonsubstitutivity in →-contexts is overwhelming, given Ramseyan orthodoxy about how in practice we make our minds up about indicative conditionals.[30] One doesn't need a semantics for $P \to Q$ to know that any plausible truth-rule will have to respect the deliverances of the Ramsey Test. Adding *Holmes is F* hypothetically to one's stock of knowledge and arguing on that basis about Q is a different exercise from adding *Venus is F* hypothetically to one's stock of knowledge and arguing on that basis about Q. Nonsubstitutivity follows since empty names are referentially equivalent.

What does the Ramsey Test tell us about the conditions expressed by (i) $Eh \to x \neq h$ and (ii) $Ev \to x \neq v$? It tells us that (i) holds of an object if, when we imagine ourselves hearing *Holmes exists* from a reliable informant, our (updated) information tells us that the object is not Holmes. (ii) holds of an object if, when we imagine hearing *Vulcan exists* from that informant, our (updated) information leads us to judge that the object is not Vulcan. The conditions are distinct (and potentially not even coextensive) if we go into one state of mind when imagining we've been told that Holmes after all exists, another when imagining we've been told that Vulcan after all exists.

No one can deny that we as a psychological matter are disposed to update one way on receiving *Holmes exists* as testimony, another on receiving *Vulcan exists*. No one can deny either that the features of o that decide for us (post-update) whether o is distinct from Holmes—say, o's relations to Doyle—are different from the ones that guide us in deciding whether o is distinct from Vulcan—say, o's relations to Le Verrier and to Mercury. But then, unless the Ramsey Test is totally off the mark, conditions (i) and (ii) ask different things of would-be satisfiers.

---

the explicit indexical in *so-called* (Quine 1956, Forbes 1997). Alternatively, the name may tweak the value of some unarticulated truth-relevant parameter, such as a parameter for counterpart relations, "normal ideas," cognitive roles, questions under discussion, or what have you. See Hintikka 1962, 1970, 1996, Lewis 1971, Kaplan 1979, Stalnaker 1986, Crimmins 1989, Zimmermann 1993, Moltmann 1997, and Forbes 2000. (Quantified epistemic logic has a lot to offer in this connection too. Relevant recent work includes Aloni et al. 2001, Holliday and Perry 2014, Yalcin 2015, Ninan 2018, Moss 2018, and Aloni 2018.)

[30] That names don't behave in standard Kripkean ways in "suppose" and "would have turned out" conditionals is a familiar point (Stalnaker 1978, Yablo 2002). For non-referential contributions specifically in indicative conditionals, see Weatherson (2001) and Santorio (2012).

This helps with the cognitive significance issue as well. Suppose that I, while continuing to think that (ii) is always satisfied, develop doubts about (i). Then I may begin to wonder about *Holmes does not exist*, while my confidence in *Vulcan does not exist* is unshaken. Imagine that Doyle's deathbed confession is discovered. He expresses regret at the factual inaccuracy of what he said about Holmes's place of work; it was really the University of Edinburgh.[31] Such a discovery might well weaken our resistance to identifying Holmes with Joseph Bell, for whom Doyle had clerked at the Edinburgh Infirmary.[32] Neither finding, however, is likely to change our minds about Vulcan's relations to a certain intra-Mercurial o observed (it is said) by Lescarbault in 1859.[33]

8.14 Objectivity

What about the worry that indicative conditionals are not objective enough? The truth is that some strike us as more objective than others, depending, perhaps, on how rationally obligatory the conditional credences $c(Q|P)$ are that fix the probability of $P \rightarrow Q$, or the availability of a factual R that "makes the difference" between P and Q (in the sense that R is what Q adds to P).[34] We have a problem if, but only if, nonexistence claims are fully objective. Should they vary in objectivity too, and the connection with indicative if/then helps us make sense of this, then we may be dealing here with a feature rather than a bug.

Phlogiston is the paradigm in philosophical discussions of something that turned out not to exist. Flammable objects do not contain a substance that gets released, or consumed, when they burn. Lavoisier is often credited with this discovery; he showed that objects *gain* weight when burned rather than losing it. He introduced the term *oxygen* for the stuff, whatever it is, whose incorporation into burning objects explains the increase in weight.

Strangely, the discovery of oxygen is also often credited to Joseph Priestley—a lifelong friend of phlogiston and opponent of Lavoisier's approach. How could a phlogiston fan like Priestley have discovered the thing that cut phlogiston out of the action? The answer is that oxygen did not in his view cut phlogiston out of the action. Oxygen for Priestley was "dephlogisticated air" rather than a substance in its own right. Of course, oxygen is not, as we see things today, a dearth or absence of phlogiston; there is no such thing as phlogiston to be

---

[31] Or that psychiatric reports are found detailing Doyle's bizarre insistence that he was a novelist rather than a crime reporter.

[32] See https://lithub.com/how-sherlock-holmes-got-his-name for more on Bell and on the origins of the fictional name. "He settled upon Holmes as his detective's surname, likely because of his and his family's fondness for the writings of Oliver Wendell Holmes." The American Holmes visited London in 1886, a year before *A Study in Scarlet*, the first Holmes novel, appeared.

[33] Le Verrier for one was convinced.   [34] Yablo (2016).

present or absent. But what about a reverse-Priestley position on which phlogiston is nothing but the absence of oxygen, or (another term I have seen) "negative oxygen"? Ridiculous as this sounds, a view somewhat like it prevailed in a neighboring field.

Benjamin Franklin introduced electric current on the model of air and water current. Like them, it flows, he assumed, from positive ("high-pressure," "high-altitude") zones to negative ("low-pressure," "low-lying") zones. He believed too that electric current's physical carrier was a charged particle—positively charged, presumably, since there are more of them at the place where current originates. You may know what happened next:

> An assumption was made that a current was positive charges moving from positive to negative....However, it was later discovered that in the most common cases, currents in metal wires, it was in fact electrons (negatively charged) flowing in the opposite direction. The convention was in place to give the direction of a current...as if it were positive charges on the move. There was no real need to change the convention, other than to help school children learning about electrical effects.   (https://www.quora.com/What-is-conventional-current-1)

Thus did southbound current turn out to consist in the movement of north-going particles. That nothing else, and certainly nothing particulate, travels in the current's supposed direction was not taken to show that current did not exist. Instead it was identified (in the case of current running through wires) with negatively charged particles moving in the opposite direction.

Suppose for argument's sake that all this occurred via standard-issue Bayesian update dictated by prior conditional credences. Those prior credences directed us to retain (positive) current in the absence of anything moving in the right direction, but not to retain phlogiston-discharge in the absence of anything moving in the right direction. It seems likely that inferential dispositions (conditional credences, →-statements accepted) varied somewhat among the experts, with the preservative dispositions winning out in the case of electric current, and the eliminative winning out in the case of phlogiston. This is in each case the proper outcome, let's assume. Positive current really does exist, and phlogiston-release does not.

Now imagine an intermediate case. The experts are evenly divided between those with preservative dispositions (credences, →-beliefs), where a certain putative substance or entity θ is concerned, and those with eliminative dispositions. This with all the details filled in looks like a case where there is no fact of the matter either way about whether θ survives the relevant discoveries. The theory that θ *does not exist* depends for its truth on facts or quasi-facts of the form θ *exists* $\rightarrow Q$ explains this nicely. Reasonable people may disagree on which conditionals of this form are correct.

8.15 Uniformity

Nonexistence claims should "say the same," whether true or false. One of Kripke's main complaints about his own account, which has *Holmes does not exist* saying that there are no true propositions about Holmes attributing existence to him, is that it fails this test:

> in some sense the analysis of a singular existence statement will depend on whether that statement is true. And this, of course, seems in and of itself to be absolutely intolerable: the analysis of a statement should not depend on its truth-value.   (Kripke 2013, ch. 6)

The content of *Holmes does not exist* for us is given by truth- and falsemakers, expressed with conditionals like *Holmes is not Mike Pence, even if Holmes exists*. We should ask whether this conditional is true for the same reason whether or not Holmes exists. It may seem that the reasons change. If Holmes exists, it holds because two existing things (Holmes and Pence) are distinct. Whereas if Holmes does not exist, it holds (loosely speaking) because Pence is a poor candidate for the Holmes role, whether or not the role is occupied.

Does this mean that the conditional holds for distinct reasons in the two cases? Yes and no. A sentence's truth may be overdetermined, we observed at the outset. The truth of *Holmes is not Mike Pence, even if Holmes exists* is overdetermined, it seems to me, should Holmes to our surprise exist. One reason *Holmes is not Pence, if Holmes exists* is true (assuming he does) is that its antecedent and consequent are both true; Holmes does exist and he and Pence are just two different items.[35]

But the truth of *Holmes is not Pence, if Holmes exists* has a second basis as well. The second basis is that Pence is, quite regardless of whether Holmes exists, distinct-from-him-should-he-exist. We may grant that *Holmes is not Pence, even if Holmes exists* does not hold for *exactly* the same reasons in either case—the overdetermination point—while still insisting that it is true in both cases for *a* shared reason, namely that Pence ≠ Holmes if Holmes exists. This in turn holds because Pence has properties (e.g. that Doyle never wrote about Pence) that unsuit him for the role.

8.16 Conclusion and Issues Outstanding

Singular nonexistence claims are true, when they are, because of facts like this: $\forall x$ (*x is not Holmes, even if Holmes exists*). Let me mention two prima facie difficulties for this proposal before concluding.

---

[35] Given *Centering*—no other worlds are as close to actuality as it is to itself—*If P then Q* is implied by *P&Q*.

Could *Holmes does not exist* be true even if it was false that $\forall x\ (Eh \to x \neq h)$? Perhaps something x exists that is so much the best *candidate* for identity with Holmes that: x is Holmes if Holmes exists? A fair question, which we cannot go into here.[36] The claim will have to be that even the best x is not good enough, when we hold fixed enough of its properties, as partition-sensitive accounts of indicative if/then allow us to do.[37]

Second, we know from elementary logic that $\forall x\ (P \supset Q)$ is equivalent to $P \supset \forall x Q$ if x is not free in P. This equivalence had better fail for the indicative arrow $\to$, or we would be forced to conclude, absurdly, from $\forall x\ (Holmes\ exists \to x \neq Holmes)$ that *Holmes exists* $\to \forall x\ x \neq Holmes$. It does fail for counterfactuals; $\forall x$ (*Pence exists* > $x \neq Pence$) is true in the empty world, but it's false there that *Pence exists* > $\forall x\ x \neq Pence$. But then it fails too on a closest-world world semantics for indicatives (like Stalnaker's). The Pence example still goes through, assuming that $\forall x\ \varphi$ is true in e even if φ contains a $\to$; for it is not true in e that if Pence exists, he is distinct from Pence.

References

Adams, Ernest W. 1975. *The Logic of Conditionals: An Application of Probability to Deductive Logic*, volume 86. Boston, MA: D. Reidel.

Aloni, Maria. 2018. 'Knowing-Who in Quantified Epistemic Logic'. In *Jaakko Hintikka on Knowledge and Game-Theoretical Semantics*, 109–129. New York: Springer.

Aloni, Maria et al. 2001. *Quantification under Conceptual Covers*. Amsterdam: Institute for Logic, Language and Computation.

Atlas, Jay D. 1988. 'What Are Negative Existence Statements About?' *Linguistics and Philosophy*, 11(4): 373–394.

Baron-Schmitt, Nathaniel. forthcoming. 'Contingent Grounding'. *Synthese*

Bennett, Jonathan. 2003. *A Philosophical Guide to Conditionals*. Oxford: Oxford University Press.

Crimmins, Mark. 1989. 'Having Ideas and Having the Concept', *Mind & Language*, 4(4): 280–294.

Field, Hartry H. 1977. 'Logic, Meaning, and Conceptual Role', *Journal of Philosophy*, 74: 379–409.

Forbes, Graeme. 1997. 'How Much Substitutivity?' *Analysis*, 57(2): 109–113.

Forbes, Graeme. 2000. 'Objectual Attitudes', *Linguistics and Philosophy*, 23(2): 141–183.

Hintikka, Jaakko. 1962. *Knowledge and Belief*. Ithaca, NY: Cornell University Press.

Hintikka, Jaakko. 1970. 'Objects of Knowledge and Belief: Acquaintances and Public Figures', *The Journal of Philosophy*, 67(21): 869–883.

---

[36] It's discussed in Yablo 2020.   [37] Khoo 2016.

Hintikka, Jaakko. 1996. 'Knowledge Acknowledged: Knowledge of Propositions vs. Knowledge of Objects', *Philosophy and Phenomenological Research*, 56(2): 251–275.

Holliday, Wesley H. and Perry, John. 2014. 'Roles, Rigidity, and Quantification in Epistemic Logic'. In *Johan van Benthem on Logic and Information Dynamics*, 591–629. New York: Springer.

Kaplan, David. 1979. 'Transworld Heir Lines'. In Michael J. Loux (ed.), *The Possible and the Actual*, 88–109. Ithaca, NY: Cornell University Press.

Kripke, Saul. 1975. 'Outline of a Theory of Truth', *Journal of Philosophy*, 72: 690–716.

Kripke, Saul. 1980. *Naming and Necessity*. Cambridge, MA: Harvard University Press.

Kripke, Saul. 2011a. *Philosophical Troubles: Collected Papers, volume 1*. New York: Oxford University Press.

Kripke, Saul. 2011b. 'Vacuous Names and Fictional Entities'. In *Philosophical Troubles: Collected Papers, volume 1*, chapter 3, 52–74. New York: Oxford University Press.

Kripke, Saul. 2011c. 'Identity and Necessity'. In *Philosophical Troubles: Collected Papers, volume 1*, 1–26. New York: Oxford University Press.

Kripke, Saul. 2013. *Reference and Existence: The 1973 John Locke Lectures*. Oxford: Oxford University Press.

Kripke, Saul et al. 1973. 'Intentionality, Language, and Translation: Second General Discussion Session', *Synthese*, 27(3/4): 509–521.

Lewis, David. 1971. 'Counterparts of Persons and Their Bodies', *Journal of Philosophy*, 68: 203–211.

Lewis, David. 1976. 'Probabilities of Conditionals and Conditional Probabilities', *Philosophical Review*, 85(3): 297–315.

Lewis, David. 1978. 'Truth in Fiction', *American Philosophical Quarterly*, 15: 37–46.

Lewis, David. 1986. *On the Plurality of Worlds*. Oxford: Blackwell.

Moltmann, Friederike. 1997. 'Intensional Verbs and Quantifiers', *Natural Language Semantics*, 5(1): 1–52.

Moss, Sarah. 2018. *Probabilistic Knowledge*. Oxford: Oxford University Press.

Muñoz, Daniel. 2019. 'Defeaters and disqualifiers.' *Mind*, 128(511): 887–906.

Muñoz, Daniel. 2020. 'Grounding nonexistence.' *Inquiry*, 63(2): 209–229.

Ninan, Dilip. 2018. 'Quantification and Epistemic Modality', *Philosophical Review*, 127(4): 433–485.

Noonan, Harold W. 1991. 'Indeterminate Identity, Contingent Identity and Abelardian Predicates', *The Philosophical Quarterly*, 41(163): 183–193.

Quine, Willard V. 1956. 'Quantifiers and Propositional Attitudes', *The Journal of Philosophy*, 53(5): 177–187.

Quine, Willard Van Orman. 1960. *Word and Object*. Cambridge, MA: The MIT Press.

Ramsey, Frank P. and Mellor, D. H. (eds.). 1990. *Philosophical Papers*. Cambridge: Cambridge University Press.

Salmon, Nathan. 1998. 'Nonexistence', *Nous*, 32(3): 277–319.

Santorio, Paolo. 2012. 'Reference and Monstrosity', *Philosophical Review*, 121(3): 359–406.

Sider, Theodore. 2003. 'What's So Bad About Overdetermination?' *Philosophy and Phenomenological Research*, 67(3): 719–726.

Skiles. Alexander. 2015. 'Against grounding necessitarianism'. *Erkenntnis*, 80(4):717–751.

Skyrms, Brian. 1994. 'Adams Conditionals'. *Probability and Conditionals: Belief Revision and Rational Decision*, 13–26. Cambridge: Cambridge University Press.

Stalnaker, Robert. 1977. 'Complex Predicates', *The Monist*, 60(3): 327–339.

Stalnaker, Robert. 1978. 'Assertion', *Syntax and Semantics: Pragmatics*, 9(4): 447–457.

Stalnaker, Robert. 1986. 'Counterparts and Identity', *Midwest Studies in Philosophy*, 11(1): 121–140.

Weatherson, Brian. 2001. 'Indicative and Subjunctive Conditionals', *Philosophical Quarterly*, 51(203): 200–216.

Yablo, Stephen. 2002. 'Coulda, Woulda, Shoulda'. In T. Gendler and J. Hawthorne (eds.), *Conceivability and Possibility*, 441–492. Oxford: Oxford University Press.

Yablo, Stephen. 2016. 'Ifs, Ands, and Buts: An Incremental Truthmaker Semantics for Indicative Conditionals', *Analytic Philosophy*, 57(3): 175–213.

Yablo, Stephen. 2020. 'Nonexistence and Aboutness: The Bandersnatches of Dubuque.' *Crítica. Revista Hispanoamericana de Filosofía*, 52(154): 77–100.

Yalcin, Seth. 2011. 'Nonfactualism About Epistemic Modality'. In Andy Egan and Brian Weatherson (eds.), *Epistemic Modality*. Oxford: Oxford University Press.

Yalcin, Seth. 2015. 'Epistemic Modality De Re,' *Ergo, an Open Access Journal of Philosophy*, 2(19): 475–527.

Zimmermann, Thomas Ede. 1993. 'On the Proper Treatment of Opacity in Certain Verbs', *Natural Language Semantics*, 1(2): 149–179.

9

Structural Pluralism

Alessandro Torza

The contemporary metaphysics literature has been going through a major shift, as some key debates are now carried out at a higher level of abstraction wherein the methodological, epistemological, and semantic presuppositions of metaphysical practice are scrutinized. That higher-level enterprise is known as metametaphysics. A major trend among the realistically minded actors in the debate has it that there is a distinguished way of describing the world, one that carves it at its joints. The gold standard of that trend is arguably Ted Sider's realism about joint-carving, which finds its most mature and systematic exposition in his *Writing the Book of the World*.

In this chapter I will define and articulate a novel form of realism about joint-carving, *structural pluralism*, which is intended as both a generalization of and an improvement on Sider-style structural monism, in which ways of carving reality at the joints are now countenanced. Section 9.1 offers a critical overview of Sider's monism about joint-carving. Section 9.2 raises a challenge to Sider's monism, and rules out a number of potential ways of addressing the challenge. Section 9.3 introduces structural pluralism, and argues that the challenge can be met within the pluralistic framework. Section 9.4 is about metaontology: it is shown that structural pluralism is compatible with a moderate form of ontological deflationism. Since one of the key consequences of Sider's view is a refutation of ontological deflationism, the moral of the section is that the deflationist threat will rear its head once ways of carving reality at the joints are countenanced. Section 9.5 is a discussion of some consequences of adopting structural pluralism, among them a fresh look at the possibility of vague existence, and section 9.6 concludes the chapter.

9.1 Realism about Joint-Carving

Lewis (1983) argued that a host of philosophical issues can be properly addressed by positing a primitive class of perfectly natural properties—intuitively, the fundamental ones, from which all the remaining properties can be defined. A Lewisian method for specifying the degree of naturalness of a property P consists in measuring the length of the shortest definition of P in perfectly natural

Alessandro Torza, *Structural Pluralism* In: *The Language of Ontology*. Edited by: J. T. M. Miller, Oxford University Press (2021). © Oxford University Press. DOI: 10.1093/oso/9780192895332.003.0010

terms.[1] Provided with degrees of naturalness, one can then define the comparative relation *being more natural than*. According to Lewis, naturalness allows us to characterize a number of key philosophical concepts, such as intrinsicality, duplication, lawhood, causation, supervenience, determinism, materialism, and reference magnetism.

Sider (2012) has defended a generalization of Lewisian naturalness. On the generalized view, the fundamental features of reality are captured by means of *structural*, or *joint-carving* terms (or notions, or meanings). Insofar as a Lewisian natural property is the semantic value of a Siderean structural predicate, and any term is structuralness-apt, Sider's view generalizes Lewis' by going beyond the predicate.[2] Moreover, since 'structural' is a generalization of 'natural', the former also is taken as primitive, and can be used to define a dyadic relation *being more structural than*.

Sider's realism about joint-carving comes with a number of postulates. A language is said to be *fundamental* if all of its primitive terms are joint-carving; it is *nonfundamental* otherwise. A true sentence is said to be a *fundamental truth* if it is expressed in a fundamental language; it is a *nonfundamental truth* otherwise. Any truth-condition expressed in a fundamental language is called a *metaphysical semantics*. The following *completeness postulate* will play a crucial role in the ensuing discussion (Sider 2012, ch. 7.1):

Comp.   Every nonfundamental truth has a metaphysical semantics.

The gist of **Comp** is that every truth is either fundamental, or holds in virtue of a fundamental truth. For example, if 'there is a table' is true, but 'table' does not carve at the joints, we are dealing with a nonfundamental truth. Assuming that terms from fundamental physics are joint-carving, and so is quantification, **Comp** tells us that we can in principle write down truth-conditions for 'there is a table' by means of some complicated sentence of the form 'there are particles so and so', where 'so and so' is an open formula in the language of some regimentation of fundamental physics.

The question as to how we get epistemic access to the world's fundamental structure has been answered in terms of a broadly Quinean *criterion of ideological commitment* (Sider 2012, p. 12; cf. Donaldson 2014, p. 1054):

---

[1] But see a critique of that criterion in Williams (2013).

[2] Or so we are told (Sider 2012, p. vii). Things, however, are not so straightforward, since Lewisian naturalness is intensional, as it applies to coarse-grained properties, whereas Siderean structure is hyperintensional. For suppose that the predicate 'having mass' is structural, and define 'having mass*' as 'having mass or being such that there are round squares'. Whereas 'having mass*' is not structural in Sider's sense, as it is defined via the nonstructural predicate 'round', mass* is natural in Lewis' sense in virtue of being numerically the same coarse-grained property as mass. Since I will be focusing on Sider's notion, I am setting this issue aside.

C.   A term should be regarded as structural just in case it (or a synonym) is a primitive in the language of the best system

where the *best system* is the axiomatic true theory of the actual goings-on that strikes the best balance of a number of epistemic virtues such as strength and simplicity (Lewis 1973). Sider deploys his criterion in order to argue that only a small elite of terms are perfectly structural: first-order logical constants, set-theoretic membership, and a handful of terms drawn from fundamental physics. It is worth stressing that C does not define 'structural' (which is primitive), but states under what conditions we are justified in regarding a term as structural.

The right-hand side of C, however, carries an unwarranted uniqueness presupposition (Donaldson 2014, p. 1054), since for all we know multiple systems are tied for best (Armstrong 1983, pp. 70–71, van Fraassen 1989, pp. 48–49); and Sider (2012, p. 221) too seems to concede the possibility of there being no unique best system. At some point Lewis (1994, p. 479) claimed—without argument— that "we haven't the slightest reason to think the case really arises." But a modicum of intellectual modesty would suggest that we have not the slightest reason to think the case does not arise, either, as we have a rather faint idea of what a best system may look like, let alone whether it is unique. Therefore, in order not to prejudge the issue, I will follow Donaldson (2014, p. 1055) in glossing the criterion of ideological commitment in a more circumspect way:

C'.   A term should be regarded as structural just in case it (or a synonym) is a primitive in the language of every best system.

9.2   A Challenge to Realism About Joint-Carving

In this section I argue that, under certain easily realized conditions, Sider's realism about joint-carving is incompatible with the conjunction of the completeness postulate (**Comp**) and the criterion of ideological commitment (**C'**). An issue very much in the vicinity has already been raised: joint-carving realism forces upon us a choice between regarding an operator or its dual as structural (Sider 2012, ch. 10.2, McSweeney 2017, Torza 2020). If we choose both, structural ideology is redundant; if we choose one, the choice appears to be arbitrary. This section's contribution consists in showing that the problem can be turned into a conclusive refutation of joint-carving realism, once that view is paired with a number of desirable semantic and epistemic constraints.

Suppose by way of *reductio* that there exists a joint-carving first-order quantifier, as argued in Sider (2012). By C', some first-order quantifier is a primitive term in the language L_T of every best system T. Without loss of generality, we can assume that quantifier to be '∃'. But for any best system T, we can write down an equivalent system T' in a language $L_{T'}$, which is just like L_T except for having '$\forall$', and not '$\exists$', as a primitive quantifier. Insofar as T and T' only differ with respect to which quantifier is primitive in their respective language, it is eminently plausible that they should be regarded as equally good systems. So, it is not the case that all best systems feature the same primitive first-order quantifier '$\exists$'. Contradiction. We must conclude that no first-order quantifier is joint-carving.

Notice that the same line of reasoning applies *mutatis mutandis* to most if not all candidate joint-carving terms, whether logical or nonlogical. If the world features some kind of mereological structure, we should expect parthood to be joint-carving, and so to occur as a primitive in the language of all best systems. Parthood and overlap being interdefinable (in some systems of mereology, at least), the latter can then replace the former as a primitive in some best system's language, against the hypothesis. Or suppose that some best system expresses nomological dependence among a number of physical quantities, such as mass, volume, and density. Since any of those quantities is definable via the others, none is indispensable to the formulation of our best systems (Fine 2001, p. 11, Thompson 2016, p. 385).

Now, **Comp** tells us that there must be a true description of reality in a fundamental language—which Sider dubs a *book of the world*—provided that there is a true description of reality at all. As we just saw, however, most logical and nonlogical terms are not indispensable to the formulation of our best theories, and should not be deemed joint-carving. Therefore, we cannot help ourselves to the expressive resources required by a book of the world. It must be concluded that realism about structure cannot be upheld jointly with **Comp** and **C'**.

In the remainder of this section I am going to consider a number of strategies for addressing the above challenge from the perspective of a joint-carving realist. First of all, one could put forward an epistemicist criterion of ideological commitment to the effect that if two theories which are tied for best only differ insofar as one features primitive '$\forall$' whereas the other features primitive '$\exists$', we are justified in believing that one quantifier is joint-carving, even though we cannot know which.[3] I simply find this view incredible, as I fail to see what the world should be like in order for it to make universal as opposed to existential quantification joint-carving (or vice versa). Although it might just be a matter of lack of ingenuity on my part, I am inclined to think that the issue lies with the epistemicist criterion making facts about structure arbitrary.[4]

Another strategy consists in revising the criterion of ideological commitment as follows:

---

[3] Sider (2012, p. 221) floats that very idea: "My response to the concern is that when [systems] are tied, we should be agnostic which [system] is correct."

[4] For further discussion, see McSweeney (2017), Torza (2020).

C⁻.   A term should be regarded as structural just in case it (or a synonym) is a primitive in the language of some best system.[5]

This condition addresses the limitations of the previous criteria. Insofar as both '∀' and '∃' would turn out to be structural, the threat of arbitrariness coming from the epistemicist criterion will not arise. Nor will we end up without any structural quantifiers, and so without a book of the world, as was the case by assuming C'.[6]

C⁻ is not without its problems, however. As Donaldson (2014, p. 1074) has observed, any best system should be able to express facts about all aspects of the world's fundamental structure—in other words, it should be structurally rich in the following sense:

S.   A theory is said to be *structurally rich* if its language can express every structural term.[7]

Donaldson's *desideratum* is eminently reasonable: if the world is fundamentally a distribution of, say, mass over spacetime, then any best system worthy of the name should be able to capture the property of being massy.

But C⁻ seems to be incompatible with S. As it turns out, it is possible to frame first-order theories in a quantifier-free setting. The *predicate-functor logic* developed by Quine (1960, 1981) is a quantifier-free calculus able to express every sentence of a first-order language without names. Roughly, a sentence such as 'there are tables' (regimented as '∃xPx', where a variable-binding operator is prefixed to a formula with one free variable) will be paraphrased as 'it is table-ing' (regimented as 'ΔP', where a predicate-functor is prefixed to a simple predicate). Now, let T be a best system defined in a first-order language with primitive '∃' (and no names). Quine's result guarantees that T is equivalent to a predicate-functor theory T_Q. Moreover, Donaldson (2014) has argued that any first-order theory is overall as good as its predicate-functor counterpart. If that is correct, then T_Q is a best system and, by C⁻, the predicate-functor 'Δ' is joint-carving. But L_T cannot express functorese ideology, insofar as first-order languages do not have any terms, simple or complex, of the same syntactic category as 'Δ', namely predicate functors, and so no terms that could be synonymous with 'Δ'. Consequently, T is

---

[5] Donaldson (2014, p. 1073).

[6] The solution of considering both quantifiers as structural would seem to be one that Sider (2012, pp. 219–220) sees favorably, as he argues against the Lewisian view that the class of structural notions has to be nonredundant.

[7] Donaldson calls this property *structural completeness*. I have renamed it in order to avoid confusion with Sider's completeness postulate **Comp**.

not structurally rich, hence not a best system, against the hypothesis. It can be concluded that C⁻ is not a viable epistemic criterion.[8]

According to the third strategy I wish to consider, being joint-carving is not a property of individual bits of ideology, such as the possibility operator '◇' or the predicate 'mass', but of semantic categories, such as Modal Operator or Mass Term. We then want to cook up a criterion of ideological commitment to the effect that, given the above scenario where every best system features either '∀' or '∃' as a primitive term, we should regard as joint-carving the First-Order Quantifier category. This strategy faces an immediate obstacle, however, as '∀' happens to belong to a plurality of semantic categories: First-Order Quantifier, Sentential Operator, Variable-Binding Operator, etc. Which of those categories is joint-carving? Ideally, we would like to be able to select exactly one such category. Let us start with a definition: a semantic category is said to be *minimally indispensable* if it has members in the primitive ideology of all best systems, and it has no subcategory with members in the primitive ideology of all best systems. For example, suppose that every best system's primitive ideology features some truth-functional operator, and that no truth-functional operator is featured in every best system's primitive ideology. The Truth-Functional Operator category will then be minimally indispensable, since it is instantiated in every system, unlike any of its subcategories such as Dyadic Truth-Functional Operator, Tautologous Truth-Functional Operator, etc. This example would suggest the following criterion of ideological commitment:

CC. A semantic category should be regarded as structural just in case it is minimally indispensable.

This criterion tells us that, to the best of our knowledge, the joint-carving semantic categories are the least general among the theoretically indispensable ones.

Let us go back to the original scenario. If each best system features either '∀' or '∃', CC correctly rules out such categories as Sentential Operator, and of Variable-Binding Operator for being too general. Unfortunately, the category of First-Order Quantifier is also ruled out. For, assuming that no first-order quantifier other than '∀' or '∃' appears in the primitive ideology of our best theories, the relevant minimally indispensable category is the one of Universal-or-Existential First-Order Quantifier (which subsumes 'all' and 'some', but does not subsume other first-order quantifiers such as 'there are at least seventeen' or 'most'). But the category of Universal-or-Existential First-Order Quantifier is disjunctive in nature, and so hardly a candidate for being joint-carving. Unless someone—not

---

[8] Could the argument be blocked by rejecting the thesis that T_Q is not as good as T? See Torza (2017, pp. 386–389) for a rejoinder to Donaldson to the effect that first-order theories are overall better than their predicate-functor counterparts.

me, alas—can come up with a better criterion of ideological commitment for semantic categories, this third strategy appears to be not worth pursuing, either.

Let us take stock. After providing a *reductio* of joint-carving realism given C' and **Comp**, I have considered a number of potential ways out associated with alternative epistemic criteria of joint-carvingness (the epistemicist criterion, C⁻, CC), none of which appear to be viable. All is not lost, however. In section 9.3 I will formulate a generalization of Sider's realism about structure in which the present problem can be adequately addressed—or so I will argue.[9]

9.3 Meeting the Challenge

In the literature, being joint-carving is usually expressed in terms of a structure operator 'S' which can apply to terms of any syntactical sort. Here is a line of thought motivating a generalization of the received view:

Let us grant that there are multiple systems of the actual goings-on which are tied for best, and which are formulated in terms of competing ideologies. If theory choice tracks structure, the multiplicity of best systems may be evidence of the multiplicity of ways of carving reality at the joints. On that view, the ideology of each best system should be regarded as capturing a way of carving reality at its joints. Insofar as a term can be joint-carving in any of those ways, then, we must countenance not one, but multiple structure operators—as many as there are ways of carving reality's joints.

By analogy with ontological pluralism, the view that there are irreducible ways of being (McDaniel 2009, 2010, Turner 2010), and with modal pluralism, the view that there are irreducible modalities (Fine 2002), I introduce *structural pluralism*, the view that there are irreducible ways of carving reality at its joints. On this view, we should investigate not simply whether but also how a term is joint-carving. In particular, different existential quantifiers may all be structural, albeit each in its own way. I will devote the remainder of the present section to articulating structural pluralism and showing how it meets the challenge to realism about joint-carving.

In order to regiment statements about ways of carving at the joints, we need a denumerable stock of primitive indexed structure operators 'S_1', 'S_2',…'S_n'… (informally: 'structural$_1$', 'structural$_2$',… 'structural$_n$'…). By analogy with Sider's

---

[9] There is in fact a further strategy, which I have not considered here, to the effect that when our best systems do not allow us to pick between joint-carving '∀' and joint-carving '∃', we should interpret that fact as evidence that it is metaphysically indeterminate whether '∀' or '∃' is joint-carving, although it is metaphysically determinate that one of them is joint-carving. A study and defense of *structural indeterminacy* in that sense is carried out in Torza (2020).

monism, the pluralist will assume that terms are ordered by a (nonprimitive) binary comparative structure$_n$ operator, for every index n. A term 's' is said to be *more structural than* a term 't' if, for every index n, 's' is at least as structural$_n$ as 't', and, for some index n, 's' is more structural$_n$ than 't'. Terms are said to be *equally structural* if, for every n, one is as structural$_n$ as the other. It follows that two terms are structurally incomparable just in case they are not equally structural, and neither is more structural than the other. A particular case of structural incomparability is given by the conjunction of '$S_i(s)$', 'not $S_i(t)$', 'not $S_j(s)$' and '$S_j(t)$', for distinct terms 's', 't', and distinct indices 'i', 'j'. This kind of scenario will play a crucial role in section 9.4.2.

What does it mean for there to be *ways* of carving nature at the joints? We can shed light on that notion by specifying the epistemic and semantic constraints on the applicability of indexed structure operators, by analogy with the monistic case. In the above speech motivating structural pluralism, I associated ways of carving nature at the joints with best ways of describing the actual goings-on. Accordingly, I submit that we should regard each way of carving at the joints as being associated with one best system, as per the following *pluralistic criterion of ideological commitment*. Given an enumeration of the best systems,

> C_p.   for any index n, a term should be regarded as structural$_n$ just in case it (or a synonym) is a primitive in the language of the nth best system.

A further issue, which was discussed in section 9.1, is whether structure is complete with respect to the class of all truths. Let us call a language *fundamental$_n$* if all of its primitive terms are structural$_n$, and *nonfundamental$_n$* otherwise. A sentence is said to be a *fundamental$_n$ truth* if it is expressed in a fundamental$_n$ language; otherwise it is a *nonfundamental$_n$ truth*. Any truth-condition expressed in a fundamental$_n$ language, for some index n, is said to be a *metaphysical semantics*. By analogy with the monistic case, I submit the following pluralistic completeness postulate:

> $Comp_p$.   A truth which is nonfundamental$_n$, for every index n, has a metaphysical semantics.

That is to say, if a truth is not fundamental$_m$, for any m, it will have truth-conditions in a fundamental$_n$ language, for some n. Since C_p guarantees the existence of a one-to-one correspondence between structural$_n$ languages and best systems, a corollary of $Comp_p$ is that each truth is either expressed in or has truth-conditions in the language of some best system.

One more question is whether any given best system is able to express facts about the joints of nature. The question can be answered in the affirmative as follows. First, a definition:

S_n.   A system is said to be *structurally$_n$ rich* if its language can express every structural$_n$ term.

For every index n, the nth best system can trivially express every structural$_n$ term (by C_p), and so is structurally$_n$ rich. That is tantamount to saying, informally, that every best theory can provide a fundamental description of reality, according to some way or other of carving reality at the joints. It follows as a corollary that, for every index n, there is some structurally$_n$ rich theory.

Now that the skeleton of structural pluralism has been laid out, we are finally able to see how the view meets the challenge to Sider's joint-carving realism in a natural and straightforward way. First of all, let us recapitulate the challenge: for all we know, there is a plurality of best systems formulated by means of competing primitive ideologies, in such a way that very few terms, if any, are theoretically indispensable. If structural monism is assumed, by C' we must conclude that we should regard very few terms, if any, as structural, and so that we have no reason to think that there is a fundamental language in which a book of the world can be written.

Let us now see how structural pluralism fares vis-à-vis the challenge. Even if very few terms, if any, are theoretically indispensable, we know by C_p that for every index n the primitive ideology of some best system T_n is structural$_n$, and so that the language of T_n is fundamental$_n$. If a *book$_n$ of the world* is any true description of reality in a fundamental$_n$ language, then for some index n there exists a book$_n$ of the world. In fact, there is a plurality of such descriptions—as many as there are ways of carving reality at the joints, since, for every index n, a book$_n$ of the world can be written in the primitive ideology of T_n. This concludes the pluralist's reply to the challenge from section 9.2.

I have argued that the challenge to joint-carving realism can be met by countenancing ways of carving reality at its joints. In section 9.4 I will further explore structural pluralism by studying its metaontological import.

9.4 Metaontology and Quantifier Structure

9.4.1 The Deflationist Threat

Ontologists enjoy keeping themselves busy with such questions as: Are there tables? Nonactual worlds? Mars outposts? Unfortunately, questions of the form 'are there *F*s?' are rarely settled either way. Eventually, some philosophers started fearing that nothing substantive is at stake; that there are multiple, equally good ways of representing reality, some entailing 'there are *F*s', others entailing 'there are no *F*s'. Let us consider a textbook case, the special composition question (SCQ): When does an object have proper parts? (van Inwagen 1987). Universalists hold that composition always takes place. On their view, the world contains not only me and the Colosseum, but also an object having me and the Colosseum as parts (Lewis 1986, 1991, Sider 2001). Nihilists believe that all there is are mereological simples (Sider 2013a, Contessa 2014; cf. Rosen and Dorr 2002). Finally, some have defended moderate answers to SCQ, such that composition takes places sometimes but not always (van Inwagen 1990, Merricks 2001).

Although the literature on SCQ is vast and sophisticated, no solution is in sight.[10] As a result of the stalemate, alongside the first-order mereological dispute a broadly neo-Carnapian view has gained ground according to which the opposing camps in the first-order dispute employ different existence meanings, thereby disagreeing only superficially. As Hirsch (2009, p. 231) puts it: "Each side can plausibly interpret the other side as speaking a language in which the latter's asserted sentences are true." For instance, when the mereological universalist says 'there are tables', the nihilist can charitably interpret that as 'there are simples arranged table-wise'; and when the nihilist says 'there are no tables', the universalist can charitably interpret that as 'no simples are tables'. This deflationist view about ontological disagreement has been articulated by Putnam (1987, 1994) and, more systematically, by Hirsch (2009, 2011) under the label of *quantifier variance*. If the quantifier variantist is right, the disagreement about mereological composition is nonsubstantive, as it would rest on the two parties speaking languages that can be regimented in terms of nonequivalent existential quantifiers.[11]

Thus, we must distinguish between first-order, ontological disputes (such as the one concerning the special composition question) and second-order, metaontological disputes as to whether first-order ontological disagreement is substantive or merely verbal. *Ontological realism* is the metaontological thesis that ontological disagreement is substantive; *ontological deflationism* (or *anti-realism*) is the denial of ontological realism. Unless the deflationist threat is conclusively defused, the ontological enterprise as a whole is bound to rest on shaky grounds.

Before delving into matters of metaontology, we first need to properly articulate the notion of ontological disagreement. Let us start with some definitions. Quantifier '∃' of L is said to be L-*unrestricted* if, for every individual term 't' of L, '$\exists x(x=t)$' is true. Also, let us say that a language is *translatable* into another if every sentence of the former language is cointensional (i.e. truth-conditionally equivalent) with a sentence of the latter. Consider now two (regimented) languages L_A and L_B spoken by A and B, respectively. According to the doctrine of

---

[10] Nevertheless, a number of contemporary philosophers have been drawn to either extreme answer, universalism or nihilism, by the conjunction of two influential lines of thought: an argument from the denial of vague existence against restricted composition (Lewis 1986, pp. 212–213), and an argument against vague existence (Sider 2013). Others have settled on either extreme answer because of the apparent anthropocentrism of the moderate answers.

[11] Alternative deflationist views about ontology have been defended in Bennett (2009), Chalmers (2009), and Thomasson (2009).

quantifier variance, A and B will have a *nonsubstantive ontological disagreement* just in case:

1. L_A and L_B are intertranslatable;
2. There is some predicate 'F' common to L_A and L_B;
3. There are quantifiers '$\exists_A$' of L_A and '$\exists_B$' of L_B such that

   i. '$\exists_A$' ('$\exists_B$') is L_A-unrestricted (L_B-unrestricted);
   ii. '$\exists_A xFx$' is true iff '$\exists_B xFx$' is false.

The above characterization aims to capture the idea that speakers of the two languages are on equal footing when it comes to describing the mind-independent world, while differing in their respective notions of existence. In particular, condition (1) is meant to guarantee that the two languages have the same metaphysical merit, insofar as the true sentences of L_A and L_B, respectively, will pick out the same coarse-grained facts, and therefore describe the same portion of logical space (Hirsch 2009, p. 235, Sider 2012, pp. 177–180, Liebesman 2015, p. 303).

Condition (2) guarantees that the disagreement is genuinely ontological, and does not instead turn on the speakers employing different interpretations of 'F'. For since L_A and L_B are interpreted languages, if 'F' belongs to both languages, their interpretations of 'F' will coincide. There is a wrinkle, however. It might be tempting to interpret (2) as entailing that 'F' is assigned the same intension in either language. That reading is too strong, however, for if A is a mereological universalist and B a mereological nihilist, the predicate 'table' has empty actual extension in L_B but not in L_A; and yet the deflationist wants to say that the disagreement rests on the two parties employing nonequivalent quantifiers. I submit that (2) should be construed to the effect that A and B agree in their use of 'F' in the sense that they assign the same truth-value to 'Fx' in their respective languages whenever the two parties agree on the value of 'x'. Accordingly, when the universalist A points at a piece of furniture and asserts 'that is a table', whereas the nihilist B does not assert 'that is a table', the disagreement is compatible with (2) insofar as B cannot utter 'that is a table' while interpreting 'that' just as does A. Therefore, (2) should be construed as follows. For every world w and speaker S, let $D_S(w)$ be the domain of w relative to L_S. Also, let $I_S(F, w)$ be the interpretation of 'F' at w relative to L_S. Condition (2) amounts then to the thesis that $I_A(F, w) \cap D_B(w) = I_B(F, w) \cap D_A(w)$, as opposed to the naïve thesis that $I_A(F, w) = I_B(F, w)$.

Condition (3.i) intends to capture the idea that '$\exists_A$' and '$\exists_B$' are ontologically relevant insofar as each of them expresses unrestricted existence relative to their respective language (Hirsch 2011, p. 64). It is worth noticing that, in order for a quantifier of L to be L-unrestricted, it suffices for it to validate classical logic. For suppose that '$\exists$' is not L-unrestricted, in such a way that '$\exists x(x=t)$' is untrue for some term 't' of L. Since '$t=t$' is a truth of L, '$\exists$' fails to validate the classical $\exists$-introduction rule.

Finally, (3.ii) tells us that the two languages assign distinct truth-values to the respective assertions of 'there are Fs', and so that the parties will relevantly disagree in matters of ontology.

Suppose now that a mereological universalist A and a mereological nihilist B disagree on the truth of 'there are tables'. Also, suppose that the two languages are intertranslatable (in particular that, necessarily, 'there are Fs' is true in L_A just in case 'there are things arranged F-wise' is true in L_B);[12] that the languages agree on the interpretation of 'table'; and, finally, that both speakers' use of 'there is' is governed by the classical rules for the existential quantifier. Since 'there are tables' is true in L_A and false in L_B, the quantifier variantist's verdict is that the two parties will nonsubstantively disagree in matters of ontology. As a consequence, ontological realism is false.

9.4.2 Metaontological Realism and Quantifier Structure

In a rejoinder to Hirsch, Sider has argued that a successful defense of metaontological realism can be mounted by appealing to realism about joint-carving. After quickly rehearsing Sider's point, in the present subsection I will explain why switching to structural pluralism leads to a moderate form of deflationism—an intermediate position that lies between Sider's realism and quantifier variance-based antirealism.

Sider's strategy hinges on the observation that, if joint-carving realism is true, the three conditions proposed by the quantifier variantist (section 9.4.1) are necessary, although not jointly sufficient to characterize the nonsubstantivity of ontological disputes. For if the ultimate goal of theorizing about the world is not just to capture the true facts but to do so by means of the right concepts, then we must aim at describing ontological facts in joint-carving terms. Accordingly, ontological disagreement can only be nonsubstantive if there is no joint-carving quantifier that both parties can refer to.

Accordingly, for any two (regimented) languages L_A and L_B spoken by A and B, respectively, A and B will have a *nonsubstantive ontological disagreement* in Sider's sense just in case:

1. L_A and L_B are intertranslatable;
2. There is some predicate 'F' common to both L_A and L_B;
3. There are quantifiers '$\exists_A$' of L_A and '$\exists_B$' of L_B such that
   i. '$\exists_A$' ('$\exists_B$') is L_A-unrestricted (L_B-unrestricted);
   ii. '$\exists_A xFx$' is true iff '$\exists_B xFx$' is false.

---

[12] Note that, in order to match the expressive power of L_A, L_B requires (at least) both plural quantification and primitive plural predicates. I am setting this complication aside.

4. '$\exists_A$' and '$\exists_B$' are equally structural, and no unrestricted quantifier is more structural than either '$\exists_A$' or '$\exists_B$'.[13]

The above definition of nonsubstantivity is brought to bear in the following *completeness argument for ontological realism* (Sider 2012, ch. 9.6.2), which takes the form of a *reductio*. If two parties are having a nonsubstantive ontological disagreement, there have to be multiple maximally structural existential quantifiers. A dilemma ensues: either those quantifiers are all structural, or none of them are. The first horn commits us to some sort of *egalitarianism* about quantifier structure, such that there are multiple structural existential quantifiers (cf. Hirsch 2013). This view, however, would produce structural redundancy, "since, intuitively, a complete description of reality can be achieved with any one of [those] quantifier meanings" (Sider 2013b, p. 750). By way of analogy, consider the case of quantities. We can describe facts about mass in any number of equivalent ways: by mass-in-grams, mass-in-kilograms, mass-in-pounds, etc. If each of those numerical mass functions were joint-carving, the fundamental mass structure of the world would be highly redundant, which seems implausible. The same line of thought applies *mutatis mutandis* to the quantifier case: the world could be described via, say, nihilist quantification, organicist quantification, universalist quantification, etc. All such descriptions would be equally good if egalitarianism were correct, and the quantificational structure of the world would therefore be highly redundant.[14]

If we take the second horn of the dilemma, no existential quantifier is structural, therefore our best theories will have quantifier-free metaphysical semantics (by **Comp**). But "no serious work on the foundations of physics and mathematics has been done in a quantifier-free setting" (Sider 2012, p. 183), which lends evidence that our best theories cannot be phrased in a quantifier-free language.[15]

---

[13] Sider (2012, p. 46).

[14] Here is a potential rejoinder on behalf of egalitarianism. The key difference between quantifier variance and egalitarianism lies in that the latter, unlike the former, would be willing to buy Sider's notion of structure, as well as his definition of ontological substantivity in terms of structure. (That is precisely what the dialectics presupposes, in fact.) Accordingly, it is reasonable to assume that the egalitarianist will take on board the key postulates about structure, one of them being the criterion of ideological commitment. But that difference is crucial, for then only those quantifiers that are theoretically indispensable should be regarded as structural; and it might well be that, even though any number of nonequivalent quantifiers allows us to express all the relevant facts, most of them are not theoretically indispensable. In other words, whereas the quantifier variantist of old will regard as good enough any quantifier meaning that allows us to express all the facts, the egalitarianist will regard as good enough only those quantifier meanings that both allow us to express all the facts and are theoretically indispensable. Consequently, egalitarian quantifier variance is compatible with there being only a small elite of joint-carving quantifiers, *contra* Sider's charge of structural redundancy.

[15] However, see Donaldson (2014), where it is argued that first-order theories are just as good as predicate-functor theories, and Torza (2017) for a rejoinder to Donaldson, as well as a defense of the superiority of first-order ideology.

Since both horns of the dilemma are precluded, the disagreement must be substantive, which concludes the argument for ontological realism. Although there appear to be a number of ways to resist the argument—an unqualified rejection of realism about joint-carving, for a start—a dissection of Sider's argument is beyond the scope of this chapter. In the remainder of this section I will argue instead that, once we go pluralist about joint-carving, deflationism is bound to raise its head, although in a moderate form when compared to the one championed by Hirsch.

Sider's definition of nonsubstantive ontological disagreement appeals to the hypothesis that quantifiers are ordered by a binary relation of comparative structure. Recall that structural pluralism admits of a plurality of such relations, one for each way of carving reality's joints, which are then employed in defining an overall comparative structure relation which, unlike in the monistic case, is not total. Accordingly, the pluralist's definition of ontological nonsubstantivity will match Sider's, except that condition (4) is now replaced with

4*.   '$\exists_A$' and '$\exists_B$' are either equally structural or structurally incomparable, and no unrestricted quantifier is more structural than either '$\exists_A$' or '$\exists_B$'.

Now, suppose that the best systems are exactly two: one defined in a classical first-order language L_1 featuring a primitive mereologically universalist quantifier '$\exists_1$'; the other defined in a classical first-order language L_2 featuring a primitive mereologically nihilist quantifier '$\exists_2$'. It follows by C_P that '$\exists_1$' and '$\exists_2$' are structurally incomparable, since '$\exists_1$' is more structural$_1$ than '$\exists_2$' (because $S_1(\exists_1)$ but not $S_1(\exists_2)$), and '$\exists_2$' is more structural$_2$ than '$\exists_1$' (because $S_2(\exists_2)$ but not $S_2(\exists_1)$). Also, '$\exists_1$' ('$\exists_2$') is L_1-unrestricted (L_2-unrestricted) in virtue of its classicality. Moreover, no existential quantifier is more structural than either '$\exists_1$' or '$\exists_2$', since any first-order language has at most one classical existential quantifier up to mutual entailment, and so no other existential quantifier is part of the primitive ideology of either best system. Assuming that L_1 and L_2 are equally expressive and share a common predicate (e.g. 'having mass greater than 1 gram', which can be satisfied by some composite object but no simple object), we must conclude that a L_1-speaker is bound to nonsubstantively disagree with a L_2-speaker in matters of ontology.

It will be instructive to see why the above scenario is not ruled out by a pluralistic version of Sider's completeness argument. Notice first of all that since neither '$\exists_1$' nor '$\exists_2$' is structural$_n$, for all n, no quantified language is fundamental$_n$, for all n. So, in order to successfully carry out the *reductio*, the realist would require a principle to the effect that some quantificational truth has truth-conditions in a language that is fundamental$_n$, for all n. However, the pluralist's completeness principle $\mathbf{Comp}_P$ only requires that every truth that is not formulated in any fundamental$_m$ language, for any m, has truth-conditions in a fundamental$_n$

language, for some n. Since every fundamental$_n$ language contains a quantifier (by hypothesis, either the universalist quantifier '$\exists_1$' or the nihilist quantifier '$\exists_2$'), the problem of formulating quantifier-free truth-conditions will not even arise, thus blocking the *reductio*.

9.5 Discussion

Once structural pluralism is adopted, or at least entertained, a number of questions will arise.

1. Which debates are nonsubstantive, if any?

This question goes beyond the scope of the present chapter, and arguably beyond the extent of our current knowledge. The main question I have addressed in section 9.4 is whether ontological disagreement can be nonsubstantive and, in particular, whether it can be nonsubstantive given realism about joint-carving. The answer I have provided is a qualified 'yes': it is possible for ontological disagreement to be nonsubstantive, given joint-carving realism of the pluralistic variety. My answer does not tell us anything about whether any particular debate is or is not substantive. That further question can be answered only in terms of the pluralistic criterion of ideological commitment: in order to know which debates are substantive, we must know which systems are best, and that is knowledge we do not happen to possess, yet. At best we could attempt to make some educated guesses based on the state of current science. I regard epistemic openness in matters of metaontology as a feature, rather than a bug, of structural pluralism, as it injects a healthy dose of methodological naturalism into metaphysical practice.

2. How does the structural pluralist's metaontology stack against the metaontologies of the structural monist and the quantifier variantist, respectively?

The pluralistic metaontology is weaker than the monistic, since the latter, unlike the former, entails ontological realism. On the other hand, the pluralistic metaontology is stronger than the one based on quantifier variance. For suppose there are languages L_1, L_2 which are equally expressive, employ nonequivalent quantifiers, and share some predicate. If the two speakers disagree about the truth-value of some utterance of the form 'there are Fs', according to quantifier variance such a scenario suffices to declare the nonsubstantivity of ontology. According to the structural pluralist, on the other hand, the same scenario underdetermines the question of ontological realism. For if '$\exists_1$' and '$\exists_2$' are structurally incomparable, and not less structural than any other quantifier, we are squarely in deflationist territory; whereas if, say, '$\exists_1$' is more structural than any other quantifier, realism is going to be true.

One might worry that structural pluralism, by making room for the possibility of ontological deflationism, undercuts the rationale for buying into fundamental structure. For a metaphysics of structure is typically justified abductively in terms of the work it is able to do. If the gains that structure was supposed to provide turn out to be illusory, in such a way that we must give up ontological realism and perhaps more of the perks that we were promised, one is left wondering why we should embark on a project that demands so much of us and delivers so little. I must confess that I find the objection to be rather toothless. First of all, as I just pointed out, structural pluralism does not allow all-out ontological deflationism, unlike Hirsch's quantifier variance. More importantly, the alleged advantages of joint-carving monism come at a hefty price, if my arguments from section 9.2 are correct. Therefore, it may well be that what structural pluralism has to offer is in effect all that can be offered by any stable and coherent form of realism about joint-carving.

3. Sider (2014, p. 566) has this to say about his defense of ontological realism:

My reply to Hirsch isn't meant to convince Hirsch or anyone else with neo-Carnapian tendencies that ontology is, after all, a substantive and worthwhile enterprise. It's rather supposed to be a stable position from which one can resist neoCarnapian arguments. It's supposed to have some independent appeal; and it's supposed to undermine the arguments if its metaphysical assumption of realism about joint-carving is true. (If this assumption is false then some form of neoCarnapianism might well be correct.)

Of course, when Sider speaks of 'realism about joint-carving', what he has in mind is structural monism. Since my critique of ontological realism from section 9.4.2 presupposes structural pluralism, it seems as though we are stuck in a dialectical stalemate: if monism is true, the ontological realist prevails; if pluralism is true, deflationism remains a live possibility.[16]

Two remarks are in order. First, structural pluralism is by no means the result of 'neoCarnapian tendencies', since it is compatible with both ontological realism and its denial, as I have already explained. My critique of realism is a consequence of adopting structural pluralism, not vice versa. Second, it would be unfair to paint the debate between monism and pluralism about structure as a dialectical stalemate, as if picking one over the other was merely a matter of philosophical inclination. Since pluralism was introduced in order to meet the challenge to Sider's proposal, the dialectics is not symmetrical—pluralism has already been shown to have the upper hand in one crucial respect.

4. Several years before publishing *Writing the Book of the World*, Sider (2003) sketched the following argument against vague existence:

---

[16] I would like to thank John Horden for pressing me to address this point.

Vagueness requires multiple precisifications; joint-carving meanings are reference magnets; there is a unique joint-carving unrestricted quantifier meaning; therefore the unrestricted quantifier is not vague.   (pp. 142–143)

I want to zero in on the premise that there is a unique joint-carving unrestricted quantifier meaning. In hindsight, Sider was in effect assuming realism about joint-carving of the monistic variety. But it should be clear by now that, if pluralism is assumed instead, the argument becomes inconclusive when suitably rephrased. For if there are multiple structrural$_n$ unrestricted quantifier meanings, for different values of the index n, and if each such meaning is a reference magnet, then an unrestricted quantifier can have multiple precisifications, *pace* Sider. Thus, appealing to structure by itself does not appear to rule out the possibility of vague existence.

9.6 Conclusion

This chapter has introduced, articulated, and defended structural pluralism, the metametaphysical view that countenances a plurality of ways of carving reality at its joints. First of all, I have raised a challenge for Sider's monism about structure, and argued that structural pluralism meets that challenge. Second, I have shown that structural pluralism does not rule out ontological antirealism, unlike its monistic counterpart. Consequently, the hypothesis that reality has a fundamental structure is unable per se to save ontology from the neoCarnapian threat, when fundamentality is construed in terms of joint-carvingness. Finally, I have anticipated and discussed a number of questions that arise once structural pluralism is adopted.[17]

References

Armstrong, D. 1983. *What Is a Law of Nature?* Cambridge: Cambridge University Press.

Bennett, K. 2009. 'Composition, Colocation, and Metaontology'. In D. Chalmers, D. Manley, and R. Wasserman (eds.), *Metametaphysics*. Oxford: Oxford University Press.

Chalmers, D. 2009. 'Ontological Anti-Realism'. In D. Chalmers, D. Manley, and R. Wasserman (eds.), *Metametaphysics*. Oxford: Oxford University Press.

[17] I would like to thank Aldo Filomeno, John Horden, Ricardo Mena, and two anonymous referees for their useful comments, as well as the audiences of the Language of Ontology Conference at Trinity College Dublin, the 9th European Congress of Analytic Philosophy in Munich, the Epistemology of Metaphysics workshop in Prague, and the *Seminario de Investigadores* at UNAM. This work was supported by the PAPIIT grant IA400316.

Contessa, G. 2014. 'One's a Crowd: Mereological Nihilism without Ordinary-Object Eliminativism', *Analytic Philosophy*, 55: 199.

Donaldson, T. 2014. 'Reading the Book of the World', *Philosophical Studies*, 172(4): 1051.

Fine, K. 2001. 'The Question of Realism', *Philosopher's Imprint*, 1(1): 1–30.

Fine, K. 2002. 'The Varieties of Necessity'. In G. Szabó and J. Hawthorne (eds.), *Conceivability and Possibility*. Oxford: Oxford University Press.

Hirsch, E. 2009. 'Ontology and Alternative Languages'. In D. Chalmers, D. Manley, and R. Wasserman (eds.), *Metametaphysics*. Oxford: Oxford University Press.

Hirsch, E. 2011. *Quantifier Variance and Realism: Essays in Metaontology*. Oxford: Oxford University Press.

Hirsch, E. 2013. 'The Metaphysically Best Language', *Philosophy and Phenomenological Research*, 87(3): 709.

Lewis, D. 1973. *Counterfactuals*. Oxford: Blackwell.

Lewis, D. 1983. 'New Work for a Theory of Universals', *Australasian Journal of Philosophy*, 61(4): 343.

Lewis, D. 1986. *The Plurality of Worlds*. Oxford: Blackwell.

Lewis, D. 1991. *Parts of Classes*. Oxford: Blackwell.

Lewis, D. 1994. 'Humean Supervenience Debugged', *Mind*, 103(412): 473.

Liebesman, D. 2015. 'Quantifier Variance, Intensionality, and Metaphysical Merit'. In A. Torza (ed.), *Quantifiers, Quantifiers, and Quantifiers: Themes in Logic, Metaphysics, and Language*. New York: Springer.

McDaniel, K. 2009. 'Ways of Being'. In D. Chalmers, D. Manley, and R. Wasserman (eds.), *Metametaphysics*. Oxford: Oxford University Press.

McDaniel, K. 2010. 'A Return to the Analogy of Being', *Philosophy and Phenomenological Research*, 81(3): 688.

McSweeney, M. 2017. 'Following Logical Realism Where It Leads', *Philosophical Studies*, 176(1): 117.

Merricks, T. 2001. *Objects and Persons*. Oxford: Oxford University Press.

Putnam, H. 1987. 'Truth and Convention: On Davidson's Refutation of Conceptual Relativism', *Dialectica*, 41: 69.

Putnam, H. 1994. 'The Question of Realism'. In *Words and Life*. Cambridge, MA: Harvard University Press.

Quine, W. V. 1960. 'Variables Explained Away', *Proceedings of the American Philosophical Society*, 104(3): 343.

Quine, W. V. 1981. 'Predicate Functors Revisited', *The Journal of Symbolic Logic*, 46(3): 649.

Rosen, G. and Dorr, C. 2002. 'Composition as a Fiction'. In R. Gale (ed.), *The Blackwell Guide to Metaphysics*. Oxford: Blackwell.

Sider, T. 2001. *Four-Dimensionalism: An Ontology of Persistence and Time*. New York: Oxford University Press.

Sider, T. 2003. 'Against Vague Existence', *Philosophical Studies*, 114: 135.

Sider, T. 2012. *Writing the Book of the World*. Oxford: Oxford University Press.

Sider, T. 2013a. 'Against Parthood'. In K. Bennett and D. Zimmerman (eds.), *Oxford Studies in Metaphysics 8*. Oxford: Oxford University Press.

Sider, T. 2013b. 'Replies to Dorr, Fine, and Hirsch', *Philosophy and Phenomenological Research*, 87(3): 733.

Sider, T. 2014. 'Hirsch's Attack on Ontologese', *Noûs*, 48(3): 565.

Thomasson, A. 2009. 'Answerable and Unanswerable Questions'. In D. Chalmers, D. Manley, and R. Wasserman (eds.), *Metametaphysics*. Oxford: Oxford University Press.

Thompson, N. 2016. 'Is Naturalness Natural?', *American Philosophical Quarterly*, 53(4): 381.

Torza, A. 2017. 'Ideology in a Desert Landscape', *Philosophical Issues*, 27(1): 383.

Torza, A. 2020. 'Structural Indeterminacy', *Philosophy and Phenomenological Research*, 101(2): 365.

Turner, J. 2010. 'Ontological Pluralism', *The Journal of Philosophy*, 107(1): 5.

van Fraassen, B. 1989. *Laws and Symmetry*. Oxford: Oxford University Press.

van Inwagen, P. 1987. 'When Are Objects Parts?', *Philosophical Perspectives*, 1: 21.

van Inwagen, P. 1990. *Material Beings*. Ithaca, NY: Cornell University Press.

Williams, J. R. G. 2013. 'Lewis on Reference and Eligibility'. In B. Loewer and J. Schaffer (eds.), *A Companion to David Lewis*. New York: Wiley Blackwell.

10

Levels of Ontology and Natural Language

The Case of the Ontology of Parts and Wholes

Friederike Moltmann

10.1 Introduction

In contemporary metaphysics, it is rather common to recognize two levels of ontology:

(1) the naïve or *ordinary ontology*, as I will call it, which is the ontology reflected in our common-sense intuitions and perhaps in cognition in general and which includes the ontology of ordinary objects[1]

(2) the *fundamental ontology*; that is, the ontology of what there really or ultimately is.

Metaphysics has been focused on those two levels as well as the relation between the two, pursuing questions such as whether and how the ordinary ontology can be understood in terms of what is fundamental and whether some or all of its items even exist.

It seems obvious that natural language reflects ordinary ontology. With its referential noun phrases (NPs), in particular, it seems to display the full range of ordinary objects and entities ontologically dependent on them, an ontology that includes material objects, artifacts, events, shadows, holes, tropes, and various sorts of 'stuff'. Philosophers discussing such entities frequently make reference to linguistic data, such as the applicability of predicates to terms putatively referring to the entities in question. Yet, clearly, the ordinary ontology is not dependent on natural language; rather, as an ontology implicit in cognition in general, it is acquired quite independently of the acquisition and use of language.

The aim of this chapter is to argue for another level of ontology besides the levels of ordinary ontology and of fundamental ontology. This is what I will call the

---

[1] There are reasons to think that there is a difference between naïve ontology, the ontology non-philosophers would accept using common sense or naïve reflection, and the ontology implicit in cognition. The latter may not be accessible to reflection in the way the former is. For the purposes of this chapter this potential difference will be set aside, however important it may turn out to be.

Friederike Moltmann, *Levels of Ontology and Natural Language: The Case of the Ontology of Parts and Wholes* In: *The Language of Ontology.* Edited by: J. T. M. Miller, Oxford University Press (2021). © Oxford University Press. DOI: 10.1093/oso/9780192895332.003.0011

language-driven ontology. The language-driven ontology is not a full alternative to the ontology of ordinary objects, but rather involves an enrichment of it. The language-driven ontology is specifically tied to language, and the implicit acceptance of that ontology strictly goes along with the use of language.

One main motivation for the language-driven ontology is the semantics of the mass-count distinction and more generally the semantics of parts and wholes involving plural and mass nouns. Recent research on the mass-count distinction converges on an agreement that the semantic distinction between mass and count nouns cannot reside in a difference in the ordinary ontology, but is more closely tied to language itself. For example, minimal pairs of a mass noun and a count such as *carpeting-carpets* appear to stand for the very same things, yet they differ semantically in the acceptability of predicates and the availability of predicate readings:[2]

(1) a. John counted the carpets
    b. ??? John counted the carpeting.
(2) a. John compared the carpets.
    b. John compared the carpeting in the two rooms /?? the carpeting.
    c. John compared the individual carpets.

Count applies only to plural, not mass NPs, as seen in (1a, b); *compare* applies to plural NPs and certain mass NPs, as seen in (2a, b). Unlike *count*, *compare* can target individuals as well as subgroups, as on a reading of (2a) on which John compared the carpets in the one room to those in an other. In addition, *compare* can apply to mass NPs when a modifier specifies a division of their denotation into parts, such as *in the two rooms* in (2b). A subgroup reading of a plural argument of *compare* becomes unavailable with the addition of *individual*, as in (2c).

Count and *compare* impose different *part-structure-sensitive semantic selectional requirements* on their arguments; that is, they carry different presuppositions regarding the part structure of an argument that a plural or mass NP may present. *Count* requires as an argument a plurality of single entities; *compare* requires an argument with contextually or descriptively distinguished parts.

In the language-driven ontology of parts and wholes, the notion of unity—that is, the property of being a single, countable entity—plays a central role. Count nouns denote sets of single entities and thus convey unity; mass nouns don't. In contemporary semantics, in the tradition of Link (1983) and others, a common view has been that for an entity to have unity means for the entity to be an atom with respect to the noun used to refer to it. On an older view, going back to Aristotle, having unity means being an integrated whole, by having a form or structure or a boundary or by being a maximal entity whose parts are connected. A situation-based version of that view has been pursued in Moltmann (1997,

---

[2] See Moltmann (1997, chap. 3) and Moltmann (2016) for discussions of such part-structure-sensitive semantic selection.

1998). On that view, a count noun characterizes an entity as an integrated whole in a (minimal) situation of reference, but not so a mass noun. This chapter rejects those views and instead adopts the view that the mass-count distinction consists in the presence (count nouns) or absence (mass nouns) of a primitive condition of unity in the language-driven ontology, the ontology from which noun extensions are made up. Besides the mass-count distinction, such a language-driven notion of unity also plays a central role in part-structure-sensitive semantic selection as well as the semantics of part structure modifiers such as *individual* and *whole*.

The language-driven ontology raises the question about its status: does it amount to another level of (conceptual) representation or can it be viewed as an ontology of what is real? This chapter will argue that the language-driven ontology, like the ordinary ontology, is an ontology of the real (though not fundamental). However, it is based on a selection of actual entities and in that sense it is perspectival. This goes along with a 'maximalist' or 'permissive' view of reality as a plenitude of entities (Eklund 2008, Hawthorne 2006, Schaffer 2009). That is, reality consists in a plenitude of entities of both simple and derivative sorts, some of which will have unity in the language-driven ontology, some of which won't, depending on what entities language selects for its ontology. Both the language-driven ontology and the ordinary ontology thus are based on a (mind- or language-dependent) selection among what is real.

The chapter takes up a number of generalizations from my earlier work on the semantics of parts and wholes within the theory of situated part structure (Moltmann 1997, 1998, 2005), which was based on the notion of an integrated whole as well as a notion of a situation of reference. Being an integrated whole generally consists in having a form, structure, or boundary, but it may also just consist in being a maximal entity whose parts share a particular property or connection in the situation of reference, which makes pluralities like 'the carpets' or quantities like 'the carpeting in the room' integrated wholes. The new view this chapter pursues sharply distinguishes the notion of unity from the notion of an integrated whole. Referring to something as a single entity may go along with characterizing it as an integrated whole (and often does), but it need not. Conversely, referring to something as an integrated whole does not guarantee that it counts as a single entity. Thus, the plurality 'the women' and the quantity 'the furniture in the room' will be integrated wholes, but not single entities. The new view no longer makes use of situations, but only of entities that come with unity or with a structure at the level of the language-driven ontology.

The language-driven ontology of parts and wholes shares important features with the light ontology of pleonastic entities of Schiffer (1996), an ontology of abstract entities that includes properties and propositions introduced on the basis of the use of predicates and sentences, respectively. They are part of the same, what Schiffer (1996) calls, 'language-created, language-independent' ontology, an ontology distinct from the ordinary ontology. They both are tied to the functional part of language (syntactic constructions or categories), rather than the lexicon.

The chapter will start with a few remarks about ontology and natural language in general. Against the background of the older view of situated part structures, it will then discuss the mass-count distinction and outline the new view of the language-driven ontology of parts and wholes. Finally, it will address the question of the status of the language-driven ontology, drawing the connection to the ontology of pleonastic entities.

10.2 How Does Natural Language Reflect Ontology?

The background assumption of this chapter is that natural language reflects ontology, though not the ontology of fundamental reality.[3] There are various ways in which natural language reflects ontology. Most importantly, natural language reflects entities by means of its referential and quantificational NPs and its predicates, at least on the most common view. Thus in a simple sentence like *John saw a tree*, assuming it is true, the referential NP *John* and the quantificational NP *a tree* stand for entities, and the property expressed by *saw* is predicated of John and one of the entities *a tree* ranges over. The standard view, in both linguistics and philosophy of language, is that referential NPs (names, definite NPs, and specificational indefinites) stand for entities, quantificational NPs range over entities, and predicates express properties of entities.

Why is this view plausible? First of all, it seems to match the intuitive functions of parts of speech: we use referential NPs to refer to entities and predicates to attribute properties to them. Moreover, the view allows for a uniform semantics of NPs and of predicates, and thereby appears to guarantee compositionality. That is, referential NPs always stand for entities, quantificational NP always range over entities, and predicates always express properties of entities.[4] Frege, in particular, was very explicit about the connection between objecthood and referential NPs. It was part of his Context Principle that a referential NP, in the context of a sentence, always contributes an object (entity) to the composition of the meaning of the sentence (Wright 1983). Compositionality and ontology thus appear to be intimately linked.[5]

The view that referential NPs always stand for entities requires recognizing a wider range of entities than many metaphysicians may be willing to accept, such as a great range of derivative and perhaps abstract entities. It also requires recognizing

---

[3] See Moltmann (2017, 2019) for more on the ontology reflected in natural language.

[4] Frege went even further and took the notion of an object (entity) itself to be tied to the syntactic function of a referential NP, introducing a syntactic notion of objecthood ('an object is what a referential NP may stand for').

[5] There is also an alternative view, though, according to which natural language does not involve reference to objects (Chomsky 1986, 1998, 2013) and according to which compositionality can be achieved without ontology, on the basis of concepts only (Pietroski 2018). However, see my remarks in section 10.7.

entities that are specifically part of the language-driven ontology, in particular, it seems, *pluralities* (denotations of definite plural NPs) and *quantities* (denotations of definite mass NPs).[6] Just as definite singular NPs stand for entities that are individuals, definite plural NPs and mass NPs should stand for entities, namely pluralities and quantities. That the three types of definite NPs stand for entities appears to be supported by the fact that they allow for the same predicates with the very same reading, for example *weigh*:

(3) a. The stone weighs 1 kilo.
    b. The stones (together) weigh 5 kilos.
    c. The material weighs 5 kilos.

Considerations of compositionality give a strong motivation for pluralities and quantities being entities on a par with individuals as elements in the denotation of nouns and as semantic values of definite NPs.

There is a debate whether pluralities should be viewed as entities, that is, as 'collections as one' (formally, sums or sets) instead of as 'collections as many', an issue that will be addressed in section 10.5. For the time being, pluralities will be considered entities.

As a terminological clarification, the terms 'individual', 'plurality', and 'quantity' in this chapter will be used for the sorts of entities that make up the extension of singular count, plural, and mass nouns, respectively, and also act as respective semantic values of definite singular count, plural, and mass NPs. The term 'entity' will be used as the more general term, applying to individuals, pluralities, and quantities.

10.3 The Mass-Count Distinction

The mass-count distinction is a morphosyntactic distinction between nouns that appears to reflect a fundamental ontological distinction: that between a single entity, an entity that has unity, and something that fails to be a single entity, but is

---

[6] The term 'quantity' for the sorts of things that make up the denotation of mass nouns and the referents of definite mass NPs is due to Cartwright (1970) (see also Ter Meulen 1981, Pelletier and Schubert 2012). It is not entirely felicitous in that it suggests those things have the status of single, countable entities, which they don't (McKay 2017). The term as used in this chapter is meant to be ontologically neutral.

The term 'stuff' is often used in the philosophical literature, but it is unsuited when talking about pluralities of such entities in the metalanguage. The term 'substance' was originally used for the denotation of kind-referring bare mass nouns such as *gold* in *Gold is shiny* (Ter Meulen 1981) and is not suited for the things that make up the denotation of mass nouns when they do not stand for kinds. Other semanticists have taken bare mass nouns to stand for intensions (Pelletier and Schubert 2012) or modalized pluralities or quantities (Moltmann 2013 chap. 1.6.3., p. 37ff).

just stuff (a quantity). The semantically relevant notion of a single entity is closely connected to the use of count nouns (or categories) in natural language and plays a central role in part-structure-sensitive semantic selection. As will be discussed, there are serious difficulties for standard semantic approaches to the mass-count distinction and thus the notion of unity. This chapter will instead take the notion of unity conveyed by count nouns to be a primitive notion and will formulate constraints on part-structure-sensitive semantic selection in terms of it.

While there has been an enormous amount of recent research on the mass-count distinction across languages and the related issue of classifier languages, for the purpose of this chapter, it will suffice to stay with standard criteria and intuitions regarding the mass-count distinction in English. The main criterion for the mass-count distinction is that count nouns take numerals, but mass nouns don't. Count nouns moreover generally display a singular-plural distinction, but mass nouns don't. Another criterion used by linguists for mass and count nouns is the selection of quantifiers (mass nouns go with *little* and *much*, count nouns with *few* and *many*).[7] The criterion that philosophers have often focused on is the choice between the predicates *being some of* and *being one of* (*This carpet is one of the carpets*/?? *some of the carpeting, This rice is some of what was offered*/?? *one of the things that were offered*) (McKay 2017). Moreover, mass nouns cannot generally be predicated of count NPs and count NPs cannot generally be predicated of mass NPs (?? *This carpet is expensive carpeting*, ?? *This carpeting is a beautiful carpet*) (McKay 2017).[8]

By tendency, the mass-count distinction goes along with the ontological distinction between objects and matter. Yet (near) minimal mass-plural pairs such as *carpets—carpeting, clothes—clothing, rice grains—rice, faculty members—faculty, animals—cattle* make clear that the distinction can hardly be one in the ordinary ontology. Mass and plural NPs in such pairs may, it seems, stand for the very same things, hardly even displaying a difference in how things are perceived or conceived.[9] The choice of mass or count often seems arbitrary, both for a given language (why the mass noun *rice*, but the plural *beans*?) and across languages (English *pasta* as a mass noun vs. French *pâtes* as a plural noun). Given those linguistic facts, there is little agreement among linguists what the content of the mass-count distinction consists in and whether it is an ontological, extension-based, information-based, epistemic, or conceptual-perspectival distinction.[10] This chapter

---

[7] See Doetjes (2012) and Pelletier and Schubert (1989, 2003) for criteria for mass and count.

[8] Sometimes in the literature, predicating mass nouns of entities referred to as countable is taken to be acceptable:

(i) This chair is wood.

As far as such examples are even acceptable, they seem to involve the *is* of constitution rather than of predication.

[9] See also Soja, Carey, and Spelke (1991). The distinction between the material and an object constituted by it is generally regarded as an ontological distinction by philosophers concerned with the ontology of ordinary objects (rather than the ontology of fundamental reality) (Fine 2003).

[10] See Pelletier and Schubert (1989, 2003) for an overview of different approaches to the semantic mass-count distinction.

will focus on the two main approaches to the semantics of the mass-count distinction:

(1) the *integrity-based approach*
(2) the *extension-based approach*.

The *integrity-based approach* takes the content of the mass-count distinction to be a distinction between entities that come with a boundary, form, gestalt, connectedness, or some other sort of integrity (count) and entities that lack integrity (mass). This way of drawing the mass-count distinction can be traced back to the Aristotelian notion of form (see also Simons 1987 for the general notion of an integrated whole). In linguistics, an integrity-based approach to the mass-count distinction was adopted by Jesperson (1924) and later Langacker (1987).[11] The theory of situated part structures (Moltmann 1997, 1998, 2005) makes use of the notion of the integrated whole of Simons (1987), but relativizes it to a situation, permitting entities to be accidental integrated wholes and to have or lack integrity just on the basis of linguistic information.

The *extension-based approach* to the semantics of the mass-count distinction takes the content of the mass-count distinction to consist in different properties of noun extensions formulated in terms of extensional mereology. The extension-based approach is due to Quine (1960) and became particularly influential in linguistics in the version it takes in Link (1983). Most importantly, the characteristic property of a singular count noun is to have an *atomic* extension; that is, for any x and y, if $x \in [N]$ and $y < x$, then $\neg\, y \in [N]$, where $<$ is the proper-part relation. By contrast, the extension of a mass noun is not atomic; instead it generally is taken to be *divisive*; that is, for any x and y, if $x \in [N]$, and $y < x$, then $y \in [N]$. The extensions of both mass nouns and plural nouns are cumulative; that is, if $x, y \in [N]$, then $x\, v\, y \in |[N]$, where $x\, v\, y$, the sum of x and y, is taken to be the least upper bound of $\{x, y\}$ with respect to $<$ ($\sup_{<}(\{x, y\})$). Being both divisive and cumulative defines *homogeneity*, the characteristic property of mass noun extensions.

Both the integrity-based approach and the extension-based approach face two general difficulties:

(1) Singular count nouns that fail to meet atomicity or convey properties of integrated wholes
(2) Mass nouns that display atomicity or properties of integrated wholes.

Let us address these in turn.

---

[11] Thus, for Jespersen (1924, p. 198): 'There are a great many words which do not call up the idea of some definite thing with a certain shape or precise limits. I call these "mass-words"; they may be either material, in which case they denote some substance in itself independent of form, such as silver, quicksilver, water, butter, gas, air, etc., or else immaterial, such as leisure, music, traffic, success, tact, commonsense'.

10.3.1   Singular Count Nouns That Fail to Meet Atomicity or Convey Properties of Integrated Wholes

There are a range of singular count nouns for which atomicity fails to hold. They include nouns like *thing, sum,* and *line* (Moltmann 1997) as well as *fence, twig,* and *wall* (Rothstein 2010, 2017). A proper part of a thing or sum generally is a thing or sum again. One might relativize atomicity to a context that selects only maximal entities falling under the noun (Rothstein 2017). However, there are fully legitimate uses of the nouns in question on which they are not atomic (philosophical uses of *thing* or *entity* including). Semantic theory should not exclude such legitimate 'technical' uses of nouns. The integrity-based approach does not make use of atomicity and thus in principle allows for count nouns to denote non-atomic entities. However, the entities in the extension of count nouns need to be integrated wholes in the situation of reference, which will hold only for maximal fences and walls. The integrity-based approach then has similar difficulties with legitimate uses of *thing, entity,* and *sum* on which integrity is not meant to play a role.

There are certain limit cases that make the difficulty for extension-based and integrity-based approaches particularly clear. These involve what I will call 'portion nouns' and 'collection nouns', nouns that fail to be atomic and need not convey any form of integrity. (5a, b) are examples with portion nouns; (6) is an example with a collection noun:

(5) a. the portion of wine John drank—the wine John drank
     b. the body of water on earth—the water on earth
(6) the collection of papers Mary proposed as reading—the papers Mary proposed as readings

In (5a, b), the singular count NP and the mass NP provide the very same identity and persistence condition for an individual and a quantity, respectively, and so for the singular count NP and the plural NP in (6). No integrity is implied by *portion, body,* and *collection* on the relevant use. Moreover, on that use, *portion, body,* and *collection* are non-atomic and thus fail to meet the extensional mereological criterion for singular count nouns. However, portion nouns and collection nouns clearly classify as singular count nouns, given the various criteria. For example, the portion of wine John drank is 'one of the portions offered', not 'some of the wine offered'; there is 'one portion of wine he drank', not 'one wine he drank', etc. (McKay 2017). Portion and collection nouns thus define something of which they are true as a single thing, but not in virtue of it being an atom or an integrated whole. Unity, the property of being a single thing, thus may, but need not, be grounded in properties such as being an atom with respect to an expression or concept or being an integrated whole. Singular count nouns, in addition to providing identity conditions, which may be the same as those of mass nouns, specify that an entity has the status as a single entity. Whatever their lexical content may be, singular count nouns convey unity and thus countability. This motivates the view that unity is a primitive notion, not reducible to atomicity or integrity.

10.3.2 Mass Nouns That Display Atomicity or Quantities Whose Parts Are Integrated Wholes

Lack of atomicity for mass nouns poses the familiar difficulty of the minimal-parts problem. It arises quite obviously for granular mass nouns like *rice* but also others such as *water*. An even more serious problem are so-called object mass nouns. Object mass nouns represent a great range of mass nouns that appear to stand for pluralities of well-individuated objects. They include *furniture, clothing, carpeting, hardware, jewelry, luggage, staff, police force,* and *cattle.*[12] Object mass nouns often come with apparent co-extensional plural nouns in the same language or in a different language. In English, we have *clothes—clothing, carpets—carpeting, policemen—police force, professors—faculty, cows—cattle.* Across languages, we have the choice of the mass noun *pasta* in English and Italian and the plural noun *pâtes* in French, the mass noun *hair* in English and the plural noun *cappelli* in Italian. The choice of an object mass noun as opposed to a plural noun across languages appears generally arbitrary, without there being an obvious perceptual difference (Chierchia 1998b).

The two approaches to the content of the mass-count distinction, the extension-based approach and the integrity-based approach, are hardly applicable to object mass nouns. Object mass nouns are atomic as much as count nouns are, and object mass nouns appear to convey integrity conditions for the individuals that make up their denotations as much as plural nouns do. But object mass nouns fulfill the main criteria of mass nouns, such as the choice of determiners *little* and *much* and the resistance of numerals.

Object mass nouns have given rise to the view that the choice among mass and count is, to an extent arbitrary, and does not align with the actual ontology of things. In Rothstein's (2010) words, 'While the mass-count distinction is clearly influenced by the structure of matter, it is not taken over from it'.

On the present view, object mass nouns convey a content that simply fails to describe an entity as a single entity (as 'one') or as a plurality of entities (as 'many'). Object mass nouns describe quantities that have parts that are single entities, but that themselves are not mere pluralities of single entities. That is because the

---

[12] See Chierchia (1998b) and Cohen (2020) for linguistic discussions of object mass nouns.

lexical content of object mass nouns focuses on overall qualities, functions, or patterns, rather than describing mere pluralities of individuals. Some apparent minimal pairs may display such differences particularly well, for example *jewelry—pieces of jewelry* or *hair—hairs*. *Colorful jewelry* can stand for differently colored, monochrome pieces of jewelry, but *colorful pieces of jewelry* requires the individual pieces to be colorful. 'Little hair' is less than 'few hairs', since the latter counts individual hairs, but the former measures an overall quantity. There are limit cases with little manifest differences (e.g. *pasta* vs. *pâtes*). Just as in the case of portion and collection nouns, in the limit cases the ordinary ontology does not seem to be reflected in the choice between mass nouns and plural nouns.

Portion and collection nouns as well as object mass nouns pose serious problems for extension-based and integrity-based approaches to the mass-count distinction and support the view that the semantic content of the mass-count distinction resides in the presence or absence of a primitive notion of unity (even if there is a tendency for that unity to be grounded in conditions of integrity or atomicity). Unity in that sense need not align with the individuation of entities as single entities in the ordinary ontology. Only entities in the language-driven ontology make up the extension of nouns, not entities in the ordinary ontology. The entities in the extension of singular count nouns have the status of single entities in the language-driven ontology, but not so the entities in the extension of mass nouns and plurals.

Let us introduce some minimal formal representation. For the time being, the denotation of a plural noun N_{plur} can be taken to be the closure under sum formation of the extension of N, as on the extensional mereological approach. The minimal structure of the ordinary ontology is then as in (7a), and that of the language-driven ontology as in (7b):

(7) a. The ontology of ordinary objects: $<I^*, Q^*>$
    b. The language-driven ontology: $<I, (Q, <), (P, <)>$

The assumption about the ontology of ordinary objects is simply that it divides into a domain of entities that are single entities (I^*) and a domain of entities that aren't (E^*) (a domain of quantities and perhaps pluralities). The language-driven ontology consists of a domain I of single entities as well as a domain Q of quantities, which is closed under sum formation (least upper bounds with respect to <) and a domain of pluralities P, which, for now, is also closed under sum formation.

The domains I^* and I need not coincide. In the ordinary ontology, unity is generally based on conditions of integrity and purpose, which also restricts the formation of sums (Simons 1987, Schaffer and Rosen 2017). In the language-driven ontology, by contrast, unity need not be grounded and sum formation appears unrestricted (mereological universalism).

The semantics of singular count, mass, and plural nouns then is subject to the following conditions:

(8) a. For a count noun N, $[N] \subseteq I$
    b. For a mass noun N, $[N] \subseteq Q$
    c. $P = \{x | \exists X (X \neq \emptyset \ \& \ X \subseteq I \ \& \ x = \sup_<(X))\}$
    d. For the plural N_{plur} of a count noun N, $[N_{plur}] = \{x | \exists X(X \neq \emptyset \ \& \ X \subseteq [N] \ \& \ x = \sup_<(X))]$

Another potential support for the distinction between the language-driven ontology and the ordinary ontology comes from classifier languages such as Chinese, though the issue of classifiers across languages is highly complex and the case of Chinese itself controversial. This is not a place to enter the debate about Chinese, but to simply make clear that one view within that debate can be cast straightforwardly within the present approach. Simplified, in Chinese, (almost) all nouns require numeral classifiers for numerals to be applicable. Numeral classifiers select either natural units (sortal numeral classifiers) or units based on measurement (mensural numeral classifiers).[13] English has something close to classifier constructions with mass nouns:

(9) a. two pieces of furniture
    b. two liters of milk

In (9a), *pieces* and *liter* act like sortal and mensural classifiers, respectively, enabling countability of the denotation of a mass noun. The view about Chinese that has sometimes been held is that Chinese nouns are always mass or at least are never specified as count (Ojeda 1993, Borer 2005, Rothstein 2017).[14] But standard ontological and extension-based characterizations of mass nouns (lack of integrity or natural unity and homogeneity, respectively) do not apply to Chinese nouns, just as they did not apply to object mass nouns. The present view can make sense of that view about Chinese: Chinese nouns never convey a notion of unity, regardless of their lexical content. (8b) then applies to Chinese nouns in general. The effect of numeral classifiers, on this view, is to impose unity, by selecting entities that have unity in the ontology of ordinary objects (sortal numeral classifiers) or by imposing a measurement (mensural numeral classifiers). The meaning of a classifier now is a function mapping an entity x in the domain Q onto another entity y in I that is minimally distinct from e by having unity (U(y, x)):[15]

---

[13] For classifiers and the distinction between mensural and sortal classifiers in particular see Cheng and Sybesma (1999), Doetjes (2012), and Rothstein (2017).

[14] For a different view about Chinese see, for example, Doetjes (2012) and Cheng and Sybesma (1999, 2005).

[15] See Rothstein (2017) for a similar view.

(10)   For a sortal numeral classifier C and a (mass) noun N,
       $[CN] = \{y | \exists x(x \in Q \ \& \ U(y, x) \ \& \ y \in [C] \ \& \ x \in [N])\}$

I will set aside the semantics of mensural classifier constructions, which will involve measurement functions applying to quantities.

10.3.3 The Theory of Situated Part Structures

The present view takes unity to be a primitive notion, at the level of ontology relevant for semantics: the language-driven ontology. Being a single entity at that level may go along with being an integrated whole, but being an integrated whole does not guarantee having unity and thus counting as a single entity. The latter holds also when integrity is relativized to a situation of reference. This constitutes the crucial departure from the theory of situated part structure in Moltmann (1997, 1998, 2005), which for the semantics of singular count nouns made use of the notion of an integrated whole relative to a situation. I will quickly review that theory.

The general idea of that theory was that the semantics of natural language involves part structures in situations. More specifically, the information content of the situation determines the part structure of quantities and pluralities based on whether entities count as integrated wholes. The semantic mass-count distinction, on that, consists in that singular count nouns convey the integrity of an entity in a situation of reference, whereas mass nouns convey the absence of it in a minimal situation of reference (that is, a situation attributing to an entity no more than the content of the noun itself) (Moltmann 1997, 1998). Part-structure-related semantic selectional requirements furthermore care about whether entities or their parts are integrated wholes in the situation of reference.

The theory of situated part structures has difficulties dealing with important aspects of the mass-count distinction, as already mentioned. Another problem is that it considers the referents of definite plural and mass NPs integrated wholes, which means that they count as one, rather than as many. This is problematic, as we will see (section 10.4.2). A further problem for the theory is that the situation associated with the utterance of definite plural or mass NP cannot generally determine the contextually relevant structure of the plurality or quantity referred to. The idea was that the information content of the reference situations tells what parts of the plurality or quantity are integrated wholes and therefore count as the only parts (given a non-transitive, situated part relation). However, as a matter of fact, it still depends on the speaker's intentions what the relevant parts are. The readings of (12) show that:

(12)   John compared the German and American students.

In (12), the descriptive content of the definite NP would determine the maximal plurality of German students and the maximal plurality of American students as integrated wholes. But (12) has also the individual-student comparison reading as well as readings on which, say, John compared the German and American physics students to the German and American math students.[16]

10.4 Semantic Selection

We can now turn to part-structure-sensitive semantic selection, where the language-driven notion of unity plays a central role. Part-structure-sensitive semantic selectional requirements are expected to be semantic universals that hold across languages.

Part-structure-sensitive semantic selection has received little attention in the linguistic and philosophical literature, which has instead focused on constraints that predicates may impose on the category of objects to which they may apply. These are presuppositions that need to be satisfied in order for the sentence to be able to be true or false, rather than resulting in a category mistake.[17] In order to avoid a category mistake, often accommodation may save the interpretability of the sentence; that is, a shift from the actual referent of the nominal argument to a closely related one. For example, *start* selects events, but not (enduring) objects, as in (11a); but still (11b) is acceptable with accommodation, mapping the book onto an event of reading:

(11) a. John started reading the book.
     b. John started the book.

There are challenges to the Fregean view that predicates apply just to objects, which have been discussed in the literature. A widely shared view, though, is that such challenges can be dealt with pragmatically, rather than requiring giving up

---

[16] Another difficulty for the situation-based approach is that it predicts that (i) and (12) have exactly the same readings, since they involve situations with the same information content (individuals being German students and individuals being American students):

(i) John compared the German students and the American students

But as a matter of fact, they don't: only (12) allows for readings of the sort 'John compared the German and American physics students to the German and American math students'. This means that descriptive information constitutive of integrated wholes does not strictly determine a configuration (but rather properties such as being a semantic value of the same definite NP; see Moltmann 2017). On the present view, structured pluralities or quantities are no longer determined by the information content of a situation. Rather, as configurations, they are determined by the speaker's intentions when uttering the plural or mass NP, subject (though of course, to maxims of cooperative communication).

[17] See Magidor (2013) for an overview of the discussion of category mistakes.

the view that predicates apply just to objects.[18] For example, *appreciate* is a predicate that appears to be sensitive to the way an object is presented even in unembedded contexts:

(12) a. (As regards Bill,) John appreciates the gardener, but not the teacher.

Predicates like *appreciate* are sensitive to the facets of an object. Yet, the predicate itself does not select the linguistically conveyed presentation itself. That is because (12b) by itself can easily have the reading on which John appreciates Bill, the gardener, as a teacher:

(12) b. John appreciates the gardener.

The focus of this chapter is on predicates that appear to be sensitive to the way the part-whole structure of an entity is presented; the linguistic presentation of entities in terms of unity, plurality, and division into relevant parts. Given the theory of situated part structures, such semantic selection requires an exceptional relativization of arguments to a situation; that is, predicates select not just entities, but pairs consisting of entities and a situation of reference. The information content of the situation, on that view, determines the part structure of the entity. This chapter, by contrast, proposes an account of part-structure-sensitive semantic selection without an exceptional relativization to a situation, making just use of structured quantities and pluralities and a primitive notion of unity.

10.4.1 The Accessibility Requirement

The first semantic selectional requirement, the 'Accessibility Requirement', concerns predicates or readings of predicates that appear to be sensitive to the distinction between singular count NPs on the one hand and plural or mass

---

[18] An example that figures prominently in the literature and for which a pragmatic account has been defended is the one below (Saul 1997):

(i) Clark entered the phone-booth and Superman emerged.

There is one case where a predicate does seem to select a particular linguistic presentation, namely the predicate *describe*, generally not recognized as such in the literature:

(ii) a. John described the object: he said it was a house.
     b. ??? John described the house: he said it was a house.
(iii) He described the gift. It was red wine from France.

Predicates like *describe* are sensitive to the degree of generality of a description. The more general description may include accidental function. *Describe* is strictly sensitive to the content of the NP. A pragmatic account does not seem plausible in this case.

Another class of predicates not just caring about objects is predicates like *high*, which are sensitive about the orientation of the object in space (Moltmann 1998):

(iv) This pole is higher/longer than that one.

NPs on the other. The generalization, roughly, is that predicates (or readings of predicates) making reference to the parts of the argument (but not the structure of the argument as a whole) can apply only to a mass or plural NP, not a singular count NP. Since only singular count nouns convey unity, this means that arguments of the relevant (readings of) predicates may not be single entities:

(13)   The Accessibility Requirement
        Predicates (or readings of predicates) that make reference to the parts but not (the structure of) the whole of an argument are true or false only of an entity that does not have unity.

Two types of predicates making reference to the parts but not the structure whole of an argument can be distinguished. First, there are numerals and related predicates, such as *enumerate* and *rank*, which I will call 'count-type predicates':

(14) a. The students are ten.
      b. ??? The class is ten.
(15) a. John enumerated the orchestra members.
      b. ??? John enumerated the orchestra.
(16) a. John ranked the students.
      b. ??? John ranked the class.
(16b) is impossible if understood in the sense of ranking the individual members of the class.

Second, there are predicates like *compare*, *distinguish*, *be similar*, and *be different*, which I will call 'compare-type predicates'. With singular count NPs, such predicates lack the sort of internal reading available with plural NPs:[19]

(17) a. John compared the students.
      b. ??? John compared the class.

---

[19] The verb *count* itself is actually not that bad with collective singular count NPs in English:

(i)   a. ? John counted the class.
      b. ? John counted the committee.
(ii) a. ?? John counted the orchestra.
      b. John counted the orchestra members.

This may be because the Accessibility Requirement allows for some amount of accommodation. It may also be because *count* is in fact a predicate making reference not just to the parts but also to the whole of the argument, involving a condition of exhaustion of the parts. In German the prefix *durch* ('through') makes that condition explicit, which leads to the contrast between (iiia) and (iiib) (Moltmann 1997):

(iii) a. ?? Hans zaehlte die Klasse.
           'John counted the class.'
       b. Hans zaehlte die Klasse durch.
           'John counted class through.'

(18) a. The male and the female students are similar.
      b. ??? The class is similar.
(19) a. John compared jewelry in the different boxes.
      b. ??? John compared the treasure.

Unlike *count*-type predicates, which strictly take into account individuals only, *compare*-type predicates can apply to a contextually or descriptively given division of a plurality or quantity into subpluralities. Thus, (17a) has an individual-comparison reading as well as a reading on which students in different classes are compared. I will come back to that in section 10.4.2.

Also, distributive readings fall under the Accessibility Requirement: they are hard to get with singular count NPs, at least with a range of predicates. Thus, (20b) can hardly have the distributive reading available for (20a):

(20) a. John evaluated the students.
      b. John evaluated the class.

The Accessibility Requirement exempts predicates making reference not just to the parts but also to the structure of the whole of an argument, such as *organize* and *restructure* (Moltmann 1997):

(21) a. John organized the collection of paper on the desk.
      b. John restructured the committee.

Predicates like *count* and *enumerate* in a way make reference to the whole by exhausting the parts of the argument in the process described, but they do not make reference to the structure of the whole, unlike predicates like *organize* (see below).[20]

In the theory of situated part structures, the Accessibility Requirement is formulated in terms of the notion of an integrated whole: predicates subject to the Accessibility Requirement can apply only to entities that are not integrated wholes in the reference situation. One problem with this account of the Accessibility Requirement is that integrity can also be imposed without count nouns, just by using a definite plural or mass NP. A definite plural or mass NP *the* N (*the children* or *the* water) refers to an integrated whole d, namely the maximal quantity or plurality falling under N (*children* or *water*). If F is the property expressed by N, d is an FF-integrated whole in the sense that all the parts are connected by sharing F (i.e. they stand in the relation FF) and are not FF-connected to anything

---

[20] In Moltmann (1997, p. 199), the Accessibility Requirement was formulated just making reference to the whole.

that is not part of d (Simons 1987, Moltmann 1997). In the theory of situated part structures, the notion of an FF-integrated whole is of course restricted to the situation of reference.[21] The important observation is that integrity in the sense of an FF-integrated whole never blocks the application of part-structure-sensitive predicates.

A second problem for casting the Accessibility Requirement in terms of integrity is that even 'ungrounded' unity, conveyed by collection and portion nouns, blocks the application of part-structure-sensitive predicates or readings of predicates:

(22) a. John compared the papers on the desk.
      b. ??? John compared the collection of papers on the desk.
      c. ??? John compared the amount of jewelry on the desk.

The Accessibility Requirement involves unity tied to the use of a singular count noun, which means it involves entities at the level of the perspectival, language-driven ontology, rather than that of the more substantive, language-independent ordinary ontology.

That the Accessibility Requirement involves a perspectival, language-driven ontology is apparent also in the semantic effect of the noun modifier *whole*. Modifying a singular count NP with the adjective *whole* semantically means mapping a single entity (the denotation of the singular count NP) to the mere plurality of its parts. The result is the applicability of predicates subject to the Accessibility Requirement, as in (23a), as opposed to (23b), as well as distributive readings, as in (24a), as opposed to (24b), which has only a collective reading (Moltmann 1997, 2005):[22]

(23) a. John enumerated the whole class.
      b. ??? John enumerated the class.
(24) a. The whole art collection is expensive.
      b. The art collection is expensive.

Whole has the function of mapping a unit to an entity that has no unity, but is a mere collection of parts.[23]

---

[21] In that theory, the notion of an FF-integrated whole is important because it restricts sum formation (which is restricted to integrated wholes in general).

[22] Note that the data with *whole* make clear that the Accessibility Requirement could not be viewed as a syntactic selectional requirement.

[23] NPs with the modifier *whole* as in (24a) permit a second, collective reading. Here the predicate applies to the collection of the parts together with a form (Moltmann 2005).

10.4.2 The Plurality Requirement

The Plurality Requirement distinguishes *count*-type predicates from *compare*-type predicates. *Count*-type predicates, we have seen, differ from *compare*-type predicates in that they cannot target contextually or descriptively individuated subpluralities or subquantities. Thus, *count* in (25a) can only target individual students, not contextually individuated subgroups, unlike *compare* in (25b), which has a reading on which John compared the students in one class to those in another:

(25) a. John counted the students.
     b. John compared the students.

Similarly, (26a) has a reading on which the women induce a partition of the jewelry, a reading that is absent in (26b):

(26) a. John compared the jewelry of the women.
     b. ??? John counted the jewelry of the women.

Count-type predicates differ somewhat in their applicability to mass NPs, especially those with object mass nouns. Numerals are strictly inapplicable to NPs with object mass nouns:

(27) a. * ten wood/ten pieces of wood
     b. * ten furniture/ten pieces of furniture

The predicate *count*, by contrast, is not entirely excluded with object mass nouns such as *luggage* and *artwork*:[24,25]

(28) a. ? John counted the luggage.
     b. John counted the pieces of luggage.
(29) a. ?? John counted the art.
     b. ? John counted the artwork.
     c. John counted the works of art.

---

[24] The data are presented in a less differentiated way in Moltmann (1997).
[25] They are much less acceptable, though, with mass nouns like *art* and *decor*, which put value rather than material individuation in the foreground:

(i) a. John counted the art.
    b. John counted the decor.

That seems to be because entities like 'art' and 'decor' are individuated primarily in terms of quality and function, in abstraction from individuals that make them up.

Count appears to permit accommodation of a quantity as a plurality of its individual parts.

Setting the possibility of such accommodation aside, the generalization is that *count*-type predicates select pluralities of single entities, at the level of the language-driven ontology:

(30)   The Plurality Requirement
Count-type predicates can be true or false only of pluralities of single entities.

Instead of (30), the theory of situated part structures made use of an 'Integrated Parts Requirement', a requirement that, basically, said that *count*-type predicates can apply only to entities that consist in parts that are integrated wholes in the situation of reference. Such a requirement faces the same problem as the Accessibility Requirement when the latter is formulated in terms of integrated wholes: *count*-type predicates cannot apply to entities whose parts are integrated wholes in virtue of the description used unlike *compare*-type predicates. *Compare*-type predicates can relate to parts of an argument that are distinguished descriptively, as in (31a, b) or contextually as possibly in (32a, b):

(31)   a.   John compared the furniture in the different rooms.
       b.   John compared the students in the different classes.
(32)   a.   John compared the furniture.
       b.   John compared the students.

In (31a) the modifier *in the different rooms* imposes a division of the furniture into maximal subquantities located in the particular rooms, and, similarly, the modifier *in the different classes* imposes a division of the plurality of students in (31b). (32a, b) can be used so as to be about the very same divisions. Such readings are unavailable for *count*-type predicates *Count*-type predicates cannot take into account contextual divisions of pluralities or quantities into subpluralities or subquantities since pluralities and quantities do not count as single entities, even if they are integrated wholes in the relevant context.

Quantities and pluralities that come with a particular contextual division into subquantities and subpluralities are entities that I will call 'configurations'. In the theory of situated part structures, 'configurations' were pluralities and quantities that come with a division into parts based on the information content of the situation of reference. Now configurations are considered entities by themselves that are as unstable as a situation of reference. Configurations are no longer determined by the 'content' of reference situations, but rather by speakers' referential intentions, just as other objects of reference.

Configurations do play a significant semantic role in that there are expressions whose specific semantic function is to set them up. In particular, the adjectival modifier *individual* sets up a configuration in which a plurality is divided just into its individual members.[26] Thus (33) has only the individual-comparison reading:

(33) John compared the individual students.

Individual is a *count*-type predicate in that it targets parts of an entity specified as countable. Its semantic effect is to ensure that a plurality has only its individual members as its parts.

10.4.3 The Strict Distributivity of Predicates of Size and Shape and of Existence

The Accessibility Requirement and the Plurality Requirement are requirements that need to be satisfied at the level of the language-driven ontology, requiring the absence or presence of linguistically conveyed unity. There is one class of predicates whose application to entities relates not just to the language-driven ontology, but also the ordinary ontology, namely predicates of shape and size. Such predicates are strictly distributive, resisting an application to a plurality or quantity as a whole (Moltmann 2004, Rothstein 2010, Schwarzschild 2011). What characterizes such predicates is that they can apply to NPs with plural nouns and with object mass nouns as heads, but target only the individuals of which their denotations are made up:

(34) a. The children are big.
      b. ??? The people are long.
      c. The furniture is large.

(34a) cannot possibly mean that the group of children is big, (34b) cannot possibly mean that the line of people is long, and (34c) cannot possibly mean that the collection of furniture is large.[27]

---

[26] See Moltmann (2005) for the semantics of *individual* within the theory of situated part structures.
[27] There are some limits as to the sorts of object mass nouns that allow for a distributive reading of predicates of size and shape. Mass nouns that put function or value into focus disfavor such readings:

(i) a. ?? The decor is large.
     b. The furniture is large.
(ii) a. The artwork is small.
     b. ?? The art is small.

Such mass nouns do not apply to quantities composed of ordinary objects, but rather to quantities that consist of concrete aesthetic or functional qualities of ordinary objects (tropes), and to those predicates of shape and size do not apply.
  Also certain mass nouns permit predicates of size applying to the entire quantity, for example *output* and *Werk* 'oeuvre' (*large output, grosses Werk*).

There is no general prohibition against collective readings of predicates with definite plurals and object mass NPs as such. Plural and mass NPs do allow for certain predicates to convey a property of the whole plurality or quantity, for example predicates of weight:[28]

(35) a. The books (together) are heavy.
      b. The furniture is heavy.

The distributive readings of (34a–c) mean that, unlike *count*-type predicates, predicates of size and shape do not require linguistically conveyed unity, but can relate to just the natural units of the ordinary ontology.

For predicates of size and form, linguistically conveyed unity will also do, even if it is not grounded, as with the collection and portion nouns below:

(36) a. The collection of unopened letters on my desk is large.
      b. The amount of alcohol he swallowed is small.
      c. The quantity of water on the floor is enormous.

Predicates of size and shape thus apply to just those entities that have unity either in the language-driven ontology or the ordinary ontology. The latter remains accessible for semantic selection, as well as, for example, the choice of sortal numeral classifiers, which depends on natural units in the denotation of nouns.

10.4.4 Constraints on Accommodation

Semantic selectional requirements regarding types of objects, as was mentioned, can sometimes be violated, allowing accommodation to ensure the acceptability of the sentence. There are significant constraints on accommodation regarding part-structure-sensitive semantic selection, which bear on the relation between the language-driven ontology and the ordinary ontology. We have seen that some *count*-type predicates are not entirely excluded with singular count NPs (?? *John counted the class*) as well as object mass nouns (?? *John counted the furniture*), though they generally select pluralities. Such predicates permit accommodation mapping an individual or quantity onto a plurality of the things that compose the individual or quantity in the ordinary ontology. By contrast, no *count*-type predicate can apply to a configuration, a quantity, or a plurality whose relevant parts

---

[28] Predicates like *enormous* can target the entire denotation of a mass NP if the denotation is a quality or trope, in which case they convey intensity rather than size in the spatial sense, as illustrated in the contrast below:

(i) a. John's excitement was enormous.
    b. The equipment was enormous.

are subquantities or subpluralities (*John counted the men and the women* cannot mean 'John counted two things: the group of men and the group of women'). This means that accommodation cannot map pluralities or quantities onto corresponding single entities. This in turn means that the use of language—that is, the use of a count noun or classifier—is necessary for adding unity at the level of the ontology relevant for semantic selection, which is thus rightly called the language-driven ontology.

10.5 The Status of the Language-Driven Ontology

10.5.1 The Status of Unity

Count nouns, unlike mass nouns, convey unity, enabling countability; mass nouns don't, and that regardless of how entities may be individuated in the ordinary ontology. The ontology of ordinary objects thus is not reflected in the mass-count distinction as such. This does not mean, though, that the mass-count distinction distorts the ontology of ordinary objects. Rather, count nouns operate at another level, that of the language-driven ontology, selecting unity as a feature of entities, possibly but not necessarily based on unity at the level of the ontology of ordinary objects. The same holds (at least on one view) for classifiers, which select unity based on natural units (as in 9a) or measured units (as in 9b). The absence of grammatically conveyed unity similarly means refraining from selecting unity that way. Unity and thus countability are language-driven and made available only by the use of count nouns or classifiers. Unity as conveyed by count nouns and classifiers, however, is not a cognitive notion, a mind-dependent condition imposed on certain parts of the world. Rather, it is a feature that entities have mind-independently, but subject to selection by the use of language. Grammatically conveyed unity is mind-dependent only insofar as it is selected among actual features of entities. In that sense, it is perspectival.

The present view is that anything in reality in a way has unity; any plurality of entities, whether it exhibits integrity or not, has unity. At the same time, any single entity is constituted by something that fails to have unity; that is, the plurality or quantity consisting of its parts (depending on whether the parts themselves are single entities or not). This is also intuitive: any collection of things can be viewed as a collection as one or a collection as many. Only a collection as one can be subject to counting.

The same holds for an entity and a particular feature it may have: the entity with that feature may be regarded as a unit or as a mere collection of an entity and a feature. Even if an entity has a form and persists with that form, it could still be viewed as a mere plurality of features and parts, rather than as a single entity.

Unity as such is not grounded in intrinsic properties of entities. In the context of cognition and the use of language, though, only certain beings will be selected as single entities, generally based on integrity of some sort. Unity may go along with conditions of integrity, but conditions of integrity do not guarantee that an entity counts as a single entity at the relevant level of ontology.

10.5.2 The Language-Driven Ontology and Reality as Plenitude

What is the status of the language-driven ontology, an ontology that includes entities such as pluralities, quantities, and the notion of unity? Should the language-driven ontology be viewed as a merely conceptual level, and thus another level of syntactic representation, as opposed to the ontology of ordinary objects, which would be part of reality? The answer is clearly no. Entities that are pluralities or quantities serve as arguments of predicates and contribute just as much to truth conditions as ordinary objects when they are arguments of predicates. The language-driven ontology must be an ontology of the real. Entities in the language-driven ontology, just as much as ordinary objects, are actual if derivative entities. The language-driven ontology thus is no less real than the ontology of ordinary objects.[29] The language-driven ontology, though, involves a selection of entities and their features. The ontology of ordinary objects in fact can be viewed in the same way, as a selective ontology of derivative entities, entities whose composition and nature are themselves based on selection (roughly, of features and matter).

This goes along with a particular view of reality of what has been called 'maximalism' (Eklund 2008), 'plenitude' (Hawthorne 2006), or 'permissiveness' (Schaffer 2009)—the view that 'for any type of object such that there can be objects of that type given that the empirical facts are exactly what they are, there are such objects' (Eklund 2008). Reality, on that view, does not just consist of what is fundamental or of ordinary objects. Rather, it consists of a plenitude of beings, whether intuitive or not, simple or derivative. It will include unrestricted sums, composites of matter and form of some sort, and composites of matter, form, and primitive unity. Some of those beings will count as ordinary objects, others won't, depending on what the cognitive ontology of ordinary objects selects. Some of them will count as single entities in the language-driven ontology, some

---

[29] There is a third option, according to which neither the ontology of ordinary objects nor the language-driven ontology is real, but only the ontology of the fundamental. The language-driven ontology and the ontology of ordinary objects would have the status of mind-dependent constructs, on a par with fiction. Unity, on that view, would be considered a cognitive notion, added on to chunks of reality. However, natural language certainly does not reflect a distinction between what is real and the sorts of derivative entities considered fictional. They both contribute to truth conditions in the same way.

of them won't, depending on what language selects for its ontology. The language-driven ontology and the ontology of ordinary objects thus will be on a par, based on a mind- or language-dependent selection among what is real. The ontology of the real thus includes both the ordinary ontology and the language-driven ontology.

10.5.3 The Language-Driven Ontology of Pleonastic Entities

The language-driven ontology, with its notion of unity, is an ontology that strictly goes along with the use of language, in particular the use of definite mass and plural NPs. The question then arises whether there are motivations for that level of ontology independent of the mass-count distinction and part-structure-sensitive semantic selection. As a matter of fact, a language-driven ontology has been discussed in other contexts, in particular by Schiffer (1996) in connection with his theory of pleonastic entities. Pleonastic entities are entities that are referents of referential NPs introduced by what Schiffer calls 'something-from-nothing' transformations. For example, properties as pleonastic entities are introduced by a transformation of the sort *John is happy* ⸱⸱⸱→ *John has the property of happiness*. There is nothing more to properties than what can be derived from such term-introducing inferences. In this sense properties as pleonastic entities are language-driven. Properties as pleonastic entities not have a substantial nature that could be subject to any further investigation. Pleonastic entities, for Schiffer, are what he calls 'language-created, language-independent' entities. This means they are made available for thought and linguistic reference by the use of certain object-introducing linguistic devices (*the property of being happy*), yet on the basis of language-independent conditions actually obtaining (John's being happy).

Non-worldly facts are another example for which the notion of a pleonastic object is particularly suited. Non-worldly facts are the referents of canonical fact descriptions of the sort *the fact that someone entered the room* or *the fact that John won the race or Mary did*. They exist in virtue of particular sentences or propositions being true and thus exist language-independently. However, we can hardly talk or think about them without using fact-introducing devices, namely canonical fact descriptions of the sort *the fact that* S.

Language-driven countability sides with pleonastic, 'language-created, language-independent' objects: countability is made available by the use of particular linguistic devices that select entities as units. As with pleonastic entities, this need not mean that linguistically conveyed unity is in fact created and thus imposed by the mind; rather, it is selected among the various manifestations of unity that in fact obtain. Language makes unity and countability available by selecting entities as units, just as pleonastic entities are not literally created but made available by the relevant object-introducing linguistic devices, in virtue of language-independent conditions obtaining. The ontology of countability and the ontology of pleonastic entities thus belong to the same level of language-driven ontology.

10.6 Challenges for Formal Semantics: Ontological Commitment to Sums

Pluralities and quantities do not have unity and thus do not count as single entities; pluralities are not 'one', but 'many', and quantities are neither 'one' nor 'many'. This means that the plurality denoted by *the children* could not possibly be the same entity as that denoted by *the sum of the children* or any other count NPs. The denotation of *the wood* could not possibly be the same entity as that of *the quantity/amount/heap of wood*.

The difference is reflected not only in the applicability of *count*-type predicates as well as the strict distributivity of predicates of size and shape. It is also reflected in the understanding of the existence predicate *exist*. The predicate *exist* behaves like predicates of shape and size in that it displays a strictly distributive reading. Thus, with plurals, *exist* can target only individual members of the plurality, not the plurality as such (Moltmann 2004, 2017):

  (38) The buildings do not exist.

(38) cannot possibly be used as a statement about the existence of the sum as opposed to just the individual members (as a statement, say, by someone express-ing doubt in the existence of a particular sum). The same holds for object mass nouns:

  (39) The furniture does not exist.

(39) can be understood only as a statement about the existence of the individual pieces, not as a statement about the existence of the quantity as such (as a statement, say, by someone doubting the existence of a quantity as an entity separate from the pieces making it up).[30]

The view that pluralities and quantities are not single entities is not captured by standard semantic theories of plurals and mass nouns, neither those based on

---

[30] One might object that sentences with *exist* should not be taken seriously for semantic purposes since *exist* is a technical expression, mainly used by philosophers. However, it appears that *exist* is subject to robust constraints, constraints that may in fact be incompatible with a philosopher's reflective notion of existence (Moltmann 2020). (38, 39) illustrate this: there are philosophers that adopt mereological universalism—the view that everything has a sum. Yet even such philosophers cannot use those sentences to convey the existence of a particular sum.

extensional mereology in the tradition of Link (1983) nor those that include conditions of integrity besides a part-of relation (Moltmann 1997, 1998). On standard semantic theories, pluralities and quantities are treated as single entities in the very same way as the elements in the denotation of singular count nouns: they all are elements in the domain of entities in any model interpreting the language. As such, they act as semantic values of referential NPs and first-order variables and are generally taken to form domains that are closed under sum formation. The standard model-theoretic semantics of plurals and mass nouns fails to capture the presence or absence of unity in entities, a notion that plays a central role not just for the mass-count distinction but also for part-structure-related semantic selectional requirements. The metalanguage of standard model-theoretic semantics does not distinguish between individuals on the one hand and pluralities and quantities on the other, as beings that have unity and beings that fail to have unity.

There are well-known motivations and advantages of the standard semantics of plural, mass, and singular count nouns, of course. The standard semantics gives a unified semantics of the three sorts of NPs. First of all, it complies with the Fregean view, treating definite singular count, plural, and mass NPs as singular terms standing for entities. Second, it allows for a uniform semantics of predicates in general as well as particular expressions that apply, it seems, with the same meaning to singular count, plural, and mass NPs, such as the predicate *weigh* mentioned earlier. The standard semantics is able to capture the way the mereology of events may reflect the mereology of their participants, with thematic relations that involve the gradual involvement of a participant in the event. An example is the object argument of *eat* (*eat the apple, eat the apples, eat rice*), which appears to impose its part structure on the event and determine the aktionsart of the VP (and thus the applicability of modifiers such as *for an hour* and *in an hour*) (Krifka 1998, Champollion 2017).

There is one alternative semantic approach to the semantics of plurals. This approach, which has been pursued especially by philosophical logicians, is that of plural reference (Yi 2005, 2006, Oliver and Smiley 2013, Moltmann 2017). It is based on the view that a definite plural NP such as *the children* does not stand for a single entity, a plurality or collection as one, but rather refers to each student at once. Pluralities, on that view, are no longer entities; instead there is only plural reference, reference to several entities at once.

Plural reference, however, does not provide an account of the semantics of mass NPs, since plural reference is based on reference to individuals and the parts of quantities (entities in the denotation of mass nouns) do not have language-driven unity.[31] How to deal with the semantics of mass nouns by giving justice to the distinction between entities that have unity and those that don't is a serious challenge

---

[31] But see Nicolas (2008) for a proposal of that sort.

that remains to be undertaken. That challenge needs to be pursued while maintaining, in some way, the insights and advantages of the standard approach.[32]

10.7 The Importance of Language-Driven Ontology and Unity for Grammar and Semantics

The ordinary ontology relates to the semantics of natural language differently than the language-driven ontology. Ordinary objects as putative semantic values of referential NPs may be subject to ontological reflection and rejection, and the lexical words used to refer to them may be subject to some degree of spontaneous modification by the user (subject, of course, to conditions of cooperative communication). By contrast, acceptance of the language-driven ontology is mandatory with the use of the language.[33] Given the perspective of generative linguistics, the notions and conditions of the language-driven ontology can be viewed as part of universal grammar more broadly understood, and that even if they are part of the ontology of the real. They can be considered part of universal grammar because they align with the functional part of grammar and need to be acquired together with it. They are part of the core of language on an extended understanding of the term, just as much as the functional part of grammar is.[34]

The central role of the notion of unity for the mass-count distinction and semantic selection shows the importance of the concept of an object for the semantics as well as the syntax of natural language. The notion of unity (the property of being a single entity) can hardly be understood without the notion of an object itself, and given that it is tied to grammar, the notion of an object must be part of language itself, its semantics.

This issue bears on Chomsky's (1986, 1998, 2013) skepticism regarding the involvement of objects in the semantics of natural language; more precisely, the view that referential NPs stand for objects, which Chomsky denies.[35] The question of whether natural language involves objects in its semantics cannot just be addressed by reflecting upon what referential NPs may stand for and what sorts of predicates they permit, in the sense of standard semantic selection. The notion of being a single entity is already intimately connected to the functional part of language and plays an important role in universals of part-structure-sensitive semantic selection. For that reason, it should be considered part of universal grammar, in a suitably extended sense. Chomsky motivates his view with various types of examples of referential NPs permitting apparently contradictory predicates

---

[32] For proposals in that direction see McKay (2017) and Laycock (2006).
[33] See Moltmann (2020) for that distinction and the related core-periphery distinction.
[34] See Yang (2016) for the view that the functional part of grammar represents core grammar.
[35] Chomsky's skepticism pertains to both actual and merely conceived objects as semantic values of referential NPs (Chomsky p.c.).

that challenge the notion of an object of reference. The challenges are due largely to Chomsky's adoption of a non-maximalist view of reality, with a particularly constrained notion of a 'real' object. Taking a maximalist view of reality that includes various sorts of highly derivative, possibly mind-dependent, entities promises a new take on the Chomskyan challenges for referentialist semantics.

10.8　Conclusions

This chapter has argued for a distinction among three different levels of ontology: the ontology of the real, the ordinary ontology, and a language-driven ontology. The latter is aligned with the syntax of natural language, forming a close tie with compositionality. The co-existence of three ontological levels can best be under-stood on a maximalist view of reality, which means reality includes not just what is fundamental but also various sorts of derivative entities that are part of the ordinary and the language-driven ontology. While the ontology of the fundamen-tal hardly plays a role for the semantics of natural language, the ordinary ontology clearly does, especially for the semantics of the lexicon.

We have seen that the language-driven ontology may select unity differently from the ordinary ontology, being tied to the functional part of language as well as syntactic constructions. The two ontologies also seem to involve different gen-eral notions. The ordinary ontology involves notions such as form, function, and persistence; the language-driven ontology involves primitive unity and, possibly, the introduction of objects by abstraction, as pleonastic entities. The language-driven ontology and the ordinary ontology differ also in cognitive status. The acquisition of the ontology of ordinary objects starts before the acquisition of language and proceeds rather independently of it, being based on perception (involving condi-tions of form and size) and functionality.[36] The language-driven ontology is acquired strictly with the acquisition of the language.[37]

References

Borer, H. 2005. *Structuring Sense, Volume 1: In Name Only*. Oxford: Oxford University Press.

Cartwright, H. 1970. 'Quantities', *The Philosophical Review*, 79: 25–42.

---

[36] See Hespos and Spelke (2004).

[37] I would like to thank Lucas Champollion, Hana Filip, David Liebesman, James Miller, Gary Ostertag, Jonathan Schaffer, and Stephen Schiffer for comments on an earlier version of this chapter as well as Kit Fine for both comments and inspiring conversations. Thanks also to the audience at the conference *Conceptualising Reality in the Aristotelian Tradition and Beyond* in Gothenburg in February 2020, where the paper was presented.

Champollion, L. 2017. *Parts of a Whole*. Oxford: Oxford University Press.

Cheng, L. and Sybesma, R. 1999. 'Bare and Not So Bare Nouns and the Structure of NP', *Linguistic Inquiry*, 30: 509–542.

Cheng, L. and Sybesma, R. 2005. 'Classifiers in Four Varieties of Chinese'. In G. Cinque and R. Kayne (eds.), *The Oxford Handbook of Comparative Syntax*, 259–292. Oxford: Oxford University Press.

Chierchia, G. 1998. 'Plurality of Mass Nouns and the Notion of "Semantic Parameter"'. In S. Rothstein (ed.), *Events and Grammar*, 53–103. Dordrecht: Kluwer.

Chierchia, G. 2015. 'How Universal Is the Mass/Count Distinction? Three Grammars of Counting'. In A. Li, A. Simpson, and W.-T. D. Tsai (eds.), *Chinese Syntax in a Cross-Linguistic Perspective*. Oxford: Oxford University Press.

Chomsky, N. 1986. *Knowledge of Language: Its Nature, Origin, and Use*. Westport, CT and London: Praeger.

Chomsky, N. 1998. *New Horizons in the Study of Language and Mind*. Cambridge: Cambridge University Press.

Chomsky, N. 2013. 'Notes on Denotation and Denoting'. In I. Caponigro and C. Cecchetto (eds.), *From Grammar to Meaning: The Spontaneous Logicality of Language*. Cambridge: Cambridge University Press.

Cohen, D. 2020. 'Activewear and Other Vaguery: A Morphological Perspective on Aggregate-Mass'. In F. Moltmann (ed.), *Mass and Count in Linguistics, Philosophy, and Cognitive Science*. Amsterdam: Benjamins.

Doetjes, J. S. 2012. 'Count/Mass Distinctions Across Languages'. In C. Maienborn, K. v. Heusinger, and P. Portner (eds.), *Semantics: An International Handbook of Natural Language Meaning, Part III*, 2559–2580. Berlin: De Gruyter.

Eklund, M. 2008. 'The Pictures of Reality as an Amorphous Lump'. In T. Sider, J. Hawthorne, and D. W. Zimmerman (eds.), *Contemporary Debates in Metaphysics*, 382–396. Oxford: Blackwell.

Fine, K. 2003. 'The Non-Identity of a Material Thing and Its Matter', *Mind*, 112: 195–234.

Fine, K. 2017. 'Naïve Metaphysics', *Philosophical Issues*, 27: 98–113.

Hawthorne, J. 2006. 'Plenitude, Convention, and Ontology'. In *Metaphysical Essays*, 53–70. Oxford: Oxford University Press.

Hespos, S. and Spelke, E. 2004. 'Conceptual Precursors to Language', *Nature*, 430: 453–456.

Jespersen, J. 1924. *The Philosophy of Grammar*. London: George Allen and Unwin.

Krifka, M. 1998. 'The Origins of Telicity'. In S. Rothstein (ed.), *Events and Grammar*, 197–235. Dordrecht: Kluwer.

Langacker, R. 1987. *Foundations of Cognitive Grammar*. Stanford University Press, Stanford.

Laycock, H. 2006. *Words without Objects: Semantics, Ontology, and Logic for Non- Singularity*. Oxford: Oxford University Press.

Link, G. 1983. 'The Logical Analysis of Plurals and Mass Nouns'. In R. Baeuerle et al. (eds.), *Semantics from Different Points of View*, 302–323. Berlin: Springer.

Magidor, O. 2013. *Category Mistakes*. Oxford University Press, Oxford.

McKay, T. 2017. 'From Mass to Plural'. In M. Carrara, A. Arapinis, and F. Moltmann (eds.), *Unity and Plurality: Logic, Philosophy, and Semantics*. Oxford: Oxford University Press.

Moltmann, F. 1997. *Parts and Wholes in Semantics*. New York: Oxford University Press.

Moltmann, F. 1998. 'Part Structures, Integrity, and the Mass-Count Distinction', *Synthese*, 116(1): 75–111.

Moltmann, F. 2004. 'Two Kinds of Universals and Two Kinds of Collections', *Linguistics and Philosophy*, 27(6): 739–776.

Moltmann, F. 2005. 'Part Structures in Situations: The Semantics of *Individual* and *Whole*'. *Linguistics and Philosophy*, 28(5): 599–641.

Moltmann, F. 2013a. *Abstract Objects and the Semantics of Natural Language*. Oxford: Oxford University Press.

Moltmann, F. 2013b. 'The Semantics of Existence', *Linguistics and Philosophy*, 36(1): 31–63.

Moltmann, F. 2016. 'Plural Reference and Reference to a Plurality: Linguistic Facts and Semantic Analyses'. In M. Carrara et al. (eds.), *Unity and Plurality: Philosophy, Logic, and Semantics*, 93–120. Oxford: Oxford University Press.

Moltmann, F. 2017. 'Natural Language Ontology'. In *Oxford Encyclopedia of Linguistics*. Oxford: Oxford University Press.

Moltmann, F. 2019. 'Natural Language and Its Ontology'. In A. Goldman and B. McLaughlin (eds.), *Metaphysics and Cognitive Science*. Oxford: Oxford University Press.

Moltmann, F. 2020. 'Abstract Objects and the Core-Periphery Distinction in the Ontological and the Conceptual Domain of Natural Language'. In J. L. Falguera and C. Martínez (eds.), *Abstract Objects: For and Against*. Dordrecht: Synthese Library., 255-276.

Nicolas, D. 2008. 'Mass Nouns and Plural Logic', *Linguistics and Philosophy*, 31(2): 211–244.

Ojeda, A. 1993. *Linguistic Individuals*. Stanford, CA: CSLI Publications.

Oliver, A. and Smiley, T. 2013. *Plural Logic*. Oxford: Oxford University Press.

Pelletier, F. J. and Schubert, L. 1989, 2003. 'Mass Expressions'. In F. Guenthner and D. Gabbay (eds.), *Handbook of Philosophical Logic*, 2nd edition, 249–336. Vol. 10. Dordrecht: Kluwer (Updated version of the 1989 version).

Pietroski, P. 2018. *Conjoining Meanings: Semantics without Truth Values*. Oxford: Oxford University Press.

Quine, W. V. O. 1960. *Word and Object*. Cambridge, MA: MIT Press.

Rothstein, S. 2010. 'Counting and the Mass/Count Distinction', *Journal of Semantics*, 27(3), 343–397.

Rothstein, S. 2017. *Semantics for Counting and Measuring*. Cambridge: Cambridge University Press.

Saul, J. 1997. 'Substitution and Simple Sentences', *Analysis*, 57(2): 102–108.

Schaffer, J. 2009. 'What Grounds What?'. In D. Chalmers, D. Manley, and R. Wassermann (eds.), *Metametaphysics*, 347–383. Oxford: Oxford University Press.

Schaffer, J. and Rosen, D. 2017. 'Folk Mereology Is Teleological', *Nous*, 51: 238–270.

Schiffer, S. 1996. 'Language-Created and Language-Independent Entities', *Philosophical Topics*, 24(1): 149–167.

Schwarzschild, R. 2011. 'Stubborn Distributivity, Multiparticipant Nouns and the Count/Mass Distinction'. In S. Lima, K. Mullin, and B. Smith (eds.), *Proceedings of the 39th Meeting of the North East Linguistic Society (NELS 39)*, 661–678. Amherst, MA: GSLA.

Simons, P. 1987. *Parts. A Study in Ontology*. Oxford: Oxford University Press.

Soja, N., Carey, S., and Spelke, E. 1991. 'Ontological Categories Guide Young Children's Inductions of Word Meanings: Object Terms and Substance Terms', *Cognition*, 38: 179–211.

Strawson, P. 1959. *Individuals: An Essay in Descriptive Metaphysics*. London: Methuen.

Ter Meulen, A. 1981. 'An Intensional Logic for Mass Terms', *Philosophical Studies*, 40(1): 105–125.

Wright, C. 1983. *Frege's Conception of Numbers as Objects*. Aberdeen: Aberdeen University Press.

Yang, C. 2016. *The Price of Linguistic Productivity. How Children lean to break the Rules of Language*. Cambridge, MA: MIT Press.

Yi, B.-Y. 2005. 'The Logic and Meaning of Plurals: Part I', *Journal of Philosophical Logic*, 34: 459–506.

Yi, B.-Y. 2006. 'The Logic and Meaning of Plurals: Part II', *Journal of Philosophical Logic*, 35: 239–280.

Index